REVISITING MEDIEVAL TELANGANA AND ANDHRA REGIONS: A HISTORICAL INSIGHT

REVISITING MEDIEVAL TELANGANA AND ANDHRA REGIONS: A HISTORICAL INSIGHT

Prof. R. VARALAKSHMI

RESEARCH INDIA PRESS
New Delhi (INDIA)

ISBN : 978-93-5171-036-3

Price : ₹ 1250/-

First Edition: 2015

This book is published with the financial assistance of U.G.C. Unit, Osmania University.

Published by :
RESEARCH INDIA PRESS
E-6/34, Sangam Vihar
New Delhi-110062
Phone: 011-26047013, (M) 9818085794
E-mail: researchindiapress@gmail.com

Dedicated

to

my Beloved Parents

LATE SRI R. KRISHNAMURTHY & SMT. R. VENKATANARASAMMA

CONTENTS

Prof. R. SOMA REDDY (Retd.)
Department of History
Osmania University

9-15, Ravindra Nagar
Habsiguda
Hyderabad-500 007.

FOREWORD

I take great pleasure in introducing the book, entitled *Revisiting Medieval Telangana and Andhra Regions: A Historical Insight*, a collection of 20 articles written by Prof. R. Varalakshmi. It deals mainly with the socio-economic and cultural history of Medieval Andhradesa. The research articles included in this book focus on different themes relating to the social history of medieval Andhradesa. The first article deals with the Historical Geography. Since Geography is the foundation of all historical knowledge the author made an attempt to provide the historical geography of some places, especially the Nadus. One article is devoted to discussing the Status of Women. It has been noted that the position of women in the medieval period deteriorated. Social evils like polygamy, concubinage and prostitution have been common. Four articles deal with certain aspects of caste structure, social system and caste groups. It has been pointed out that as in other parts of India, the society in medieval Andhradesa was basically divided into four main castes. On the basis of epigraphical and literary sources, the author has examined the social composition and distinctiveness of the caste groups. The cultural and religious aspects are dealt with in six articles. They throw light on Village Deities, Festivals and Fairs, Religious Institutions like Temple and Dargah. The growth of composite culture in the medieval period is attributed to the growth of Sufism and the graves of the famous Sufi saints became the Dargahs. Prof. R. Varalakshmi pointed out that the Sufis of 16th & 17th centuries (Qutub Shahi period) were the torch bearer of composite culture. Dargahs have played a significant role in the lives of the people, irrespective of caste, creed and community not only in the past but also today.

Economic conditions and growth of urbanization are the subject matter of seven articles. Various aspects of economic history like Material Culture, the Cropping Pattern, Tanks, Water Ways and Commerce, Means of Transport and Communication, Inland and Overseas Trade and the Dynamics of Urbanization are discussed. The cultural dimension of medieval Andhra society pertaining to Games and Amusements is discussed in one article. The author noted that the establishment of the Muslim rule in medieval Telangana and Andhra has its impact on the society. Interestingly, in the field of games and amusements, the two communities influenced each other. Two examples of Polo and Chess have been cited as evidence of mutual interface between Hindus and Muslims. This article also provides information about several forms of entertainment like Hunting, Gambling, Ram fight, Cockfight, Acrobatic feats, Snake charming and so on. All the articles included in his book are based on primary and secondary sources and they are a welcome addition to the growing literature on the socio-economic history of medieval Andhradesa.

Therefore, I congratulate Prof. R. Varalakshmi for bringing out the book and making it available to the scholars. It will become a reference work for research scholars of medieval Telangana and Andhra History.

(Prof. R. SOMA REDDY)

Prof. E. SURESH KUMAR
M.A. (English),
M.Sc. (Psychology), Ph.D.
Professor of English
&
REGISTRAR

e-mail: registrar@osmania.ac.in

: 040-27098043 (O)
: 040-27682363 (O)
Fax : 040-27090020 (O)

OSMANIA UNIVERSITY
HYDERABAD - 500007

February 18, 2015

MESSAGE

I am happy to note that Dr. R. Varalakshmi, Professor of History, University College of Arts and Social Sciences, Osmania University is bringing out the collection of her articles presented in the various National and International Seminars and Conferences in the form of a book entitled **"Revisiting Medieval Telangana and Andhra Regions: A Historical Insight"**. I extend my greetings and good wishes to her in this scholastic venture.

To bring out the deliberations in a book form is a worth appreciating attempt and it would be of great help for the present generation and useful for the posterity.

I wish all the best in her up-coming endeavours.

[PROF. E. SURESH KUMAR]

Mahamahopadhyaya, Desikottama
Dr K. Sivananda Murty
D.Lit (GITAM Uni), D.Lit (PS Tel Uni)
Peethadhipati,
Sri Saiva Maha Peetham,

'Anandavan'
Bheemunipatnam
Visakha District
Andhra Pradesh - 531 163
Ph (08933) 229505
email:ksivanandamurty@gmail.com
Dt.14/10/2015

To

Dr. R. Varalakshmi

Madam

Your letter dt.21/11/2014.

The proposed publication on Medieval Telangana consisting of your articles on various occasions is certainly a most welcome publication. It can certainly throw light on various aspects of Medieval Telangana. Its arrival in book form will be a permanent asset to the students and scholars.

Yours Truly

(K. Sivananda Murty)

PREFACE

This book is intended to contain an interesting range of collection of my 20 research articles, which throw a flood of light on the socio-cultural and economic aspects of medieval Telangana and Andhra areas. Most of these research articles were presented in several seminars and conferences and published in journals and proceeding volumes. I aspired to bring all the articles into a book form in order to make it useful to students and researchers.

The medieval period was marked by the rise of Sudras, who claimed Kshatriya status. The most interesting trait of this period is that some of the Dependent communities such as Vipravinodis, Viramushtis and Dommaras emerged as prosperous class and offered gifts to temples. Regarding the stature of women, it is clear that she no more enjoyed that great respect that she held in earlier times. No respectable person ever considered it as beneath his dignity to be a patron of a courtesan.

In the realm of religion, the existence of a mosque in Orugallu shows appearance of the new Islamic faith in medieval Andhra Desa. The worship of village deities was a significant aspect of popular religion. During this period, it was temple that dominated the life of even the lowest class of people. During the medieval times Dargahs, the tomb-shrines of Sufi saints, played an important role in the lives of people of distinct castes, creeds and communities.

In this period, there was tremendous urban growth. Though the process of urbanization was a result of the interplay of social, religious, economic and political factors, the economic elements such as surplus, industries, trade and commerce and guilds contributed largely to the acceleration of urbanization in medieval Telangana and Andhra. Burton Stein aptly pointed out that trade and urban life became much more significant in South India. During the study period, villages were found self-sufficient as all things yielded in abundance and it gave impetus to internal trade. Hectic external trade was carried out and the advent of Europeans gave fillip to it. After the Mughals conquered Andhra, the affluent Persian merchants faded into oblivion.

Thus, the present study has endeavoured to give much authentic and fascinating picture of the socio-cultural and economic aspects of medieval Telangana and Andhra.

ACKNOWLEDGEMENT

I gratefully acknowledge my appreciation to several individuals and institutions, who rendered unstained help in the publication of my work. I am greatly beholden to my *Guru Satya Sai Baba* for His Divine blessings in the completion of the proposed book. I express my respectable gratitude to Guru K. Sivananda Murthy for his precious message. I also express my gratitude to our Honourable Registrar Prof. E. Suresh Kumar for his message with the words of admiration. I profoundly thank Prof. R. Soma Reddy (Retd.), Department of History, Osmania University, who has been magnanimous in writing foreword.

I am extremely grateful to my teachers, Prof. Y. Vaikuntham (Retd.), Late Prof. P. Sree Rama Sharma, my M.Phil. Supervisor and Prof. K. Sarojini Devi (Retd.), my Ph.D. Supervisor, whose precious advise helped me to reach the position I am in today.

I am very much thankful to Prof. Sunitha, Department of English, Osmania University for helping me in the completion of work. I thank all my faculty members for extending cooperation and giving valuable suggestions in upbringing this book. I also thank my supporting staff for assisting me in finishing the work at various stages.

I sincerely acknowledge my indebtedness to UGC unit, Osmania University, for extending financial assistance for the publication of this book.

It gives me great pleasure to express my gratitude to my younger sisters Smt. K. Vijaya, Smt. B. Renuka, Smt. R. Uma, Smt. T. Padmaja, brother Mr. R. Naveen Kumar, son Mr. R. Venkata Sai Rakesh and his wife Mrs. Neha and her sister Miss. Namitha for their moral support and persistent encouragement. A special word of thanks to my most beloved eight month old grand-daughter Shaunika Sai Ramisetty, whose infant smiles gave me strength to complete my work successfully.

My thanks are due to Mr. Suman Pathak and Mr. Ganga Ram Sharma, Research India Press, New Delhi for their finesse in publishing this book.

1

HISTORICAL GEOGRAPHY OF SOME PLACES

We come across with the names of many places of medieval Telangana and Andhra in the contemporary sources. Geography forms foundation of all historical knowledge. Hence, I made an attempt to give the historical geography of some of the places, with special reference to the Nadus. In Medieval period the word Nadu was much in vogue. A group of villages from 1 to 60 was constituted into a Sthala or Sima and several Sthalas were combined to make one Nadu. The area of the Nadu depended on the number of villages it consisted of. Though its usage has disappeared, still it has left its mark on the divisions prevalent in Brahmin community such as Velanadu (Velanati), Kasalnadu (Kasalnati) and Mulkinadu (Mulkinati) etc.

Orugallu

Orugallu or Ekasilanagara was the capital city of the Kakatiyas. Orugallu of the medieval times is modern Warangal. Now it is the headquarters of a district named after it. Warangal is situated about 86 miles north-east of Hyderabad. In olden days it is referred to as Oragallu, Varungallu and Vorugallu both in literature and inscriptions. General Alexander Cunningham called it as Varankol and identified it with Vorunkula of Ptolemy.[1] According to Kolani Ganapathi Deva's '*Sivayogasaram*',[2] Rudradeva-I left his first capital Hanumakonda and built Orugallu and began ruling from that place. The Bekkallu inscription[3] of 11th century confirms the information given by this work. But how Rudra proceeded to build it is described in the Ganapesvaram inscription, which belongs to the time of Ganapathideva.[4] It is stated that the towns which he razed to the ground were known by the quarter which he founded in the city of Orugallu under their respective names and people with their respective inhabitants.

Orugallu appeared as the abode of Lakshmi (house of the wealth–goddess), enemies apprehended it as a mine of valour, scholars and poets dreamed of it as the theatre where Vani (the goddess of learning) danced.[5] *Kridabhiramam*, a Telugu contemporary work, says that Prataparudra was recognized and respected as '*Andhrorvisudu*'[6] (Supreme Lord of Andhradesa). Further, the same source gives a vivid description of the fort. It describes Orugallu as a city having a deep moat, high walls and gold covered doors shining with all their beauty.[7] Besides, it mentions the temples of Bhairava, Virabhadra, Chamundeshwari, a Buddhist monastery, a temple dedicated to Heroes of Palanadu, as well as a mosque.

The fort at Orugallu had two moats, one outer and the other inner, two rampart walls, made as mud and stone, eight gateways four in each wall and a number of bastions at some intervals. The four gateways in the mud rampart, are known locally, as the Peddama gate in the east, Talla Gandi gate in the south, Talupula Bhavi Gandi gate in the west and Lanjapatra Gandi in the north. The stone fort of Orugallu was rectangular in structure and highly formidable. It was built of crude and irregular blocks of black granite. There are four gateways in the middle of four cardinal points and several bastions at regular intervals. These four gates are locally known as Bandi Darwaja on the east, Chini Darwaja on the south, Hydari gate on the west and Michili Darwaja on the north. The rock fort can be climbed over only from inside and from outside it is totally inaccessible.

Polasa

It was originally the capital of Polavasadesa ruled by some chieftains. The village was named after the deity Poulastya Brahma, whom the local villagers regard with great respect. An inscription engraved on the pillar of Poulastyesvara temple in Polasa dated 1186 A.D. reveals that one Meda Raja of Rashtrakuta affiliations was the ruler of Polavasa country.[8] Rudradeva, the Kakatiya ruler, defeated Meda Raja.[9] Polavasa region corresponds to Jagatial then the taluq of Karimnagar district of Telangana State. At present we see only the enclosed wall of the Polavasa fort around the village with the four gates in dilapidated condition.

Draksharamam

Draksharamam is the famous Saiva Kshetram in Ramachadrapuram then the taluq of East Godavari District of Andhra Pradesh. It is recognized as one of the five Aramakshetras of Andhradesa. Its old name was Dakiremi. In the inscription of Draksharamam Bhimeswara Swamy temple dated 1084 A.D., it was mentioned as 'Pedda Dakiremi'.[10] In another inscription of 1087 A.D., it was merely called 'Dakiremi'.[11] In the later inscriptions of the last quarter of 11th century, it was called 'Dakshapuri', 'Daksharamam' and 'Draksharamam'. Thus,

Dakiremi became 'Daksharamam' and this came to be known as 'Draksharamam'. Vidhyanatha Kavi in his work *Prataparudra-yasobhushanam*[12] said that the country in which the three famous Saivaite Shrines of Srisailam, Draksharamam and Kaleswaram are situated is known as 'Trilinga Desa' (i.e. Telugu country). Draksharama temple is rich in inscriptions pertaining to various kingdoms of medieval Andhra and their ministers and generals.

The Reddi ruler Anavema built a *Natya Mantapa* (an open hall for dance) in the temple of Bhimeshvara in 1385 A.D. and also built a *Sanivara Mantapa* in 1452 A.D. for Lord Bhimeshvara, Draksharamam. In 1494 A.D. certain Erramanayaka dug a canal from the stream named Ela, brought it up to Govada and joined it to Gurugadda and presented it to the deity Bhimeshvara of Draksharama.

Velanadu

The first inscription that mentioned 'Velanadu' was dated in 763 A.D. This inscription belonged to the time of Vijayadithya. In this inscription it was called 'Vilanandu'.[13] Perhaps the word 'Vilanandu' might have become Velanadu later. Originally Velanadu corresponded to the modern Tenali and Repalle then the taluqs. A part of Guntur was also in Velanadu. It was one of the famous places in the coastal area of the river Krishna.[14]

Palanadu

In one of the famous Chatus of Srinatha, it was rendered as 'Pallenati Sima Palletullu'.[15] The Koneki inscription of Vishnuvardana-II,[16] the Eastern Chalukyan king, mentions 'Palli Rashtri Koneki Nama Gramam'. In the Macherla inscription of Chagi Betharaju,[17] it is referred to as 'Palli Desa Satatrayantarvarthi Nageshwari Nadi'. Durgi inscription of Kakati Rudramadevi[18] mentions it as 'Pallinatiloni Dugya Patnam'. The villages mentioned in the above inscriptions, such as Koneki (Konamki), Dugyapatnam (Durgi) are in modern Palanadu then the taluq. As per the observation cited above, Palanadu is situated towards the south of the river Krishna, westward of Sathenapalli then the taluq and northwards of Vinukonda.

Mulkinadu

Kridabhiramam indicates that Vallabharaya ruled over Mopuru estate consisting of three villages in Mulkinadu.[19] In one of the Kannada inscriptions of Kannara Deva-III[20] of Rastrakuta dynasty, found in Pushpagiri of Cuddapah district, it is stated that he was ruling over Mulikinadu in Honnamadi. In one of the Telugu inscriptions[21] found in Atthanala of Rajampeta then the taluq, it is mentioned that the king Ambadeva ruled over Gandikota and Mulkinadu etc., with Vallur city. From the aforesaid evidence, we can safely conclude that the term 'Mulikinadu' gradually changed into 'Mulkinadu'. The Srisailam inscription[22] refers to the villages Rajavolu, Mallaiah Vemulu, Perakapadu, which belonged to Mulkinadu. The Bitragunta inscription of Sangama-II,[23] a representative of Vijayanagara kings describes Mulkinadu to a certain extent. In this place there is a temple known as Pushpachalam and to the north of it there is the river Penna. From the above data it can be inferred that Pulivendala, Rajampeta, Proddutur then the taluqs of Cuddapah and the northern region of Bellary, Chittoor and Anantapur belong to Mulkinadu.

Kasalnadu

Srinatha in one of his Chatus described a Kasalnati beauty (Kasalanativari kanakangi) at the bathing ghat.[24] Ameen

Khan was a relation of Ibrahim Qutb Shah of Golconda. Ponniganti Telanganacharyudu dedicated his work '*Yayati Charitra*' to Amin Khan, and in his work he says that Potlacheruvu the place Ameen Khan ruled was part of Kasalnadu.[25] Potlacheruvu is in Sangareddy then the taluq of Medak district. In one of the inscriptions,[26] in the temple of Mallikarjuna in Srisailam, 'Kasalnadu' is mentioned as 'Kusalanadu'. The villages 'Kalu Cherulu', 'Sasurala' and 'Devarapally' of Kusalanadu are the present 'Kaluvacherla' of Sultanabad then the taluq, Sirsilla and 'Devarapally' of Sirsilla then the taluq of Karimnagar district. From this it is clear that Kusalanadu might have changed as Kasalnadu. It corresponds to the modern Karimnagar and part of Medak districts.

Karnadu

In an inscription of Srisailam[27] some of the villages of Karnadu are mentioned such as Shivapuram, Nandikunta, Tatipadu, Siddeshwaram etc., of Nandikotkur then the taluq. Some villages like Pesaravaya (Pesaravayi) and Gandivemula (Gadivemula) are of Nandyal then the taluq. From this data, it can be inferred that the Karnadu of medieval times corresponds to the present Nandikotkur and Nandyal then the taluqs of Kurnool region.

Nellore

The name Nellore is variously drawn. One explanation of the name, Nellore, is that the town was so named after the extensive cultivation of paddy in and around (Nell, means 'Paddy' and 'Ore' or 'ur' means town). Even today this town is famous for rice and husked paddy.[28] A large town is said to have existed once on the suburb of Nellore, now known as Durgametta, occupied by the houses of the

European residents and the name of this town was Vikrama Simhapuram (brave lion town). Srinatha, a great Telugu poet of medieval times dedicated his work *Haravilasam* to a rich merchant name Avachi Tippaya Setti of Simha Vikrama Pattana (i.e. Nellore). All the medieval Andhra kingdoms had their sway over Nellore in different periods.

Nellore became a prominent town during the 12th century A.D. It was the capital town of the Telugu Chodas. In 1573 A.D. Venkatappa Naidu, the governor at Nellore, made the Sthala-Karanams (village officers), Kapus (farmers), Settis (merchants) and Pakareddis (landlords) accept the arrangements for showing honour to the Panchanas (goldsmiths, blacksmiths, braziers, carpenters and stone –cutters) during the festival days of Lord Pallikondanatha.[29] The Chittrameli guild developed in Southern Andhra with Nellore as its headquarters. At present Nellore is headquarters of Nellore district in Andhra Pradesh.

Rajamahendravaram

It is a large town, situated on the left bank of the river Godavari and had a hoary past. It is said to have been constructed by the Eastern Chalukyan ruler Rajaraja Narendra[30] in 1022 A.D., and hence named after him as *Rajaraja Narendrapuram* or Rajamahendravaram which was shortened as Rajahmundry in course of time. The earliest mention of Rajahmundry is found in the introduction to the *Andhra Mahabharata* rendered by Nannaya during the reign of the Eastern Chalukyan king Rajaraja Narendra (1018-1061 A.D.). It served as a capital town to a branch of Reddi kings. It came to prominence during the rule of Eastern Chalukyas and the Reddi kings. After the decline of the Reddi kings, it went into the hands of Gajapathis of Kalinga. Rajahmundry has some traces of fine palaces, fort walls etc. The ruins of this capital city can still be seen from Sarangadhara Metta. The temple of Kotilingeshvara, situated on the bank of the Godavari, is one of the reputed temples. In Rajahmundry the Reddi kings built a splendid palace of Trailokya-Vijaya with several floors, on the banks of the Godavari. Srinatha, a contemporary poet, reports that the bronze doors of its fort were very strong.[31] Rajahmundry is now in the East Godavari district of Andhra Pradesh.

Bejawada

Bejawada or Vijayawada is an ancient town that has existed since the post-Satavahana period. It is surrounded by picturesque hill, like Sitanagaram, Kanakadurga and Indrakila hills. It became a famous pilgrim centre on account of its situation on the bank of the holy river Krishna and there are three important temples, namely Kanakadurga, Bhramaramba - Malleshvara and Vijayeshvara at Vijayawada. No information is available regarding the construction of the first temple, but the second and the third are believed to have been built by Dharmaraja and Arjuna of the *Mahabharata.* The Teliki-Vevuru or the merchant guild of oil-millers, built a Mukhamantapa in 1426 A.D. in front of Lord Malleshvara at Bezawada.[32] At present Vijayawada is situated in the Krishna district of Andhra Pradesh.

Kondapalli

Kondapalli is situated 16 kms. east of Vijayawada in Krishna district of Andhra Pradesh. The river Krishna is flowing about 3 kms., South of Kondapalli. The earliest inscription pertaining to Kondapalli mentioned it as Kondai.[33] The name Kondai has been identified with

Kondapalli. It is said that the fortress of Kondapalli was constructed by Anavema Reddi,[34] the ruler of Reddi dynasty. There is a legend regarding the origin of Kondapalli. It goes to say that the word Kondapalli had been derived from the name of a shepherd Kondadu, who showed the site to a Reddi king and therefore the place obtained the name after the shepherd Kondadu.[35] During the time of Gajapathis of Orissa, Vidhyadhara Gajapathi constructed a great reservoir at this place.[36] The illustrious ruler of Vijayanagara Empire, Krishnadevaraya during his eastern campaigns conquered Kondapalli from the Gajapathis and it is said that for some reason or the other he restored it to Gajapathis.[37] The founder of Qutb Shahi Kingdom, Qutb-Ul-Mulk occupied it and named it as Mustafanagar.[38] Kondapalli had been described as, "one of the greatest forts of Tilang had quite a number of wells and water tanks as well as fruit and other trees along with large rice fields".[39] Kondapalli functioned as second capital to the Reddis of Kondavidu. It also constituted as the southernmost frontiers of the Gajapathis.

There are three ways to go into the fort from the main entrance, viz. Rachabata (vehicle road), Rallabata (stone-passage) and the Kalibata (foot-way). To the right of the road, at a distance of 200 metres from the main entrance, there is Jumma Masjid said to be built during the Qutb Shahi period. To the north of Jumma Masjid, there lies a building in a dilapidated condition called 'Thope Khana', meant for preserving ammunition etc. It consisted of a stone stair-case and 18 rooms in three rows constructed with trimmed granite stones. After passing through three gateways of the inner fortification, there is a Dargah of Galib Shah, a Muslim missionary. The fort was built on the hill top in a 50 acres leveled area. It consisted of a Darbar hall, which was a two-storeyed construction of 40 x 45 metres. From this hall, the visitor can have a beautiful panoramic view of the entire Kondapalli. The ground floor had many chambers with arched stone pillars. There were also elephant stables or Gajasalas. To the east of Darbar hall, there is an open place with a stone enclosure or wall, used as gymnasium with a stage. Near the second fortification wall, there is a dilapidated Sivalayam. The idol of Lord Siva with Parvathi seated on his right thigh, and statues of Dwarapalakas can be seen there. Ruins of houses are seen in the grounds. There are two natural rock tanks called as Attha-Kodalu tanks. They supplied water to all the inhabitants of the fortress. There is a bastion known as *Durgam* adjoining the second fortification wall. To the north, on the Durgam is a Hanuman Mandapam with the figure of Lord Hanuman carved on a rock.

Kondavidu

It is situated about 12 miles south-west of Guntur district. It flourished as a strong capital city of Reddi kings till their decline. It was termed as Kundinapura.[40] Kondavidu played a prominent role in the Vijayanagara – Bahmani wars. It was under the rule of the Vijayanagara, Gajapathi, Bahmani, and Qutb Shahi rule. The Qutb Shahis renamed it as Murtuzanagar. The Gopavaram[41] and the Komaragirivaram grants[42] of Kataya Vema Reddi dated in 1395 A.D. and 1408 A.D. that state the king Kumaragiri Reddi, constructed many pleasure houses (Lilagruhams) with gold and precious stones, a lofty palatial mansion termed Griharaja Prasada with pinnacles, pleasure ponds (Kridasarams) and pleasure chariots (Keli-radhams), and sported with his beloved women. References to his Griharajameda are also found in a Chatu verse current in the Telugu country.

This fort was constructed in a great strategical place that forms its central position. It commands a view from all quarters and hence it was made the capital of Kondaviti Reddi kingdom. The fortifications raised on these hills are extensive and highly strong. The bastions are strongly built with largely hewn stones well-connected with one another. The main entrance to the fort was praised by poets of those times. It is said to have had 44 storeys, 44 ramparts and 77 entrances. The main entrance was 20' high and 12' wide.

Srisailam

It is the most important of Saiva centres from times immemorial. It is situated in Kurnool district of Andhra Pradesh. This place has a bewitching scenic beauty with hills and the holy river Krishna. Its ancient antiquity is referred to in Aranyaparva of the *Mahabharata*. Kammanadu was specified to be situated to the east of Srisailam in a record dated 1108 A.D. A place named Kolla (Kollapaka) was referred to as having been at the western entrance to Srisailam. According to tradition that the Siva Linga there came to be known as Mallikarjuna Linga, as it was held that a certain Chandravati, daughter of a Gupta king called Chandragupta, was in love with Swayambhu Siva. She offered daily a bunch of Malli (Jasmine) flowers to Him. He was pleased with the sincere devotion of her and wanted to marry her. Finally she was wedded to Him and from that time onwards the Siva Linga came to be known as Mallikarjuna Linga. The same account is given by Palkurki Somanatha in his *Panditaradhya Charitra*.[43] An inscription from Chebrolu of 1118 A.D. records that Gonka-II of Velanadu installed Kalasa (vessel) made of gold on Sri Parvatha.[44]

Adishankara, the great Advaita teacher, visited this sacred place, stayed for sometime and composed verses in praise of Lord Mallikarjuna in his celebrated work *Sivanandalahari*. He sang in admiration of goddess Bhramaramba in his *Bhramaramba Ashtaka*. There are innumerable inscriptions in and around the Srisailam temple, pertaining to the Kakatiya, the Reddi, and the Vijayanagara periods. The Reddi king Prolaya Vema, built steps to the holy Tirtha Patala Ganga.[45] The Vijayanagara rulers and others greatly improved the temple. The temple with its many excellent bas-reliefs depicting Saivite stories and legends attracts archaeologists, sculptors and devotees.

Notes & References

1. Alexander Cunningham, *The Ancient Geography of India,* Varanasi, 1975, p.444.
2. M. Rama Rao, *Kakatiya Sanchika*, Anubandam, Rajamahendravaram, 1935, p.12.
3. *Warangal District Inscriptions*, No. 42.
4. *Epigraphia Indica*, III, p.90.
5. Vidhyanatha, *Prataparudrayashobhushanam,* Arthalankara Prakarana, Vol. 10.
6. Vinukonda Vallabharaya, *Kridabhiramam,* published by V. Prabhakara Sastry, Hyderabad, 1960, v.155.
7. *Ibid.,* v.112.
8. *Karimnagar District Inscriptions*, No. 66.
9. *Warangal District Inscriptions*, No. 36.
10. *South Indian Inscriptions*, IV, No. 1015.
11. *Ibid.,* IV, 1016.
12. Vidhyanatha, *Op.Cit.*, Nataka Prakaranamu, Prataparudra Kalyanam, V, v.22.
13. K. Iswar Datt, *Prachinandra Charitraka Bhugolam,* Hyderabad, 1979, p.306.

14. *Ibid.,* p.308.
15. V. Prabhakara Sastry, Compiled, *Chatupadyamanimanjari,* Chennapuri, 1949, p.126.
16. *Epigraphia Indica,* Vol. XXXI, No. 12.
17. *South Indian Inscriptions*, Vol. X, No. 66.
18. *Ibid.,* Vol. X, No.422.
19. Vinukonda Vallabharaya, *Op.Cit.,* v.22.
20. *South Indian Inscriptions*, Vol. IX, Part-I, No. 69.
21. *Ibid.,* Vol. X, No. 448.
22. *Ibid.,* Vol. X, No. 504.
23. *Epigraphia Indica*, Vol. III, p.24.
24. V. Prabhakara Sastry, *Op.Cit.*, p.124.
25. Ponnikanti Telaganarya, *Yayati Charitra*, v.31.
26. *South Indian Inscriptions*, Vol. X, No. 504.
27. *Ibid.,* Vol. X, No. 503 & 504.
28. *Nellore District Gazetteer*, pp.2 & 3.
29. *Nellore District Inscriptions*, II, No. 54.
30. N. Venkataramanayya, *Eastern Chalukyas of Vengi,* Ch. XII, p.163, and also *South Indian Inscriptions*, VI, No. 662.
31. Srinatha, *Kashikandam,* I, v.56, VI, v.309.
32. *South Indian Inscriptions*, IV, No. 796.
33. G. Yazdani, *History of Deccan,* Parts VII-IX, Oxford University Press, 1960, p.344.
34. Gordon Mackhenzie, *Krishna District Manual,* p.10.
35. K. Chandramouli, *Kondapally through the Ages*, Hyderabad, 1989, p.15.
36. Gordon Mackhenzie, *Op.Cit.,* p.10.
37. *Ibid.,* p.11.
38. N.S. Ramachandra Murthy, *Forts in Andhra – A Study*, Delhi, 1996, p.168.

39. H.K. Sherwani & P.M. Joshi (eds.) *History of Medieval Deccan (1295-1724),* Vol. I, Hyderabad, 1973, p.472.
40. N.S. Ramachandra Murthy, *Op.Cit.*, p.167.
41. *Journal of Andhra Historical Research Society,* Vol. XI, p. 213, v.30.
42. *Ibid.,* p.205 ff.
43. A. Vaidehi Krishnamurthy, *Social and Economic Conditions in Eastern Deccan (From A.D. 1000 to 1250),* Secunderabad, 1970, p.236.
44. *South Indian Inscriptions,* Vol. IV, No. 1164.
45. M. Somasekhara Sarma, *History of the Reddi Kingdoms,* Waltair, 1948, p. 452.

2

CASTE SYSTEM

The caste system is the unique feature of the Hindu society. It is the independent and self-sufficient units called castes that distinguish Hindu society from others. As in other parts of the country, the society in Medieval Andhradesa was basically divided into the four main castes- the Brahmins, the Kshatriyas, the Vaisyas and the Sudras. Each of these divisions have numerous sub-divisions. The Chandalas or the Panchamas, i.e. the fifth caste constituted a separate section of the society.

Brahmins

By virtue of his supposed origin from the head of Brahma (the creator), the Brahmin was considered the highest of the castes. Superiority in every respect is claimed for a Brahmin, though emphasis is laid on the superior knowledge and qualifications on which that status rests. A Brahmin was supposed to be well versed in his grasp of the absolute or Brahma *(Brahmadharana),* observed vows *(Niyamadharana)* and cultivated universal love. The life of a Brahmin was conceptually duty bound towards the society and the gods and himself.

The Brahmin community was divided into several sects. The Brahmins of those days were mainly followers of the *Rigveda* or the *Yajurveda*. The Kapalur Grant[1] dated 1258-1336 A.D. gives some of the names of the Brahmins following the *Rigveda* and the *Yajurveda*. The votaries of the *Samaveda* were few, and obviously the followers of *Atharvanaveda* were very few. Another basis of distinction among the Brahmins was the Gotra. The contemporary sources[2] mention the names of the Gotras such as:

1. Agnivesya	2. Atreya
3. Badarayana	4. Bharadvaja
5. Bhargava	6. Cikitasa
7. Devarata	8. Garga
9. Gautama	10. Harita
11. Jatukarna	12. Kalyana
13. Kamakayana	14. Kanva
15. Bhargava	16. Kasyapa
17. Kata	18. Kaundinya
19. Kausika	20. Krishnatreya
21. Kutsa	22. Lohita
23. Maitravaruna	24. Martanda
25. Maunabhargava	26. Mosa
27. Mudgala or Maudgalya	28. Nagasya
29. Nitundi	30. Parasara
31. Purukutsa	32. Putimasa
33. Radhitara	34. Rohita
35. Salankayana	36. Salavata
37. Sandilya	38. Sankruti
39. Sata	40. Sathala
41. Sathamarsana	42. Saunabhargava

43. Saunaka
44. Srivatsa
45. Sungabharadvaja
46. Upamanya
47. Vadhula
48. Valakhilya
49. Vardhyasava
50. Vasistha
51. Visvamitra
52. Visnuvardhana
53. Visnuruddha
54. Vrusa
55. Yaksa.

There were other sub-divisions among the Brahmins based on territorial origin. Velanadus, Venginadus, Telinganas, Kasalnatis and Mulkinatis are a few such sub-divisions.

The contemporary sources contain references to Brahmins proficient in the *Vedas, Vedangas, Agamas, Dharmasastras, Mimamsa, Ayurvedam, Dhanurvedam* and poetry.[3] It is evident that the Brahmins not only promoted Vedic studies but also secular learning. The royal priests used to be well versed in Atharvana Veda. *Madhura Vijayam* explains how the priests chanted the hyms from Atharvana Veda, emphasizing their meaning and wishing him all success, when the king rode out for the conquest of Madhura. Hence, it was said that royal priests must be well versed in Atharvana Veda.[4] A section of Brahmins sought to enter the Government service, which offered them bright career. The imperial secretariat was almost entirely manned by men of this class. They filled the highest office of state by virtue of their character. They enjoyed the position of ministers, generals, superintendents, Durgadhipatis and governors.[5]

Other Brahmins lived mostly on the patronage of kings and the charity of the public. They were given Agraharas by the kings and the nobles. Agrahara was the home of scholars devoted to learning and intellectual pursuits. An inscription,[6] dated 1378 A.D., mentions the grant of a village as an Agrahara to some Brahmins. In *Kridabhiramam* there is a reference to Jonnagadda Agrahara.[7] Brahmins were denied the right of receiving gift from men outside the caste-structure. Officiating as a priest for him also was considered to be a sin.[8] The contemporary literary works refer to the unworthy Brahmins also who had fallen low and neglected their ordinary duties.[9] However, Brahmins steeped in learning desirous of teaching were very much esteemed. Even the foreign travellers did not fail to notice the reverence shown to them. Abdur Razzack says in his account that "the Brahmins are held by him (the king) in higher estimation than all other men".[10]

Kshatriyas

The Kshatriyas practised essentially the profession of warfare. Protection of the state from external aggression and internal trouble, maintenance of peace and order were considered as the duties of the Kshatriyas. In the middle ages, after the decline of the Eastern Chalukyas of Vengi, the power and prestige of Kshatriya community started declining. Within two centuries, political power passed almost completely into the hands of the Sudras. A few continued to rule over small territories. The Telugu Codas of Nellore, the Calukyas of Vengi and the Haihayas of Palanadu were some of these Kshatriyas.

The Kshatriyas as a class were subjected to many vicissitudes. As kingdoms grew, normally the privileges of the ruling class could be enjoyed only by a few. Their numbers were obviously restricted. In times of danger anyone, even Brahmins, could take up arms according to the Sastras. But in actual practice the fourth class took to arms, whenever there was a chance to enlist, and obtained a real change from their humdrum life of everyday. The latitude allowed by the Sastras in the matter of Kshatriyas marrying women of lower classes must have also added to the increase in the number of persons who were partly Kshatriya in blood. They were anxious to play the role of Kshatriyas when a chance presented itself. Any discussion about the caste of any ruling family is futile. Many of the dynasties of Medieval India were of low origin. The Kakatiyas of Warangal claimed themselves to belong to Kshatriya caste though they were Sudras. Mailamba and Kundamba the two daughters of the Kakatiya king Mahadeva married Nattavadi Rudra, a Kshatriya chief. Rudramadevi, the daughter of Ganapathi Deva, married the Eastern Calukyan Virabhadra, a Kshatriya.

Vaisyas

The Vaisya's duty was to increase the prosperity of the country. Agriculture, cattle keeping and trade were under their social care. The Vaisyas were inferior to the Brahmins and the Kshatriyas in social hierarchy. In Medieval Andhradesa they were called Komatis and Settis.[11] Members of the Vaisya caste generally bore suffixes like Setti, Sresthi and Gupta etc. Acquisition of wealth is commendable in a Vaisya and he is encouraged to make money by all legitimate means. Donations, gifts to the Brahmins and generous contributions for the building of temples and shrines formed some of the best means of spending money. We find such charitable Vaisyas during this period. The lithic record[12] of Alampur of Prataparudra-II, dated 1299 A.D. refers to the gift of land and a pond by a number of merchants (Settis). *Haravilasam* refers to Avaci Setti, who was a great devotee of Siva and made innumerable *danas*.[13]

The subsequent growth of population led to a vast increase in the number of occupations, and the fragmentation of many to prevent unemployment. This resulted in skill becoming the criterion of a particular occupation rather than the limitations dictated by caste. The social order of the human community was seen as a biological law. We find some of the Vaisya community distinguishing themselves as soldiers, writers, linguists and lords.[14] Most of the trade and commerce was under the control of the Vaisyas. The deceitful merchants were given severe punishments.[15] On the whole, the Vaisya community maintained trade and commerce very well during this period. Most of the trade and commerce was under the control of the Vaisyas. The deceitful traders were given severe punishments.

Sudras

The Sudras formed the real bulwark of Hindu society. Their status according to the Hindu law books is very low in the social scale. They formed the back-bone of the nation and the prosperity of the state depended upon their welfare to a very great extent. The main occupation of the Sudras was to work as agricultural labour, render military service and take recourse into handicrafts. Several classes of people following diverse professions were included in the Sudra caste. They were known as *Ashtadasavarnas* (18 *Jatis*). *Pratapacharita*[16] gives us a detailed list of the houses of the *Ashtadasavarnas* profession-wise.

1. Visvakarmalu (Gold-smiths)
2. Gollalu (Shepherds)
3. Kapulu
4. Edugula (Toddy man)

5. Siva Brahmins (Tamballas)
6. Kummara (Potter)
7. Sale (Weaver)
8. Padmasale (a clan in weavers)
9. Medara (Bamboo workers)
10. Chittaruvu Vrasevaru (Painters)
11. Uppara (the mining caste, who dig tanks & wells)
12. Mera (the measuring caste)
13. Besta (Fisherman)
14. Tenugu
15. Bukka (Perfumers)
16. Sangara
17. Rajakulu (Washermen)
18. Vesyas.

The Sudra community was divided into a number of clans. Occupations and territorial divisions were the main factors deciding the sub-division among them. Kamma and Telaga are example of caste groups formed on a territorial basis, while Velama, Balija, Virabalija and Reddi are the example of such occupational groups. The Tamballas, who officiated as priests in temples of Siva, were classified as the Sudras. They used to bring leaves for the choultries attached to the temples. It is said that the Tamballas of Rayalaseema area bring flowers and betel-leaves on auspicious occasions.[17] This is a remarkable age in the history of the Sudras for they gave up the plough for the sword and rose to the high position in the service of the state. All most all the states that had come into existence during this period were founded by the members of the fourth caste.

Chandalas

Chandala is an out caste, a person of the lowest of the mixed tribes; particularly one born of a Sudra father and a Brahmin mother. Persons guilty of bad conduct were supposed to have been reborn in the womb of a dog, swine and Chandala.[18] Whatever be the origin of the Chandala, they have all along been the victims of Hindus social tyranny. The area in which they lived was called Velipalam.[19] This is used to be on the outskirts of the village. The Chandalas were divided into two groups viz. (i) the *Mala* and (ii) the *Madiga*. The Malas constituted the bulk of agriculture labourers. Shoe making was the legitimate trade of the *Madigas.* They also supplied the cultivator with ropes, leather-buckets etc. needed to carry on agricultural operations.

Unfortunately all the social customs were strictly enforced against the Chandalas to keep them degraded with no self-respect. Chandalas as a rule were not allowed to use the water of general tanks of the villages and towns. They were rarely allowed to enter the residential localities of the high castes. *Sivaratrimahatyam*[20] reveal the agonies of a Brahmin who married a Chandala woman. Unable to face the rigorous opposition of the society, the newly married couple led their lives in great secrecy. However, we find some liberal tendencies shown towards the Chandalas during this period. The Malkapuram inscription[21] dated 1261 A.D. states that Vishweswara Sivacharya established a *matha* called *Golaki Matha*, to which a *choultry* was attached for feeding all people from the Brahmins to the Chandalas.

The contemporary literary work, *Rukmangadacharitra,*[22] says that it was a pious and meritorious act to provide Chandalas with food. Both the Saivite and Vaishnavite religions took the Chandalas into their regular fold and made them enjoy equal status with others. Brahmanayudu, a Vaishnavite and the minister of the king Mallideva adopted a Chandala by name Kannama as his son and elevated him to the rank of the commander in the army of his master.[23] Virasaivism preached spiritual equality of all classes of the society including that of the Chandalas.

The above discussion shows that the traditional caste system was in operation in medieval times. The society was hierarchical and did not mark with any drastic change in the system so far social structure and professions were concerned. However, there was occasional mobility of the people within and outside the caste system.

Notes & References

1. *Nellore District Inscriptions*, Part-I, No.15.
2. R. Narasimha Rao, *Life in Medieval Andhradesa: 1000-1450 A.D.*, (Unpublished) Thesis, Osmania University, 1956, pp. 163-164.
3. Pillalamarri Pinavirabhadra, *Sringara Sakuntalam,* I, v.76; Srinatha, *Kasikhandam,* III, v.80.
4. Gangadevi, *Madhuravijayam*, IV, v.19.
5. Vinukonda Vallabharaya, *Kridabhiramam*, published by V. Prabhakara Sastry, Hyderabad, 1960, vv.4, 17, 20 & 33.
6. Annual Report on Indian Epigraphy, 1940-41, No.18.
7. Vinukonda Vallabharaya, *Op.Cit.,* v. 245.
8. Srinatha, *Kasikhandam*, VII, vv. 250-252.
9. Srinatha, *Sivaratrimahatyam*, II, v. 102.
10. Elliot and Dowson, *History of India as told by its own Historians,* Vol. IV, p. 103.
11. *South Indian Inscriptions,* Vol. IV, No.1014 & Vol. X, No. 373.
12. *A Corpus of Telangana Inscriptions*, Part-II, No.55.

13. Srinatha, *Haravilasam,* Preface, v. 20.
14. *Nellore District Inscriptions,* Part-II, No. 54.
15. Mancana, *Keyurbahucharitra,* II, v. 201.
16. Ekamranatha, *Pratapacharitra*, p. 54.
17. S. Pratapa Reddy, *Andhrula Samghikacharitra*, Hyderabad, 1950, p. 207.
18. Margaret and J. Stutley, *A Dictionary of Hinduism*, Bombay, 1977, p. 59.
19. Vinukonda Vallabharaya, *Op.Cit.*, v. 67.
20. Srinatha, *Sivaratrimahatyam,* III, vv. 83-89.
21. *South Indian Inscriptions*, X, No. 395.
22. Mallana, *Rukmangadacharitra,* II, v.77.
23. R. Narasimha Rao, *Op.Cit.*, p. 183.

3

DEPENDENT COMMUNITIES

The Indian society, composed of distinct groups of people with each dependent on others, is a complicate social organisation. The original Varna system with four fold division, in course of time, divided into castes and sub-castes distinct from each other, and at the same time complimentary to each other. The various castes in India developed a complex and complicate social structure. What distinguishes Hindu society from others is its intricate and inter-dependent units called castes. The castes, with increasing specialization, each group confined itself to a particular activity that crystallized into a definite sub-caste. Thus, the society during this period was divided into various castes and sub-castes.

One remarkable feature of this period is the emergence of several groups of entertainers and dependent communities. They led a semi-nomadic life and depended for their livelihood on the other castes. They used to sing and praise the family histories and *prasasti* of certain castes and sub-castes, besides entertaining the people. The interaction of social and economic factors culminated into more concentration of wealth during this period. It indirectly promoted the rise of dependent communities. The most unique feature of the society under review is that the dependents too became highly prosperous and made donations for the cause of religion. Some of these communities like Vipravinodis, Dommaras and Viramushtis flourished into a prosperous class, some others like Pichchikuntlu, Bavanilu, Rumjalu, Kommulu etc., remained poor.

Vipravinodis

The most important semi-nomadic tribe which rose to significance during this period were the Vipravinodis. They were one of the major dependent communities. They earned their living by entertaining a particular caste, which they are attached. The Vipravinodis were attached to the Brahmins. They entertained them by displaying various acrobatic feats, in return receiving contributions known as "*Tyagavartanalu*". There are different of opinions regarding their origin. Some evidence makes them Brahmins who took up jugglery as an occupation. Others point out their Sudra origin. Mr. Brown explained them as a class of "Brahmin Jugglers", where as in the Ganjam and Vishakapatnam districts, the Vipravinodis are Sudras and Brahmins.[1]

On the basis of epigraphical evidence it can be safely concluded that the Vipravinodis were a section of Brahmins. They were forced by circumstances or poverty to take up an occupation for their survival, which was considered despicable and assigned to the lowest strata of society. Inspite of their economic and social degeneracy, they seem to have not forgotten their proud lineage. Hence, they entertained and received alms only from their brethren. An epigraph dated 1554 A.D. for example, records that the Vipravinodis and jugglers of the place gave their local allowance from the Brahmins to God Chennakesava.[2] A record from Chamaluru in Cuddapah district recorded in the *Chamaluru grama Kaifiyat* refers to them directly as Vipravinodi Brahmins.[3]

Infact that like the Brahmins, the Vipravinodis too had Gotras and belonged to various Sakhas and Sutras. It supports the view that the Vipravinodis were originally Brahmins. The inscriptions of the period, for instance, refer to Vipravinodis of Kasyapa Gotra,[4] Bharadvaja Gotra,[5] Vasishtha Gotra,[6] and Srivatsa Gotras[7] belonging to Katyayana,[8] Apastambha[9] and Asvalayana Sutras[10] well-versed in various Vedas, especially Atharva[11] and Yajur Vedas[12] also Rig Veda.[13] But there are no references to say that Vipravinodis belonged to Sama Veda. Perhaps the Vipravinodis gave more importance to Atharvana Veda as its contents directly helped them in their profession by preaching magic and Tantricism. In an inscription dated 1544-1545 A.D., the Vipravinodis claim to have belonged to Atharvana Veda and call themselves "Aruvela-Telungalu" or 6000 Telungas.[14] The fact that the profession of Vipravinodis was similar to that of Dommaras, jugglers and acrobats is proved by an inscription which was issued jointed by them reflecting their occupational association. An epigraph dated 1554 A.D. records that Vipravinodis and jugglers of the place gave their local allowances from the Brahmins to god Chennakeshava.[15]

The religious leanings of the Vipravinodis are known from the inscriptions they issued. Majority of the donations made by them were to God Vishnu. Their names also show that they were in general Vaishnavites. The names of Kesavayya, Govindayya, Vallabhayya, Madhavayya etc., all associated with Vishnu prove the point. However, some of them had Saivaite inclinations also.[16] The inscriptions of the period furnish us with the information about the contributions they received from the Brahmins. An inscription[17] from Gorajapuram Agrahara mentions their Vartana as one Mada per annum. Their Vartanas also seem to have included various commodities as the inscription[18] from Kalamalla mentions food, Tambula, clothes, ornaments, sandal, flowers, utensils, vehicles etc., donated to Vipravinodis. The Vipravinodis became prosperous enough to make donations. An inscription[19] dated 1553 A.D. records that Vipravinodis granted their local allowance to the deity Gopinatha. Like-wise the Vipravinodis of Kasinepalle donated their income to Lord Tiruvengalanatha.[20]

Many donations made by the Vipravinodis reveal to us about their prosperity. The improvement in their economic position might have made them to aspire for a better social position. Thus, along with few other communities like barbers, artisans, etc., a rise in social consciousness was manifest among the Vipravinodis. The Vipravinodis appears to have been organised under a head, as most of the inscriptions contain the name of a particular person, who makes donations on behalf of the community. An epigraph[21] dated 1554 A.D. issued during the reign of Sadasivaraya, records that Bolanamantri Parvadayya granted the taxes of Vipravinodis in the village to God Panduranga.

Viramushtis

The Viramushtis were an important community of medieval Andhra. They depended on some particular castes for their survival. The word Viramushtis is derived from Sanskrit 'Vir' warrior and 'Mushti' fist, and is said to refer to the proficiency of their ancestors in boxing.[22] They are professional acrobats and mendicants attached to Devangas and Komatis. The legend tells us that when Lord Siva cursed the Viramushtis for having killed a devout Viramushti named Chikkayya on suspicion, the Devangas took compassion of them and promised to give them a small sum of money annually and give towards their marriage expenses. The Viramushtis earned their living by displaying acrobatic feats. The amount collected by the Viramushtis as their Vartana or allowance seems to have been three Gadyanas per annum. An inscription[23] dated 1549 A.D. for example, records the gift of three Gadyanas per annum derived as *Virmushtipannu* for conducting offerings and monthly festival to the gods Vireshwara of Narasimhapuram Agrahara, the other name of Bedaduru and Rameshwara of Gari by certain Puranatakas (Viramushtis).

The Viramushtis were the followers of Saivism and made considerable grants to the temples of Siva. An inscription[24] dated 1551 A.D. records the gift of *Viramushti-pannu* for the lamps to the god Someshvaradeva of Mudiyam alias Trilochanapuram in Renati Sima of Gandikota Rajya by Chenna Basavayya, son of Bhumayya and disciple of Bhikshavritti-ayyavaru. An inscription[25] of the reign of Sadasiva, for instance, records that the Viramushtis of Bandalakunta donated the tax due to them from the place to Lord Visveshwara of Srishaila. There are several contemporary inscriptions which throw light on the donations made by the Viramushtis to temples.

The Viramushtis appear to have had a chief pontiff for their sect. He levied taxes on the members of the community and spent that amount on social and spiritual welfare of the community. An inscription[26] dated 1551 A.D. records the gift of income derived as *Viramushtipannu* to the Ganachari named Virayya serving the God Mukti Rameshwara by the ascetic Virasaiva Bhikshavritti (who must have been the chief pontiff of the sect). The reference to Ganacharis also throws light on the other profession of the Viramushtis, that of religious mendicancy, besides jugglery.

Dommaras

The Dommaras are a tribe of tumblers, athletes, and mountebanks, some of whom wander about the country, while others have settled down as agricultural labourers, or make combs out of the wood and horn. Their name may possibly be connected with the Doms of North India.[27] The etymology of their name is obscure. It is said to be derived from the words "Dimari" and "Dulmar", but their meanings are uncertain.[28]

Thus, the Dommaras earned their livelihood by the performance of acrobatic feats by moving place to place. The Dommaras are tall and well-made, varying in complexion from white colour to very dark. The Dommaras performed various dangerous feats like walling on ropes and climbing on the top of the bamboo sticks without any support. A great extent of the hazard was involved in performing these feats. The women of the community also seem to have performed the acrobatic feats. They were known as "Goraga-yuvatulu". By bending on their back they picked-up the nose-stud from water and put it on their nose. They also displayed their keen sight and steadfast action by picking up very small black-beads scattered over the ground and arranging it in the form of a string.[29]

As a reward for their entertainment the people seem to have gifted them abundantly in cash and kind. The tax which the Dommaras collected from a village was known as *Dommaripannu*. It was collected annually and also known as *Tyaga Vartana*. The Vartanalu that were collected by them were high. So, Dommaras of various places donated their Vartanalu to several temples to acquire religious merit for their community. An inscription dated 1553 A.D. records the gift of *Dommaripannu* to the gods Hari and Hara of Valluru renamed as Timmasamudramu Agrahara near Pushpagiri in Gandikotasima of Udayagiri rajya by Kaki Padmaraju, Misarigandani Pammareddi, Tippiraju, Turukanyam Basavaraju and Vodipotinayudu all belonging to Dommari caste.[30] The Dommaras appears to have been divided into twenty four seats. An inscription[31] dated 1527 A.D. records the gift of *Dommaripannu* to the god by the Dommaris in the village of Tippaluru for the merit of the king and twenty-four castes of Dommaris. The Dommaras seems to have accepted the authority of a person of their own community as their head. The head was empowered to gift the taxes that were due to the whole community.

An inscription[32] dated 1589 A.D. records the gift of *Dommari-pannu* for burning tiruvalike (perpetual lamp) to the gods Chennakesava and Sakalanathalinga of Kokadam-Agrahara in the Gandikotasima by Saluva Misaraganda for the merit of his community. Sometimes the gifts were made jointly by the members of the Dommara community. The Dommaras were the followers of both Saivism and Vaishnavism. Most of the gifts were made by them to Vaishnavaite temples, especially to god Chennakesava. However, some of them professed Saivism. At present the Dommaras in Telangana are living in poor conditions. Men in the community are lazy and depend on women earnings. They are not bothered how women are earning. They are happy if women provide money for their entertainments. So, most of the Dommara women are patronizing commercial sex activities.

Pichchigunta

The name Pichchigunta means literally an assembly of beggars, who are described as being, in the Telugu country, a class of mendicants, who are herbalists, and physic people for fever, stomachache, and other ailments.[33] They beg only from Kapus and Gollas by reciting their Gotras and family history of which they are believed to be the custodians.

The Pichchiguntas were beggars who were usually handicapped. Palkurki Somanatha[34] refers to the Pichchigunta who begged alms by singing that they have no hands to work, no legs to walk and no eyes to watch and thus, sought alms from the well-to-do. The fact that Pichchigunta were handicapped is also proved by the account of Koravi Goparaju in his *Simhasanadvatrimsika*.[35] The author says that aspiring to climb the throne of Vikramarka, without courage, valour, fortitude, truth and honesty is like a Pichchigunta, who is without legs, hands and eyes aspiring to climb a mountain.

Bavanis

Among the Madigas there are 25 sub-castes. The Bavanis are one of them. Bavani-eedu = Bavaneedu, which means a person who sings songs and goes around during the village festivals (Jataras). Bavanis (Pambalavaru) were the worshippers in the village temples of Ellamma, Maisamma, Pochamma and Balamma. They were named after their musical instrument called Jamidika, Javanika and Pamba. It is said in *Kridabhiramam*[36] that the chief of the Bavanis stood before the temple of Goddess, Ekavira and sang the stories of Parasurama. They go for begging reciting the stories of Goddess Ellamma and Pochamma in the present Telangana area.

The Bavanis are spread across the entire state of Andhra Pradesh. However, regional variations in their religious practices and life styles could be found. In the Telangana districts the Bavanis lead their lives from the gifts they get from the Madigas at the time of marriages. They are experts in charms and demon worship. They act as Magicians and perform magic spells. They ward off ghosts and drive away evil spirits. During village fairs (Jataras) they tour the villages, narrate stories in the nights and collect alms in the morning.[37]

Bhatrajus

Bhatrajus were another important caste of bards of the period under review. They seem to have been a mixed caste of Brahmins and Velamas. The legends connected with their origin reveal us that the caste made its appearance when Prataparudra of the Kakatiya kingdom was ruling the land. Prataparudra, who had special inclination towards the Velamas, offered asylum to the fugitives of this caste and conferred them high positions. But the Brahmins had doubts about their origin. So, they showed less interest in performing any religious ceremonies in the houses of the Velamas. The Velamas then appealed to Prataparudra, who attracted the Brahmins with various incentives that made some of the Brahmins to accept work in the religious ceremonies of the Velamas. However, the orthodox Brahmins still considered it as irreligious and boycotted those who worked in the Velama houses. The boycotted Brahmins, left with no alternative, had to go for marriage alliances with the women of lower castes. Thus, denied of a better position they took up the occupation of singing songs glorifying certain castes like the Velamas and Kapus. Thus, the Bhatrajus emerged during the medieval Andhra Desa. They seem to have had the honour of visiting the imperial courts like the Kakatiyas of Warangal and the Vijayanagara empire and sang songs in the glory of these respective kings.[38]

Bud-Budkevaru

It is a community of beggars. They wander from place to place begging alms in summer and return to their homes in the rainy season. The nomenclature "Budbudke" is derived from (bud-bud) gurgle like sound of Daphada (a sort of drum), which they beat while asking for alms. They are both Hindus and Muslims.[39]

Dichchulu

An important sect of this community were "Dichchulu". They appear to have been a prosperous caste. A Telugu contemporary work, *Simhasanadvatrimsika*,[40] describes a person belonging to this caste to have come along with his servants after decorating himself with sandal and wearing fashionable foot-wear.

Rumjalu

The name "Rumjalu" was derived from the instrument they played. They earned their livelihood by playing this instrument. A reference to this community is found in the contemporary Telugu works such as *Kridabhiramam* and *Palanativira Charitra*.

Thus, the dependent communities of medieval Andhra as the professional conjurers earned their livelihood by collecting contributions both in cash and kind from other castes. They became remarkably prominent by virtue of their activities and attracted the people of those days. The dependent communities, inspite of themselves being dependents were in a position to donate to temples reveals their prosperous condition.

Notes & References

1. *Annual Reports on Indian Epigraphy*, (hereafter A.R.E.), 1911-14, No. 961, 2nd August, 1913, p. 60.

2. V. Rangachari, *Topographical List of Inscriptions from the Madras Presidency*, Vol. II, No. 396, p.947; Inscriptions of Ceded Districts, No. 101.
3. *Chamalurugrama Kaifiyat*, Vol. 99, pp.72-73.
4. *South Indian Inscriptions* (hereafter S.I.I.), Vo. XVI, Nos. 156, 182, 186, 196, 203 & 209.
5. *Ibid.*, Nos. 203, 215 & 243.
6. *Ibid.*, Nos. 195, 209 & 215.
7. *Ibid.*, Nos. 156 & 190.
8. *Ibid.*, Nos. 182, 186, 195 & 203.
9. *Ibid.*, Nos. 215 & 293.
10. *Ibid.*, Nos. 215 & 243.
11. *A.R.E.*, 1959-1960, B. 14.
12. *S.I.I.*, Vol. XVI, Nos. 156, 182, 195, 203, 215 & 227.
13. V. Rangachari, *Op.Cit.*, Vol. I, Cuddapah, No. 66 of 1977.
14. *A.R.E.*, 1959-1960, B. 14.
15. V. Rangachari, *Op.Cit.*, No. 396, p. 947.
16. N. Vanisri, *Society in Medieval Andhra 1300-1600*, Ph.D. Thesis (unpublished), Department of History, Osmania University, Hyderabad, p.121.
17. *S.I.I.*, Vol. XVI, No. 203.
18. *Ibid.*, No. 176.
19. V. Rangachari, *Op.Cit.*, Vol. II, No. 216, p.926; Inscriptions of Ceded Districts, No. 37.
20. *Inscriptions of Andhra Pradesh, Cuddapah*, No. 238.
21. V. Rangachari, *Op.Cit.*, Vol. II, No. 216; Inscriptions of Ceded Districts, No. 37.
22. Syed Siraj-ul-Hassan, *The Castes and Tribes of H.E.H., The Nizam's Dominions*, New Delhi, 1989, p.641.
23. N. Vanisri, *Op.Cit.*, p. 130.
24. *Ibid.*, 224, No. 40 of 1960.

25. *Bandalakunta Kaifiyat*, p.284.
26. *Inscriptions of Andhra Pradesh, Cuddapah*, 217, No. 280 of 1967.
27. Edgar Thurston & K. Rangachari, *Caste and Tribes of Southern India*, Vol. II, New Delhi, 1993, p.185.
28. Syed Siraj-ul-Hassan, *Op.Cit.*, p.178.
29. N. Vanisri, *Op.Cit.*, pp.122-123.
30. *Inscriptions of Andhra Pradesh, Cuddapah*, 228, No. 61 of 1967.
31. *Ibid.*, 95, No. 252 of 1967.
32. *Ibid.*, Vol. I, 128, No. 266 of 1967.
33. Edgar Thurston & K. Rangachari, *Op.Cit.*, Vol. IV, p.195.
34. Palkurki Somanatha, *Panditaradhya Charitra*, Vol. II, p.348.
35. Koravi Goparaju, *Simhasanadvatrimsika*, IV, V, 162.
36. Vinukonda Vallabharaya, *Kridabhiramam*, published by V. Prabhakara Sastry, Hyderabad, 1960, v. 30.
37. Ch. Yadaiah, *Janapada Vignanamlo Bavanilu Oka Parishilana*, Hyderabad, 1990, pp. 32-35.
38. N. Vanisri, *Op.Cit.*, pp. 132-33.
39. Syed Siraj-ul-Hassan, *Op.Cit.*, p. 134.
40. Koravi Goparaju, *Op.Cit.*, X, pp. 83-84.

4

POSITION OF WOMEN

The status accorded to women in the early texts[1] is of a high order, almost equal to that of man in the family. Later, since the days of Manu, Hindu law has assigned to woman a dependent but by no means dishonourable position in society. In medieval times we find the situation with regard to the status and rights of the woman greatly changing not for the better but to her disadvantage. There are also exceptions in regard to the general attitude displayed towards women. Under the exceptions come the ladies, who played a distinguished role in the affairs of the state and society – Palanadu Nayakuralu distinguished herself as a minister of the king Nalagamaraju,[2] queen Rudrama who ruled the Kakatiya kingdom and whose conspicuous success won the admiration of the contemporary Venetian traveller Marcopolo.[3]

The position of women during the period under review registered a decline from her earlier status. Polygamy was prevalent. Concubinage and prostitution have become matters of common knowledge. Thus, from the high pedestal of being the sole queen of her house, woman has to share her position with others. Women may be classified into two classes, the family women (*Kulastrees)* and the courtesans (*Vesyas)*.

Kulastree

The family woman, to whichever community she might belong, was under the control of her husband. A Kulastree was expected to be a maid while serving, a lover while entertaining, a minister while advising and a mother while serving food.[4] For the services obtained from his wife, the husband must honour his wife. Where the woman was subjected to suffering making her cry and shed tears, it was believed that Goddess Lakshmi refuses to reside.[5] The family women of higher class rarely come out. When they did come out, it was generally in the company of their relations. The contemporary works reveal that she was taught to believe her husband as God and a saviour without whom she had no business to exist. [6] It was this belief that was at the root of Satisahagamana, one of the cruel customs of the age.

There was some change from the extreme dependence of women on men in the Vira Saiva society. This society came into existence as a consequence of militant Saivism. Interestingly, the Vira Saiva teachers proclaimed that women had a right to ignore their husbands if the latter did not believe in the supremacy of Lord Siva and also in Linga worship. Further, if the wife fails in bringing her husband round to her religious beliefs, she might abandon him. Infact, the general dependence of women on men did not become an obstacle in the way of women making religious endowments in their own names. The contemporary sources throw a flood of light on women of different castes and of various ranks making endowments either to temples, choultries or other works of public utility and to Brahmins. The blessings of the mother on all occasions were sought. For example, in *Palanativira Charitra*, Balachandra goes to his mother to seek her blessings before going to the battle field.

One important aspect was that the codes of ancient and medieval writers contained provision for entertaining women in Royal service, agriculture and industry. There were women advisers to kings. For instance, Nayakuralu, who by her talent for intrigue, state-craft and organisation became virtually the ruler of Palanadu. There were some women, who were trained to become rulers. In the Kakatiya dynasty Rudramadevi, the eldest daughter of king Ganapatideva, during the life time of her father received training both in administration and art of fighting. She and her younger sister Ganapamba were endowed with exceptional abilities. Rudramadevi fought many wars bravely and also promoted the welfare of the people. It was during her reign that the Venetian traveller Marco Polo visited Andhra country and made his observations on the flourishing state of trade and prosperity of the country. Kakati Ganapamba ably carried on the administration of the 'Six-thousand country' in the absence of her husband Beta. After the death of her husband in about 1253 A. D., she ruled the principality for forty years as its undisputed ruler.

The ordinary family women led a simple life. They could move about freely without any restrictions. They used to bring drinking water in pots from outside. [7] The Kapu women prepared cakes of dung infront of their houses. [8] Srinatha mentions in one of his famous Chatus that he saw a Kasalnati beauty near bathing place. [9] He also refers to a Balija woman[10] (a woman of trading community), Sale woman[11] (a woman of weavers' community), Machekanti[12] (a woman of fishermen community) and others who were going freely in the streets. We do not find the practice of Sati among them. They could remarry another man after the death of their spouse. Thus, there appears a definite difference in the customs and life of the family women of different classes.

Education

Girls were given education by their parents from childhood. Practically no attention was paid to the formal education of women. The women who belonged to the Royal families or other aristocratic families and those belonged to the class of courtesans and prostitutes received formal education. The girls of those days learnt dancing, music, drawing and painting, making dolls and images of mud, ivory and glass, stringing of rosaries and garlands, cooking and preparation of drinks. Music and dance played a very important role in their educational curriculum. The beautiful dances of seven sisters find mention in *Kridabhiramam*.[13] The girl of the courtesan classes was well-educated. Several acquired a very sound knowledge of the Sanskrit and the Vernacular literature. A reputed courtesan, Machaldevi, participated in the intellectual debates at the court of king Prataparudra-II.[14] Some courtesans were adepts in music and dance. Lakumadevi, the concubine of Kumaragiri Reddi, was a renowned danseuse.

Marriage

Marriage was an important event in the social life of any people. Marriages in those days were arranged by parents and elders. If the choice was made by the girl, the consent of the father was absolutely essential. Interestingly, sometimes marriages among the ruling classes were arranged by parents on political grounds. The Raja of Tsandavolu was defeated by Anugu Raju in a war. So, he gave his daughter Mailamadevi in marriage to Anugu Raju to strengthen the relations between them. During this period marriages were celebrated with great pomp and show. On marriage occasion abundant money was spent and many guests were invited and entertained for several days. Generally, marriage was performed in the house of the bride's parents. During medieval period it was believed that the meritorious deeds performed in the previous birth ensured a good husband. A woman was not supposed to raise her voice against her husband inspite of his misbehaviour. Further, a woman was expected to be highly devout to her husband than to God. Inspite of the cruel behaviour of her husband, she was expected to live under his protection. In order to ensure the long-life and development of her husband, a woman was required to do several deeds such as constantly adorning herself with turmeric, *tilak* and flowers. Women of those days were rarely unfaithful to their husbands.

The contemporary work, *Simhasandvathrimsika*[15] refers to a marriage among Brahmins, where the bride was only eight years old. By this period, several social changes appeared due to the conquest of the country by the Muslims. Perhaps child marriage might have become a necessity in the changed circumstances. *Kridhabhiramam*[16] describes the romantic antics of young widows in connection with the celebrations of the annual festival of Sri Maha Vishnu of Srikakulam and the beautiful Brahmin widows of Orugallu city. This information raises the legitimate question whether woman of higher classes were ever allowed to remarry after the death of their husbands. Enforced widowhood obviously led to such immoral practices as depicted in our source. It is thus clear that moral rules unrelated to nature and age resulted in social evils.

Sati

The cruel custom of 'Sati' was widely prevalent in medieval India. This was the expression of the idea that woman had no independent existence except as the wife of some man. So, her only duty as a wife was to make her husband's life happy both here and hereafter. This evil practice found place in the soil of medieval Andhra Desa. Woman chastity became main reason of honour of the families and they saw to it that it was preserved and maintained at all costs. Further, it was believed that a woman should not live on the demise of her husband. A reading of works[17] like *Palanativira Charitra* and *Kasikhandam* makes this very clear. Regarding this custom Friar Odoric says "when any man dies, they burn him, and if he leaves a wife they burn her alive with him, saying that she ought to go and keep her husband's company in the other world".[18] In *Palanativira Charitra* it is mentioned that Ratnala Peramma, the daughter of Nalagamaraju and wife of Rachamallu gained the Amaraloka by performing Sati. Some of the women of those days proceeded to the funeral pyre joyfully and laid themselves on the pyre as if they were sleeping on the bed. The institution of Sati appears to have been exclusively practised with vigour by the royalty. Yet there were some instances, where the commoners followed the examples of their rulers and performed Sati. Most of the foreign travellers, who visited medieval Telangana and Andhra, described vividly the institution of Sati in their accounts.

Occupation of Women

Women belonging to the higher classes led their life by attending to the house-hold duties. They never took up any profession. But poor women of any class were compelled by economic necessity to take to some professions. The women of low castes undertook the professions prescribed for their castes. There were women who belonged to the caste of 'Medars'. They skillfully wove cane baskets and mats. They resided in a separate locality called 'Medaravada'.[19] In 'Mailasanta' (a fair meant for the lower class people) a sales woman was selling a medicine called '*Susarabheth*'.[20]

Selling of flowers was one of the professions followed by women in those days. These women were known as 'Pushpalavikalu',[21] (flower girls). *Srungara Sakuntalam*[22] refers to jester women among the flowergirls. They had several ways of attracting buyers. Women, belonging to Telika caste, took to the profession of manufacturing and sale of oils. They prepared oil from the 'Sampangi' flowers. Oils thus extracted were sold in the streets by these women themselves.[23] In one of his Chatu verses, Srinatha makes mention of a woman shop keeper selling betel leaves.[24] In Palanati Sima even beautiful women, we are told, were in the habit of weaving yarn.[25]

Some women established inns known as 'Putakuti Illu', where they served food for money to the travellers. Most of these inns were run by the Brahmin widows. [26] In temples the pounding of paddy and removing leaves were undertaken by women. [27] Apart from these women, some ladies were entertained in royal service. *Srungara Sakuntalam*[28] mentions that the king was attended by maid servants, when he sat on the throne. They were attentively serving him with fans, perfumes and betel leaf box. The other women who were employed as guards to the queen's palace are referred to in *Palanativira Charitra*. [29] Ofcourse, the number of women working in royal palaces must have been small in number. Needy women can be employed in royal establishments and other professional establishments. It was a well recognized principle approved even by our ancient seers like Manu and Sukra.

Courtesans

The courtesans were well known members of the society. They may be divided into two categories: (1) Those who were attached to temples and royal courts, (2) those who lived independently. To whichever class the courtesans might belong, she plied the trade of her class quite regularly. Prostitution was open for women of all castes. *Kridabhiramam* and other contemporary sources refer to the Vesyas of all categories – Medarakarana Vesya,[30] Tamballa Vesya,[31] Karnataka Vesya,[32] Vaisya Vesya,[33] Brahmin Vesya[34] and Satani Vesya. It is clear that courtesans were a professional group in which women of all castes were found. The contemporary sources refer to Devadasis that were attached to the temples. Everyday they had to sing and dance before the deity during the time of worship and these courtesans were highly honoured. Some of them were taken as wives or concubines by kings and nobles.[35]

The section of courtesans who lived independently were known by various names such as Vesya, Sanulu and Varakantalu. A small section of these Vesyas were rich and learned. They were patronized by kings, nobles and rich citizens. *Kridabhiramam* mentions one Macheldevi, who was a prominent figure in the Gosthis at the court of Kakatiya monarch Prataparudra-II. There is no direct evidence to point out whether the lady was the concubine of Prataparudra-II, or not, though some scholars have written to that effect. A lady of this class by name Kamamanjari was patronised by certain Govinda Mancana Sarma.[36] An epigrapy[37] from Mogallu, dated S'

1237 (1315 A. D.) registers a gift of land of the fields belonging to the concubine of certain Pramadakavi Sirigiri Ayyangaru. Another inscription[38] dated S' 1359 (1437 A. D.) mentions a gift to that local temple by the Bhogastrilu of king Narasimhadeva. Some of the ruling monarchs and their vassals had the titles like 'Rayaveshya Bhujanga'[39] and 'Varavadhujana Pushpa Bhallulu'.[40] All these instances indicate that no one suffered social ignominy for maintaining concubines besides his legitimate wife.

The concubines lived in respectable localities, called Aryavatikas.[41] The majority of this class of women, ofcourse, were public prostitutes and lived in Vesyavatikas.[42] This custom of prostitutes living in a separate locality was in vogue since the times of Kautilya.[43] Abdur Razzak and Paes, who visited Vijayanagara Empire, observed that the ladies of this class lived in the best streets of city and were of very loose character. Their streets had the best rows of houses.[44] A Telugu work, *Pratapacharitra*[45] mentions that there were 1,27,000 Vesya houses in the city of Orugallu. Even though an element of exaggeration is there in this statement, it reveals that women of this class were substantially large in number. Perhaps the large number of this class of women in the city is accounted for by the fact that the military camps had Vesyavatikas.[46]

Among the Vesyas, there was the custom of Mukuradikshotsavam[47] (showing mirror) in those days. This ceremony relates to the initiation of a virgin into prostitution. It was celebrated on the full moon day in the month of Madhu (Chaitra). On that day all those belonging to their community were invited. The girl was seated on the lap of her father and was shown the mirror by him. The mirror was considered as 'Mahalakshmi' (wealth) by the prostitutes. The father used to recite some Mantra which indicated his blessings. These blessings conferred on her long life, grace, proficiency and wealth.

The visitors had to pay Rovattu[48] (money payment) to the Vesyas. So many were ruined by addiction to this vice. *Kridabhiramam* refers to Sridhara, who mortgaged 'Jonnagadda Agrahara' for two hundred rupees for the sake of the prostitute, Madalasa.[49] As the main aim of the Vesyas was to earn money, they used to attract and deceive men cunningly. On the contrary there were some visitors,[50] who avoided artfully the payments. When a Vesya grew old, she retired from the profession but she never deserted the business, which was highly profitable. She kept guard over her daughters to protect them from impecunious customers. '*Palanativira Charitra*'[51] gives a detailed description of the ugly mother of Balachandra's concubine, who extorted lots of money from him. One of the most reproached women of those days was courtesan's mother. During this period, there was prostitutes' court known as 'Jara Dharmasana'. A Dravida Brahmin went to the house of a prostitute in Orugallu. The mother of the Vesya showed her daughter to a Dravida Brahmin and received money payment, but afterwards she sent her servant maid dressed up as her daughter to him. He exposed the deceit of the mother in the prostitutes' court and it was decided that the punishment for Vesyamata was to chop off her nose and ears and pull out her teeth.[52] Thus, it is clear that during the period under review the prostitution was in a flourishing condition. No dishonour was shown to them and the society accommodated them by giving a place in the caste-hierarchy. The state too recognized the profession and levied professional- tax on them.

While it is true that there is a certain decline in the status of women, it is also a fact that in this age, for the first time, economic security was sought to be provided for the woman by the law maker. The gold ornaments and other costly presents by way of land and other materials given to a woman at the time of her marriage by her parents and husband were described as her property 'Stri-dhana', over which she was given exclusive rights. Even her husband, had no right to tamper with her 'Stri-dhana'. In this respect, this age certainly marks an improvement in the position of woman with regard to her rights.

Women in Muslim Society

Like any other medieval society, the society in medieval Telangana and Andhra was male dominated one. The social ethics were so fabricated as to undermine further the already declining position of women. About the position of women Fryer says that Hindu women moved freely, whereas the Muslims guarded their wives from the sight of others.

It was believed in the Muslim community, as in the Hindu community, that woman was to be subordinate to man. Even if she possessed of remarkable qualities, she was considered as inferior to man. Muhammad, the Prophet, did not look upon women as equal to men. The Muslim women in India were to be content with a lower status. The system of polygamy lowered the position of women still more. All efforts were made to maintain their chastity. They were even prepared to sacrifice their lives while defending their honour. A chaste woman was much honoured though she belonged to a lower class in society. Regarding the partition of the ancestral property among the children, the Muslim women received a good treatment as compared with the Hindu women. In the Muslim community, half of the share due to the brother went to his sister.

In medieval period the Purdah system became more acute. In Hindu society the traces of this system could be seen since the Epic Age, where by the ladies of royal families remained under seclusion. In medieval times, when the alien invaders cast their evil eyes on the Indian women, the Purdah system became essential to protect them. This system was more pronounced in Muslim society than Hindu society. The Purdah system was mainly followed by the women of royal house-hold. The common women could not adopt this system, as they have to perform other activities besides their domestic work, in order to support their families. The contemporary literary sources furnish us with information about such women engaged in their caste – professions which made them to mix freely with other people including men. The account of Thevenot reveals us the fact that Purdah was less rigid among the common women. He says that at the time of marriage, the bride-groom was obliged to promise the parents of the bride that he would allow her to move about freely in the town and visit her neighbours. [53] The Purdah system seems to have existed only among the royal ladies among the Hindus, and in case of Muslims it was strictly followed both by the common women and the upper class women.

Qutb Shahi women played a prominent role not only in the social and religious spheres but also in political field. They took keen interest in the welfare of their subjects and in religious matters. The important Qutb Shahi women are Bibi Khedija, Khanum Agha, Hayat Bakshi Begum, Khairatunis Begum, Kulthom Begum, Bade Bibi and Choti Bibi.[54] Bibi Khedija was believed to be the paternal aunt of Sultan Abdullah Qutb Shah. The Mosque at Khairatabad was built at the behest of Khairatunisa Begum, the daughter of Sultan Muhammad Qutb Shah, as a mark of respect for her tutor Akhund Mulk Abdul Malik. Kulthoom Begum, the grand-daughter of Muhammad Qutb Shah, built a nice mosque in Kulthoompura, which is in an excellent state of preservation. Khanum Agha, the mother of Muhammad Qutb Shah constructed a wonderful Ma-Saheba Tank (1624 A. D.). Khanum Agha was ever conscious of public good and always endeavouring for the comfortable life of the people. She is said to have wielded much power during her son's reign.

Hayat Bakshi Begum was the wife of Muhammad Qutb Shah. She was only daughter of the king Muhammad Quli. On the death of Sultan Muhammad, the state administration was carried by a Council of Regency during the minority of the boy king Abdullah Qutb Shah. The council worked under the sole guidance of the Sultan's mother, Hayat Bakshi Begum. She must have co-operated with her husband in handling the state affairs. She participated actively in the political life of the kingdom. As Abdullah was only 12 years boy at the time of accession, his mother Hayat Bakshi Begum administered the kingdom most efficiently. It was she who maintained law and order in the realm. A local historian speaks of her "as a woman with wits and shrewd understanding and sound reason, who handled state affairs on her own initiative and brooked no interference from any quarter". [55] In 1655 A. D. Aurangzeb invaded Golconda and plundered the city of Hyderabad. The early negotiations with Aurangzeb failed. When Hayat Bakshi Begum, the aged mother of Sultan, went to Aurangzeb with request, he accepted the peace terms in 1656 A. D. Hayat Bakshi Begum built a village, Hayat Nagar, which was then called Hayatabad. The Mosque at Hayatabad is a grand monument.

During the Qutb Shahi period, according to Tavernier, there were 20,000 prostitutes in the city and fort of

Golconda and men used to visit them without any inhibition.[56] Further, he says that at Gandikota the French gunners, who received their arrears of wages, spent "more than half" of their earnings on public women.[57]

Sarangu Tammayya, the author of *Vyjayanti Vilasamu*[58] describes how two prostitute sisters tried to entice a Brahmin youth, Vipranarayana. One of them Deva Devi, succeeds in her attempts and the youth falls into disrepute. But ultimately he was saved due to his faith in Vaishnavism. Before the Qutb Shahi period the State levied a professional tax on the prostitutes but the Qutb Shahis didn't collect any tax from them. Bhagmati was a great lady-love of Sultan Muhammad Quli Qutb Shah. Taramathi and Premamati were the favourite courtesans of Sultan Abdullah Qutb Shah.

Notes & References

1. A. S. Altekar, *The Position of Women in Hindu Civilization*, Delhi, 1973, pp. 9, 10, 49, 118, 197 & 214.
2. Srinatha, *Palanativira Charitra*, p. 50.
3. K. A. Nilakanta Sastry, *Foreign Notices of South India*, University of Madras, 1939, p. 174.
4. Baddena, *Sumati Shatakam,* v. 61.
5. *Ibid.,* v. 33.
6. Srinatha, *Kasikhandam*, II, vv. 71-92 and Pillalamarri Pinavirabhadra, *Srungara Shakuntalam*, IV, vv. 74-82.
7. Vinukonda Vallabharaya, *Kridabhiramam*, Published by V. Prabhakara Sastry, Hyderabad, 1960, v. 75.
8. *Ibid.,* v. 82.
9. V. Prabhakar Sastry, Compiled, *Chatupadymanimanjari*, Chennapuri, 1949, p. 124.
10. *Ibid.*, p. 130.

11. *Ibid.*, p. 133.
12. *Ibid.*, p. 134.
13. Vinukonda Vallabharaya, *Op. Cit.,* v. 138.
14. *Ibid.*, v. 180.
15. Koravi Goparaju, *Simhasanadvatrimsika*, II, VI, v. 74.
16. Vinukonda Vallabharaya, *Op. Cit.,* vv. 209-217.
17. Srinatha, *Palanativira Charitra*, p. 286 and *Kasikhandam*, V, vv. 169-170.
18. K. A. Nilakanta Sastry, *Op. Cit.,* p. 195.
19. Vinukonda Vallabharaya, *Op. Cit.,* vv. 67-72.
20. *Ibid.*, v. 77.
21. *Ibid.,* v. 173.
22. Pillalamarri Pinavirabhadra, *Op. Cit.,* I, v. 83.
23. Vinukonda Vallabharaya, *Op. Cit.,* vv. 101-104.
24. V. Prabhakara Sastry, *Op. Cit.,* p. 123.
25. *Ibid.*, p. 125.
26. Vinukonda Vallabharaya, *Op. Cit.,* vv. 166-172.
27. A. Vaidehi Krishna Murthy, *Social and Economic Conditions in Eastern Deccan (1000-1250 A. D.)*, Secunderabad, 1970, p. 64.
28. Pillalamarri Pinavirabhadra, *Op. Cit.,* I, v. 96.
29. Srinatha, *Palanativira Charitra,* p. 295.
30. Vinukonda Vallabharaya, *Op. Cit.,* v. 68.
31. *Ibid.*, v. 286.
32. *Ibid.*, v. 87.
33. *Ibid.*
34. Srinatha, *Palanativira Charitra,* p. 369.
35. *South Indian Inscriptions*, X, No. 151.
36. Vinukonda Vallabharaya, *Op. Cit.,* vv. 281-286.
37. *South Indian Inscriptions,* V, No. 510.

38. *Ibid.*, VI, No. 668.
39. Srinatha, *Kasikhandam,* Preface, v. 12.
40. Vinukonda Vallabharaya, *Op. Cit.,* v. 10.
41. *Ibid.*, v. 41.
42. *Ibid.*, v. 177.
43. M. Venkatarangaiah, *Kautilyuni Arthasastram,* Secunderabad, 1968, IV, p. 80.
44. T. V. Mahalingam, *Administration and Social Life under Vijayanagar*, Part-II, University of Madras, 1975, p. 44.
45. Ekamranatha, *Pratapacharitra*, p. 54.
46. Srinatha, *Palanativira Charitra*, p. 347.
47. Vinukonda Vallabharaya, *Op. Cit.,* vv. 194-197.
48. *Ibid.,* v. 240.
49. *Ibid.*, v. 245.
50. *Ibid.*, vv. 248-251.
51. Srinatha, *Palanativira Charitra*, pp. 402-406.
52. Vinukonda Vallabharaya, *Op. Cit.,* vv. 265-270.
53. Thevenot, *Indian Travels of Thevenot and Careri,* edited by Dr. Surendranath Sen, National Archives of India, New Delhi, 1949, p. 66.
54. K. Chandraiah, *Hyderabad 400 Glorious Years,* Hyderabad, 1996, p. 44.
55. *Ibid.,* p. 45.
56. Tavernier, *Travels in India by Jean-Baptiste Tavernier, Baron of Aubonne,* translated by Dr. V. Ball, edited by William Crooke, Vol. I, Oxford University Press, London, 1925, p. 128.
57. *Ibid.*, p. 231.
58. Sarangu Tammayya, *Vyjayanti Vilasam*, II, v. 75.

5

MATERIAL CULTURE

The material culture constitutes a significant aspect of human life. The study of society is incomplete without studying the material conditions as they reflect the living patterns of the people. The tastes, preferences and inclinations of the people form the core of human life. The material culture or the external culture is mostly reflected by the dietary habits, dressing designs, decorations and dwelling structures of the people. The material evidence in the form of artefacts like cloth, fabric, household goods, art and buildings etc., provide us with unique and exciting insights into the past and present cultures. The material culture reveals the variations in life-styles of the people belonging to different classes leading to cultural analysis. It is concerned with the intrinsic link between artefacts and social dynamics.

During the period under review, the material conditions of the people underwent a drastic change due to the influence of *Islam*. Almost all aspects of material life experienced a change because of the assimilation and understanding of the two religions. New items of food came into vogue - fruits like grapes and sweets like Jilebi under the influence of *Islam*. The *Hindus* adopted *Muslim Kullahs* as the head dress and coats known as

Mahakurpasam or *Qabas*. Similarly, the *Muslims* used the turbans of the *Hindus*. In the field of decoration also the mutual influence was felt. The *Muslims* were influenced by the ornamentation of the *Hindus*. Thus, an attempt is made in this research paper to portray the material culture of the people during the medieval times of Andha Desa.

The idea of social life may be said to be epicurean in medieval Andhra. The people particularly the upper classes were desirous of extracting maximum *bhoga* or enjoyment from life. They aimed at securing pleasures and cared little for the rest. However, they were not fully materialistic in their outlook on life but paid considerable attention to spiritual life also. *Bhogas* or pleasures of life were classified into eight kinds known as the *astabhogas*. They were habitation, dress, ornaments, perfumes, flowers, *tambula*, bed and women. The other kinds of *bhogas* may be added to the list viz. bath, food and drink.[1] The material culture of the people is well reflected in these aspects of life.

Diet

The dietary habits of the people varied accordingly to geographical, social, economic, religious and seasonal factors. However, rice constituted as the staple food of the people. *Kodrava* and *Vrihi* are the two varieties of paddy mentioned in inscriptions of early dynasties in Coastal Andhra. The contemporary literature furnishes the names of some varieties. Srinatha mentions in some of his works the various varieties of paddy like *kalama, Sali, Siramukha Sastika, patanga* and *hayana*. Varieties of *prasangu* and *rajanam* seem to be common. Another good variety of rice is *Kappurabogam*.[2] Paes said that rice, wheat, grains, Indian-corn, and a certain amount of barley and beans, moong, pulses, horse-gram, and many other seeds were the food of the people.[3]

The people of Coastal Andhra, where the land was very fertile subsisted on fine rice, whereas in Rayalaseema, where the land being infertile the people mainly used millets. Srinatha says that millets constituted the staple food – stuff of the people of Palanadu.[4] The rice grown in Tulunadu belonged to some varieties, which may be classified under two heads - the white rice and the black (red) rice. The former was superior and consumed by the well-to-do people. The Rayas and nobles ate the best kind of white rice known as *rajana*. The black rice was cheap and the poor used it extensively. All the people were not rice eaters. The Muslims ate wheat. The Reddis and perhaps other cultivating classes of the inland districts subsisted upon *cholam*, *ariga, ragi* etc.[5] *Amuktamalyada*[6] refers to the diet of Reddis that consisted of *Ambali* which seems to have been made with millets. It appears that green gram was in greater use in those days. Srinatha's works *Srungaranaishadam*[7] and *Haravilasam*[8] refer to its use. Use of turmeric, both in the form of powder and paste by women is noticed. During this period eating curd-rice with mango pickle was the favourite food of the people of Andhra Desa.[9]

The social position of the people denoted by the caste further determined the food habits of the people. Brahmins were strict vegetarians. They used to take simple food devoid of garlic and onion. When they visit the houses of other caste people, for the fear of pollution, they took only fruits and nuts.[10] Like Brahmins, the Vaisyas too were totally vegetarians and took simple food. On the other hand, the ruling class took a rich and delicious vegetarian and non- vegetarian food items. Nuniz furnishes with a curious list of food stuffs that constituted the dietary of the Vijayanagara kings. He says: "These kings of Bisnaga eat all sorts of things, but not the flesh of oxen or cows which they never kill in all the country of the heathen because they worship them. They eat mutton, pork, venison, partridges, hares, doves, quail and all kinds of birds, even sparrows and rats and cats and lizards, all of which are sold in the market of the city of Bisnaga".[11] Further, he said in another place that king Achyuta Raya had ten women cooks for his personal service who prepared food for no one except the king.[12] Even the Muslim rulers had highly rich and delicious food. The Sudras took meat with vegetables.

There is much difference between the food of the rich and that of the poor. The rich could afford to eat varied types of food, whereas the poor satisfied with the basic necessaries. Srinatha in one of his works gives a long list of the food items like Laddus, Idli, Kudumulu, Appadams, Dosa, Dalroti, Chakkilam, Arisalu, Payasam, Pickles, Vadiyalu, Anumulu, Minumulu, Chalimidi, milk, sugar, ghee etc.[13] The food of a poor man was *ganji*, a juice obtained from boiling rice. The better-off among them ate *chaldi* (rice mixed with curd). From tamarind, all the people irrespective of economic status prepared a favourite dish known as *pachchipulusu*.[14]

The food of the people varied according to seasons. The food in rainy season consisted of rice, dal, four types of curries, Vadiyams, a curry of dried vegetables, curd, ghee etc.[15] Butter-milk, Ambali, sweet Rasam, cane-juice, coconut-water, fruit-juice, sweet smelling water, ripe mangoes were the food items taken during summer. Butter-milk was more preferred in summer as it saves from the heat of the sun.[16] The food in winter season consisted of hot rice, curries made with pepper powder and pickles especially of mango.[17] The rich used to take fruits like mangoes, grapes, jack, plantains, cucumber etc., along with rice.[18]

Meat constituted as the favourite dish of the Muslims. Wheat was their staple food. Srinatha mentions that the Muslims even ate raw-meat.[19] They prepared with wheat - Parate, Phulka, Nan, Chapati, Reshmi Parate, Kulcha etc., with meat - Kabab, Seekh Kabab, Kufta Kabab, etc., Biryani and Palao appears their favourite dishes. They took happiness in eating sweets like Jilebi, Halva, Barfi, Khir, Peda etc. The poor Muslims took food with Jowar and rice.

The materials used for cooking food varied between the highest and lowest. The rich took their food in golden and silver utensils, while the poor used the leaves of bananas and areca palm. The Brahmins also took their food from leaves because of the fear of pollution by the other castes.[20] Besides meals the people seemed to have taken fruits. Hyderabad was famous for its grapes. According to Thevenot they were available in plenty during the months of February, March and April.[21]

Betel

It occupied a prominent place in the lives of people of those times. It helps in easy digestion. Abdul Razzak, who visited Vijayanagara court says "it relieves hunger, stimulates the organs of digestion, disinfects the breath and strengthens the teeth".[22] The habit of taking *tambulam* immediately after meals was quite common during this period. The betel leaf was considered not only as a luxury but also as a mild tonic, which helps for stimulating the digestive organs.[23] It was used for all ceremonial functions and it was the first thing offered to visitors.[24] Besides the hygienic purpose, it also had cultural significance. Interestingly it was served as a token of friendship, for mutual agreements and in marriage ceremonies.

During the Qutb Shahi period, Mir Jumla "ordered betel to be presented" when Tavernier, a French traveller, took leave from him after their first meeting.[25] A contemporary work, *Tutinama* refers to the use of betel among the Muslims. The *tambula* acquired a significant place in the social customs of medieval Andhra Desa. To receive *tambula* from the king was considered a special honour.[26] It was taken along with lime and arecanut.

Drinks

The common drink that was within the reach of all, of course, is water. The well-to-do particularly took in summer *panaka*, a beverage made of sugar and water, and *niru-majjiga* or watery-buttermilk.[27] The other liquors were Tala-madhuvu, Sura-rasam, Ikshavam and Varuni.[28] The Muslim rulers of Telangana and Andhra had a special liking for wine. They preferred strong wine of burning quality as they were capable of withstanding it. On certain festive occasions it was a custom among the *Muslims* to offer a drink made of creamy milk and ghee, garnered with dates, almonds and other condiments mixed with sugar called Shir-Kurma.[29] Thevenot, a French traveller, said that coffee and tea were favourite drinks of the people. The common beverage used by all people appears to be toddy. Thevenot said that toddy was copiously consumed by some men and women.[30]

Dress

Along with food and shelter, clothing is one of the three basic necessaries of life. Since the evolution of civilization man used something to cover his body, which also would protect the body from fury of heat and cold. In the beginning, man covered himself with leaves and hides of animals and later made clothes out of cotton, wool and silk. The aesthetic sense in man prompted him to find beautiful designs, colours and patterns. The people of medieval Telangana and Andhra during the period under review showed great interest in dressing and attract others. The alien Muslim culture added to the variety of dresses worn by the Hindus. An interaction between the Muslims and the Hindus contributed to a change in the dressing of the both.

There is ample information in the contemporary literature regarding the dress of all people manufactured from cotton, silk and wool. A Telugu work *Simhasanadvatrimsika,*[31] mentions not less than forty-two varieties of clothes plain, printed and dyed with different borders and colours and six sorts of silk cloth. The other works like *Haravilasam* and *Basavapuranam* also refer to many other varieties of cloth. It appears to have existed caste-wise and wealth-wise differences in the mode of dressing of the people. The people of those days liked coloured garments very much. The rich loved silk fabrics with borders of gold lace. They paid special attention to the texture of the cloth. The common folk had to be satisfied with cotton cloth only. The coarse cloth was worn by rude people or lower class people in the society. Generally, men wore Dovati and Uttariyam. Women wore *cira* (saree) and *raika* (badice). The sarees of the women of the cultivating class had on them squares and other designs printed in bright colours.[32] The Madiga women wore Chengavi saree or red saree in the form of a Kase round the loins and blue bodice.[33] The Brahmin women wore Kase, a long cloth around the loins and down to the ankles covering the upper part of the body by resting on the shoulders. The Sudras, who constituted the bulk of a common populace, wore Dhotis or Challadams and turbans. The use of shirts was limited during this period. The dress of Malas consisted of leather coats and Tekki or cap.[34]

The ruling class wore rich, beautiful and attractive dresses. Their dress was elaborate and exquisite. Paes says that Krishnadevaraya was dressed in "white clothes embroidered with many roses in gold".[35] The kings to display their grandeur never wore the dress which was once used by them. The dress of a Muslim consisted of long coats and turbans. The cultural interaction between the two communities, the Hindu and Muslim, led to the dovetailing of cultures and incidentally, to the similarity in apparel. The *Kuleh* (Persian kulah, cap) and the *cabaya* (Arab qaba, long coat) became the dress of elite, both Hindu and Muslim. Srinatha says in his Chatu verses that he wore Kulla and Mahakurpasanam (long-coat). The Gagra, a variety of garment must have been adopted from the Muslims. Among the Muslim women the dress was the Dopatta of about four and a half yards of cloth, one end of which was tucked on to the Paijama, which were embroidered and kept in check by girdles with embroidered ends.[36] The Qutb Shahi rulers wore the Hindu turbans and put on bracelets and other ornaments.

Foot-Wear

During the period under review, both men and women used sandals. The use of footwear was limited to the higher classes of the society. The common people moved about barefooted. Nikitin also said that the people of the Deccan went about barefooted.[37] Paes says, "the shoes have pointed ends, in the ancient manner, and there are other shoes that have nothing but soles, but on the top are some straps which help to keep them on the feet. They are made like those which of old the Romans were want to wear, as you will find on figures in some papers or antiquities which come from Italy[38]". The Muslims also used footwear.

Decoration

The material culture of the people can best be known by their ornamentation, cosmetics, hair-styles etc. The people of medieval Telangana and Andhra had high aesthetic sense and they developed a good taste for beauty and glamour. They decked themselves with different types of ornaments designed to beautify various parts of the body like head, neck, hands, waist, legs etc. To fill their surroundings with a fragrance, they used perfumes. Cosmetics were used to make the skin shine. Further, various hair-styles were allowed to improve their appearance. It appears that there was a difference in the ornaments used by various castes.

Most of the ornaments were the same for both the sexes. Only a few were exclusively used by women. The Brahmins seem to have worn the Haras of Tulasi or basil plant round the neck, silver rings to fingers and Kundalalu or ear-ornaments.[39] Their women wore ear-rings made with leaves. The Kshatriyas being ruling class wore many ornaments for decorating various parts of the body. *Rayavachakam*[40] furnishes a detailed list of ornaments worn by Krishnadevaraya. The Vaisyas put on ear-ornaments, finger-rings of sapphire and waist belt or *mola-nulu* of silver. The *Medaras* (bamboo-workers) seem to have worn finger-rings made of iron. The Jangamas wore copper rings on their fingers with the emblem of Nandi.[41]

Ornamentation became popular among the Muslims. They wore finger rings, bracelets and chain anklets. There were innumerable ornaments worn by the people in those days. They used jewels to the different parts of the body for which they were designed. They were the head-ornaments, neck-ornaments, nose-ornaments hand-ornaments, waist ornaments and anklets. Though each caste had its own way of adornment but their economic position decided the extent of their ornamentation. The rich used costly and expensive materials like gold, diamonds, emeralds, sapphires, rubies, pearls etc. for their ornaments. But the poor satisfied with the cheap and less expensive materials such as leaves especially of basil, Guriginja, brass, iron, glass, and beads etc., which are amply available in the nature.

During the period under consideration, there was ornamentation for the animals also. The bull, the horse and the elephant only were considered to be worthy of ornamentation. The bull is the vehicle of Siva. The horns were capped with gold and fore-feet were decked with anklets and bells were tied to the neck. Horses were supposed to have their origin from Gandharvas. The horse on which the king rode was fully decorated. Its body was covered with Mukhamal strewn with precious stones. On the head, there was a cluster of feathers. There was a belt studded with gems which were hidden in the middle of the body. On the neck, there were pendants of various kinds.

The elephant among animals was considered to be of royal status and the state elephant was profusely decorated. On the body, there was a silken cloth of many colours and on that the seat of the king was fixed. It was a rectangular four corned palanquin called 'Chowdolu' without outer covering. It was made of gold and studded with precious stones. Bells were hung to the elephant not only from the trunk and neck but also from both sides of the body. Gold rings were set with the tusks. All the bells and chains were made of gold.[42]

The people used perfumes for fragrance and they varied according to the season. Aloe wood was used during the cold weather. Civet, camphor and several other kinds of perfumes were in great demand. People anointed themselves after their bath with white sandalwood, aloes, camphor, musk and saffron. The women used to apply saffron or musk to their breasts in winter.[43] They also used scented flowers.

Dwelling Structures

In the primitive times, man protected himself in the caves, the natural rock formations. With the remarkable development of human mind, the nature of these residences underwent a change. The art of house construction reached its zenith by this time. The magnificence and splendor of the royal palaces were beyond description. However, the poor people lived in the huts.

There was a gulf of difference between the houses of the elite and the poor. The poorer classes lived in thatched huts without windows. These huts had only a single opening for air, light and entrance. According to Linschoten the doors of these houses were so small that men had to creep in and out. The floor of the houses was of pounded earth spread over with cow-dung. Thevenot says "the common man lived in very low and ill-contrived huts built of earth and thatched with straw".[44] Among the commoners, those with better position lived in Matti Meddelu (houses built of mud). Bamboo canes, branches of trees, ropes, palm leaves, grass of different kinds were used in the construction of huts.

The houses of the middle-class people were modest in appearance when compared to that of nobles. Most of these houses seem to be one storied and flat roofed and has a low surrounding wall. These houses had separate rooms for devotion, dining, dressing and drawing rooms and verandahs. Further, they were white-washed and shined with brilliance. To the front doors a rectangular block of wood was placed known as Kadapa. Divinity was attributed to it and none was allowed either to sit or step on it.[45] Platforms were constructed for sitting purposes infront of the houses. Paes was impressed with these houses and says that their general plan was good and they were like terraces.[46]

The houses of the nobility and rich were quite spacious. The palaces of the nobility were like those of the kings. The rich merchants also lived in well-equipped mansions. The foreign travellers had left brilliant accounts of the cities and the palaces. The kings having financial resources at their disposal spend lavishly on the construction of huge buildings with their aesthetic sense and innovative spirit. During those days buildings were constructed on a single pillar known as 'Onti Stambapu Medalu'.[47] The palace of Reddi king Virabhadra Reddi was called 'Trilokyavijayam'. Paes gives a wonderful description of the palace of the Krishnadevaraya. The kings seem to have been rich that even the walls and steps of their houses were coated with gold and silver and studded with precious stones. The houses of the kings and nobles had swings which were richly decorated. They were made of ivory and were painted with pearl parrots and golden flowers. Another interesting feature of the palaces relates to the pictures on the walls.

The Muslim houses were similar to that of Hindus, except a few variations. They used the carpets to cover the floors for which Talar golden strings were used.[48] The Muslims constructed windows and also balconies.[49] The palaces of the Qutb Shahis were magnificent and splendid.

Ghawwasi says that the palaces were so lofty that they seemed like touching the abode of Allah.[50] A number of royal palaces were constructed in Hyderabad city and of them Dad Mahal and a four storeyed palace Aman Mahal were built by spending huge amounts. To the south of the city, on the Koh-e-Tour hillock, Muhammad Quli built a three storeyed building, with large corridors, platforms and ventilators.[51]

Ghosha Mahal[52] was the most elaborate palace. Its construction commenced during Abdullah's reign and completed during the reign of Abul Hassan. It must have been a vast structure, as it is said to have consisted of as many as 100 halls and its cost was 3,40,000 hons. Qutb Shahi reign may be regarded as the high water-mark of paintings in the portraits of the rulers and other nobles. These palaces were adorned with a number of pleasant gardens. Both the Hindu and Muslim palaces were decorated and beautified exhibiting their pomp, grandeur and splendour. Tavernier states that Hyderabad city was "nearly the size of Orleans, well built and well opened out".[53]

The glories of this splendid city have been sung through the centuries. A historian, Muhammad Saqi, who accompanied the Emperor Aurangzeb during the siege of Golkonda in 1687 A.D. admired the city thus: "It is a resort of heavenly peace and world comfort; it gives solace to the human heart, and comfort to human body; its population is even larger than the human mind can think of; its buildings are loftier than the human intelligence can imagine, its air is so refreshing and flow of fountains so sweet and its verdure so pleasant and invigorating that the glowers and the vegetation of the land may be compared to the glitter and colour of emeralds and rubies".[54]

Hayatabad was a sub-urban town of the imperial capital Hyderabad. The town is situated about 9 miles to the east of Hyderabad and about 16 miles from Golkonda. Hayat Bakshi Begum constructed this town in 1626 A.D.[55] with several palaces like Hayatnagar Palace and big gardens. One among them known for its beauty was "Khas Bagh". She also built a mosque with Madarsa, Maa Sahiba Sarai, Ashur Khana and Hathi Bowli. In addition, she got constructed a water tank named "Hayat Maa-ka-Talab" near Hayat Nagar.

Hayat Bakshi begum was instrumental in the construction of many beautiful palaces in Hyderabad. The ruins of palaces are still there and reflect the past grandeur of these palaces. The royal palace was the principal and rich palace among them. Tavernier[56] compares the palace of Hayatabad with the Palais Royal of Paris, while Thevenot says that "It consisted of large piles of stone buildings two storey high and adorned with porticoes, halls and galleries".[57] The palace now is in ruins.

Thus, it is obvious from the above discussion that the aspects of material culture in medieval Andhra were distinct and high of order.

Notes & References

1. N. Venkata Ramanayya, *Studies in the History of the Third Dynasty of Vijayanagara,* Delhi, 1986, p. 362.
2. M. Somasekhara Sarma, *History of Reddi Kingdoms*, Waltair, 1948, p. 373.
3. Robert Sewell, *A Forgotten Empire*, Madras, 1924, p. 257.
4. Srinatha, *Chatupadyamanimanjari*, compiled by V. Prabhakara Sastry, Chennapuri, 1949, v. 322.
5. N. Venkata Ramanayya, *Op.Cit.*, p. 389.
6. Sri Krishnadevaraya, *Amuktamalyada*, IV, v. 134.
7. Srinatha, *Sringaranaishadham*, IV, v. 120.

8. Srinatha, *Haravilasam*, VI, v. 56.
9. Srinatha, *Sringaranaishadham*, VI, v. 130.
10. Chintalapudi Ellanarya, *Tarakabrahmarajiyamu*, v. 110.
11. Robert Sewell, *Op.Cit.,* p. 375.
12. *Ibid.*, p. 382.
13. N. Vani Sri, *Society in Medieval Andhra (1300-1500)*, Ph.D. Thesis (unpublished), Department of History, Osmania University, Hyderabad, 1996, p. 203.
14. *Ibid.*, p. 204.
15. Sri Krishnadevaraya, *Op.Cit.*, I, v. 74.
16. Srinatha, *Chatupadyamanimanjari, Op.Cit.*, p. 126.
17. Sri Krishnadevaraya, *Op.Cit.*, I, v. 82.
18. *Ibid.*, II, v. 73.
19. Srinatha, *Chatupadyamanimanjari,* p. 170.
20. N. Vani Sri, *Op.Cit.*, pp. 206-207.
21. Jean de Thevenot, *Indian Travels of Thevenot and Careri,* (ed.) Surendranatha Sen, New Delhi, 1949, p. 145.
22. Elliot and Dowson, *The History of India as told by its own Historians,* p. 114.
23. N. Venkata Ramanayya, *Op.Cit.,* p. 378.
24. T.V. Mahalingam, *Administration and Social Life under Vijayanagar*, Part-II, Madras, 1975, p. 66.
25. Jean Baptiste Tavernier, *Tavernier's Travels in India, 1640-67*, V. Ball, London, 1925, p. 229.
26. N. Venkata Ramanayya, *Op.Cit.,* p. 378.
27. *Ibid.*, p. 390.
28. N. Vani Sri, *Op.Cit.*, p. 210.
29. H.K. Sherwani, *History of the Qutub Shahi Dynasty*, New Delhi, 1974, p. 336.
30. Jean de Thevenot, *Op.Cit.*, pp. 115 & 136.
31. Koravi Goparaju, *Op.Cit.*, I, III, v. 188.
32. N. Venkata Ramanayya, *Op.Cit.,* p. 373.

33. Kadiripati, *Shukasaptati*, II, v. 425.
34. Sri Krishnadevaraya, *Op.Cit.*, VI, v. 6.
35. Robert Sewell, *Op.Cit.*, p. 251.
36. H.K. Sherwani, *Op.Cit.*, p. 521.
37. R.H. Major, *India in the Fifteenth Century*, London, 1858, p. 12.
38. Robert Sewell, *Op.Cit.*, p. 252.
39. Sarangu Tammayya, *Vyjayanti Vilasam*, II, v. 56.
40. Sthanapati Visvanatha Nayaka, *Rayavachakam*, p. 105.
41. N. Vani Sri, *Op.Cit.,* pp. 221-222.
42. A. Vaidehi Krishnamoorthy, *Social and Economic Conditions in Eastern Deccan (from A.D. 1000 to A.D. 1250)*, Madras, 1970, pp. 278-279.
43. Sri Krishnadevaraya, *Op.Cit.*, II, v. 60.
44. Thevenot, *Op.Cit.*, p. 131.
45. Sri Krishnadevaraya, *Op.Cit.*, IV, v. 26.
46. Srinatha, *Kasikhandam*, II, v. 75.
47. Srinatha, *Chatupadyamanimanjari,* II, v.1.
48. Ghawwasi, *Saif-ul-mulk*, v. 328.
49. Ghawwasi, *Qutbmushtari*, v. 1314.
50. *Ibid.*, v. 1305.
51. Nizamuddin Ahmed Mirzah, *Hadiqat-us-Salatin*, Hyderabad, 1961, p. 24.
52. H.K. Sherwani, *Op.Cit.*, p. 614.
53. Tavernier, *Op.Cit.,* Vol. I, p. 123.
54. Raza Ali Khan, *Hyderabad a City in History, Hyderabad*, 1986, p. 22.
55. A.A. Bilgrami, *Landmarks of the Deccan*, Hyderabad, 1927, p. 55.
56. H.K. Sherwani, *Op.Cit.*, p. 544.
57. *Ibid.*

6

GAMES AND AMUSEMENTS

The favourite games and amusements of a community reveal the standard of culture which the members of that community have attained in their tastes and their fancies. They contribute to the health and proper development of intelligence and individual skills. The games and amusements, by providing entertainment, enable the individual to overcome the dullness of monotonous routine life. They could infuse a new spirit and enthusiasm into life and without them the life would become gloomy. During the period under review various games and amusements were played according to the age, sex and place. Among the amusements some were outdoor and some other were indoor games. Besides the games, various shows, such as magic show, puppet show and snakes charming etc., were displayed for the entertainment of the people.

The establishment of the Muslim rule in Medieval Telangana and Andhra had its impact on the society. The two distinct Hindu and Muslim communities divided the society into two separate units. Interestingly, in the field of games and amusements, the two communities influenced each other. For example, the Muslims brought with them the game of Polo which was played by riding on the horse-back and striking ball with a stick[1]. However, this game could not reach the masses, but confined to the rich urbanities. Similarly, the Hindu game of chess became popular among the Muslims, especially the ruling class.

Hunting

It was an important entertainment of the then society, specially a popular pastime to kings and nobles. Most of the contemporary Telugu sources furnish graphic description of the hunting of wild birds and animals and a variety of weapons used in it. The ruling class was experts in hunting in those days. *Rukmangada Charitra,*[2] for example, refers to daggers, axes, bows and arrows, nets of clothes, cages for catching wild animals and certain herbs etc., as hunting instruments. Regarding hunting, Abdur Razzak observes that "the king of Hindustan spend more than a month in jungles for hunting elephants and celebrated if they capture them".[3]

In sculptural panels also several scenes depicting hunting were presented. In a panel, a king standing from a higher base is aiming at several wild animals including deer, wild boar and tiger. Two ladies are standing behind him. From this scene it is evident that the ladies too participated in hunting expedition. Further, a group hunting a hoard of wild animals is also represented in the panels.[4] *Manucharitra*[5] describes the dress of the princes that went on for hunting. They wore trousers and tied a cloth at the waist upon it. They tucked daggers at their waists and carried dangerous hawks in their hands.

Gambling

This amusement was known by different names like Pachi-kalata,[6] Nettamu,[7] Aksha-Kreeda,[8] Pachchis etc. It appears that the game became popular as Pachchis in the regions under Muslim rule. Ketana in his *Dasakumara Charitra*[9] praises the player's skill in getting the desired numbers by manipulating the dice. This game was widely played by both the rich and the poor. *Kridabhiramam*[10] describes the ways of the gamblers. The place of gambling was surrounded by prostitutes and others. People who lost in gambling were offended and participated again. Those who accepted the bet in the gamble lost everything. In *Maduravijayam*,[11] it is said that gambler, who gambles will lose his rich fields of corn, his valuable ornaments, his wife and children. Finally, he himself will become forfeited.

Chess

This game alone helped in the development of intellect of individual. The *Maddirela Kaifiyat* refers to the game as one that assists in enriching the intellect.[12] It became so popular that the aristocrats used to send the chess as one of the articles that were sent along with the girl after her marriage.[13] It seems that Krishnadevaraya was an expert in this game. He seems to have given as much respect to good chess players as to poets and philosophers.[14] Amir Khusrau also notices the game and says "Chess is a unique contribution of India to the world. It is a wonderful art which has countless moves".[15] It was played on a square board divided into sixty four blocks and eight rows and played by only two individuals.

Pulijudamu

Pulijudamu,[16] a kind of gambling, was also popular and played by the commoner even now in the interior villages. The game is played with stones on a ground by drawing a diagram.

Ram Fight

Among the public amusements of the period, special mention must be made of ram, buffalo and cock fight. The author of *Kridabhiramam* gives a spirited description of the ram and cock fight, acrobatic feats, magic and jugglery and snake charming that were displayed in the city of Orugallu. The people used to arrange ram fights in the open grounds. The rams, participating in the fights, followed their masters as the calf follows the cow. While they were going to participate in the war-game, the iron and copper ornaments around their necks and at the top of the horns, produced the sounds of bells. The rams faced their opponents bravely. After striking its enemy, the ram retreats a few steps and comes forward running and strikes again. Though blood dripped from their foreheads, they continued to fight bravely till the last moment.[17] In *Abhilashitartha-chintamani,* the author devotes one full chapter to amusements and entertainments of the time. He describes some games and snake charming, ram fight and cock-fight etc.[18]

Cock Fight

The cock fight described in *Kridabhiramam* is very interesting. They brought famous cocks for fighting. The cock, waving its wings, striking the ground with the legs, staring at the other cock with its star-like red eyes, jumped on it and struck on its head, with its sharp nose that made the other cock bleed. By bloating the upper part of the neck, the cock with its sharp and bent nose pierced the other cock's stomach and raced behind it. The cocks bled heavily and finally fell unconscious.[19] *Palanativira Charitra*[20] gives a lively description of cock fighting, as practiced in the medieval period. Cock-fighting was one of the main reasons for the annihilation of the Ekanga heroes of Palanadu. It is obvious that the institution of cock-fighting was common both to India and the island of Java, by the account of Nicolo de Conti.[21]

Acrobatic Feats

The other sources of entertainment were the acrobatic feats exhibited by the communities like the Dommaras and Vipravinodins. They walked on the ropes and mounted at the top of bamboo sticks without any support. Some of the beautiful maidens entertained audience by their physical feats. A contemporary Telugu work, *Kridabhiramam*[22] says "arching herself backwards, a young danseuse picked up a nose ornament, which was placed at the bottom of a trough of water and adorned her nose with it; and that she threaded quickly small black glass beads into a necklace".

Magic and Jugglery

Magic and jugglery were also popular in the period under review. They had red sandal wood paste on their fore-head in a circular shape. They used to knit their hair just above the eyes and held an instrument made of clay in their armpits. To the accompaniment of the pot instrument, producing some peculiar sound, they used to dance.[23] *Amuktamalyada*[24] mentions the things such as grass, peacock feathers and 'Vibhudi', which were used in the display of magic. The magic was also referred as Mahendrajala.[25] Abdur Razzak,[26] who visited Vijayanagara court, gives a detailed description of the feats of the jugglers in his account.

Snake Charming

Eventhough it comes under the amusements, it was one of the occupations of the people. *Kridabhiramam*[27] gives a charming description of the snake charmer. When the snake-charmer played on his instrument, the snakes opened their hoods and swayed to the melodious music. The charmer had thin 'Kasturi tilakam' on his forehead. He put one big snake across his body like holy-thread. While his anklets were producing tinkling sounds, the charmer, who was a scholar in snake-bites and poison came and started his snake-charming.

Duelling

Duelling was another amusement of the period. Even though it was a deadly one, which some times took out the blood or lives was observed by the viewers with great interest. The permission of the king appears to have been prerequisite for those who participate in duels. *Simhasanadvatrimsika*[28] vividly describes a duel fight and states that Kalahakantha and Ekangavira sought the permission of the ruler and it is corroborated by the account of Barbosa, a Portuguese official, who mentions that, "they are accustomed to challenge one another to duels and when a challenge has been accepted and the king gives his permission, the day for the duel is fixed by the person challenged".[29] Like duelling, wrestling was also in vogue during the period under review.

Swimming

Jala-krida or swimming was a sport that became popular both among men and women. It was a source of entertainment also. Errana, in his *Harivamshamu,*[30] describes the beautiful spectacle of women swimming or played Olata in water. He gives a clear picture as to how the game of Ola was played. He states that it could be played by any person capable of swimming in water, and by any number of people.[31] There is reference of Olata in the contemporary literary sources.

Music and Dance

The arts like music and dance also served as important entertainment of the people. Among all the fine arts music held a high and unique position. *Kridabhiramam*[32] mentions different types of musical instruments. Among them are stringed instruments and instruments made of leather. They are known as 'Maddela', 'Veena', 'Kanjira', 'Damaruka', Dindima', 'Javanika', and big 'Talas'. It also refers to the different 'Ragas' (tunes) known as 'Suddha', 'Saluva', 'Sankirna', 'Gandhara',[33] etc. The common people used to sing the ballad of Palanati heroes, the stories of Parasurama and goddess Ekavira, very melodiously. The literary sources of the contemporary period give full details about the development in vocal and instrumental music.

It was the classical music which delighted immensely the upper classes. During this period, it adequately received both the royal and temple patronage. The rulers of medieval Telangana and Andhra were not only proficient in music but wrote outstanding works on it. Devaraya-I, the Vijayanagara ruler, was expert in music. Pedda Komati Vema Reddi was not only adept in music but wrote a treatise on it entitled *Sangitacintamani*. Singa-II of the Velama family attained mastery in the Science of Music. Among the chiefs, Pratapavira Gangaraju of the Surabhi dynasty of fourteenth century and Visvesvara of the Chalukya family of fifteenth century etc. were also experts in music. The temple served as a great auditorium on account of its rich festivities, which furnished the musicians with an opportunity of exhibiting their gifted skills.

During the time of the Qutb Shahis, the laxity in the morals of the court and people led to the increase in the number of public women in the capital and consequently music and dance had become the monopoly of the prostitutes.[34] They were invited to sing or dance not only at social functions, but also when a large vessels arrived at a port and the religious celebrations such as the Prophets birthday. Music and dance were allied arts and they go hand in hand. Gondli,[35] a type of the Sanskrit Kundalinrutya, was played in both the '*marga*' and '*desi*' styles, by young women and girls arranging themselves in circles.[36] *Nruttaratnavali* states that the Western *Chalukyan* king, Bulokamalla Somesvara, was the originator of this variety of dance.[37] *Kridabhiramam* refers to the play, 'Kolatam',[38] before processional deities. The 'Kolatam' is a type of play with hand sticks in which men and women participate. Girls are adept in Kolatam and Kandukakrida (the play with a ball). *Kridabhiramam* gives a very fine description of young girls playing with a ball with both their hands.[39] *Palanativira Charitra*[40] also refers to this play. Such were the games and amusements of those people and there might have been many more means of recreation.

Notes & References

1. N. Vanisri, *Society in Medieval Andhra 1300-1600*, (Unpublished Ph.D. thesis), Osmania University, Hyderabad, 1997, p. 246.
2. Mallana, *Rukmangada Charitra*, III, v.70.
3. Elliot and Dowson, *The History of India as told by its own Historians*, Vol. IV, p.111.
4. Y. Nirmala Kumari, *Social Life as Reflected in Sculptures and Paintings of Later Vijayanagara Period* (A.D. 1500-1650) (with special reference to Andhra), Madras, 1995, p. 91.

5. Peddana, *Manucharitra*, IV, v. 30.
6. Surana, *Kalapurnodayam,* III, v. 132.
7. Nachana Somanatha, *Uttara Harivamsham*, III, v. 109.
8. Ketana, *Dasakumara Charitra,* V, v. 66.
9. *Ibid.*, v. 64.
10. Vinukonda Vallabharaya, *Kridabhiramam*, published by V. Prabhakara Sastry, Hyderabad, 1960, vv. 97-99.
11. Gangadevi, *Madhura Vijayam*, III, v.28.
12. *Maddirela Kaifiyat*, Vol. III, pp.128 & 129.
13. Sankula Narasaiah, *Kavikarna Rasayanam*, III, v.195.
14. N. Venkata Ramanayya, *Studies in the History of the Third Dynasty of Vijayanagara,* Delhi, 1986, pp.418-419.
15. Amir Khusrau, *Nuhsiphr,* p.170.
16. Koravi Goparaju, *Simhasanadvatrimsika*, X, v.91.
17. Vinukonda Vallabharaya, *Op.Cit.*, vv.227-231.
18. A. Vaidehi Krishnamurthy, *Social and Economic Conditions in Eastern Deccan (A.D. 1000-1250)*, Madras, 1970, p.283.
19. Vinukonda Vallabharaya, *Op.Cit.*, vv.234 & 235.
20. Srinatha, *Palanativira Charitra*, pp.79-85.
21. R.H. Major, *India in the Fifteenth Century*, p.16.
22. Vinukonda Vallabharaya, *Op.Cit.*, v.144.
23. *Ibid.,* v.226.
24. Sri Krishnadevaraya, *Amukthamalyada,* IV, v.193.
25. Koravi Goparaju, *Op.Cit.,* II, v.112.
26. Elliot and Dowson, *Op.Cit.,* IV, pp.118-120.
27. Vinukonda Vallabharaya, *Op.Cit.*, v.223.
28. Koravi Goparaju, *Op.Cit.*, II, VII, vv.27-71.
29. *The Book of Duarete Barbosa*, (Translated by Longworth Dames), Vol. I, pp.190 & 191.
30. Errana, *Harivamshamu*, VI, v.101.

31. *Ibid.,* VI, v. 134.
32. Vinukonda Vallabharaya, *Op.Cit.,* vv.100, 140 &147.
33. *Ibid.*, v. 143.
34. Jean De Thevenot, *The Indian Travels of the Thevenot and Careri,* (ed.), S.N. Sen, New Delhi, 1949, p. 135.
35. Vinukonda Vallabharaya, *Op.Cit.*, v. 143.
36. Srinatha, *Kashikhandam,* VI, v. 169.
37. M. Somasekara Sarma, *History of the Reddi Kingdoms,* Waltair, 1948, p. 431.
38. Vinukonda Vallabharaya, *Op.Cit.,* v. 117.
39. *Ibid.,* v. 258.
40. Srinatha, *Palanativira Charitra*, p. 358.

7

THE VILLAGE DEITIES AND THEIR WORSHIP

The numerous references in the inscriptions and literature during the period throw light on Jainism, Buddhism, Vaishnavism and Saivism. Jainism was a prominent religion in the pre-medieval period. The rulers of this time were the followers of Jainism and extended their patronage to it. The kings of the later period transferred their allegiance to Saivism. Of all the schools of Saivism, that were prevalent during this period, the Pasupata cult was the dominating cult. The main reason for the quick spread of the Pasupata Saivism in Andhra country was the vigorous efforts of the Acharyas of several Mathas. The growth of the Pasupata cult was also due to the active support and personal interest taken mostly by the kings (Royal pupils), by their subordinates and officials. In addition to these religions, there were many other primitive forms of religious practices prevalent among the masses, like the worship of village deities, offering sacrifices to them and celebrating festivals in their honour.

Kridabhiramam mentions the popular forms of Siva - Mailaradeva, Bhairava and Virabhadra. These deities had temples constructed in their honour. They were worshiped by the masses. People offered sacrifices[1] to these gods. Mailaradeva is the companion of Lord Bhairava of Orugallu. It is believed that, He confers prosperity on his devotees, when they worship him on Saturday. The deity is said to be the king of Inavrolu[2] (Inavroli Ayya). There is a pilgrim centre, by name Involu, ten miles away from Warangal. Here is a temple of Mailaradeva. In *Skandapuranam*,[3] there is a chapter by name "Mailarakanda", which describes the power of Mailaradeva.

Bhairava is an inferior manifestation of Siva, showing himself on a terrific form. The Bhairavas are in eight number. All the forms are in frightening postures: (1) Asitangam, black limbed; (2) Samhara, destruction; (3) Ruru, a dog; (4) Kala, black; (5) Krodha, anger; (6) Tamra – Chuda, red crested; (7) Chandrachuda, moon crested; and (8) Maha, great.[4] Maha Bhairava[5] and Kala Bhairava[6] are well described in *Kridabhiramam*. The worship of Kala-Bhairava appears to have been wide spread.[7] Virabhadra is a formidable being created from the mouth of Siva, for the purpose of spoiling the sacrifice of Daksha. *Vayupuranam* gives the full description of Virabhadra.[8] The Tamballas were the priests in the temples of Virabhadra.[9]

Next to Saivism comes Vaishnavism. This faith is known to us chiefly from the records of the construction of temples to god Vishnu in his different aspects. *Kridabhiramam* refers to the temple of Kesava.[10] Srikurmam, Simhachalam, Srikakulam and Ahobalam were the principal Vaishnava Kshetras of this period. There was a special shrine constructed for Buddha in Orugallu. Buddha had by this time become merely one of the Avatars of Vishnu and was thus reabsorbed into Hinduism. Still Jainism appears to have maintained to some extent its individual character. A reading of works like the *Basavapuranam* and *Panditaradhya Charitra* give the impression that the Jains were bitterly persecuted. But there is enough evidence to show the patronage extended to Jains by several kings like Pratapa Rudra-II. However, on the whole, Jainism appears to be on the decline during this period. Shakti worship was prevalent in the period under review. The most popular form of Shakti was Durga, the spouse of Siva. Durga was known by several names, such as Kakatamma, Ekavira and Chammundeshwari. In *Kridabhiramam* there is a reference to these goddesses.

Kakatamma was the tutelary deity of the Kakatiyas. According to some scholars, she is the deity of the Jains. But, there is no proper evidence in any of the Jaina scriptures or literature to confirm it. *Pratapa Charitra*[11] traces the origin of Kakatiyas to the worship of goddess Kakati. We are told that the child born as a result of her grace was named Kakati Prolaraju. In the commentary of Ratnapana,[12] it is mentioned as '*Kakatirnama Durga Shakti Ekasilanagaresvaranama Kuladevata......*'. The Telugu work, *Simhasanadvatrimsika*[13] described the deity Kakita (Kakati) as the basic energy. It is clear that the deity Kakati is Goddess Durga herself. Ekavira is said to be the companion of Kakatamma. Ekavira was worshipped as Renuka, the wife of Jamadagni and Mother of Parasurama. She was praised as Adi-Shakti (the primordial energy) and Akila- Janani (the universal mother). She had the serpents as ornaments.[14] In the folk-songs of the Bavani's, it is mentioned that she wore serpents as ornaments.[15] Ekavira was described as the Goddess Yellamma of Orugallu. A classical Dictionary of India says that Yellamma is identified with Renuka, wife of Jamadagni and if any one is bitten by a poisonous serpent he calls on Yellamma for aid.[16] It is obvious that Ekavira and Yellamma must have been the same.

The existence of the Tantric cult during this period is known by the contemporary Telugu literature. The Tantras enunciate the worship of Shakti, the female energy of Siva, chiefly devoted to Ananda Bhairavi. This worship, being centred in mystic circles, is known as Bhairavatantra or Chakrapuja. During the Puja there is the free use of the five M's[17] – Madya (liquor), Mamsa (flesh), Mastya (fish), Mudra (corn) and Maithuna (communion with women). Bhairavatantra is alluded to in *Kridabhiramam*.[18] Bhairavayogini is referred to in *Vikramarka Charitra*[19] of Jakkana. Offering sacrifice was a Tantric practice and the existence of *Campudigudis*[20] (temples to commit suicide) bespeaks of the spread of Tantric cult in Andhra Desa.

The worship of heroes and hero-stones also became part and parcel of popular religion. A temple was constructed to the heroes of Palanadu in Orugallu. The record from Karempudi[21] dated 1424 A.D. states that a certain merchant built a temple for Virakoti (obviously the heroes of Palanadu). The kings and nobles of the country patronised the worship of heroes. An inscription[22] dated 1314 A.D. at Macherla registers a grant of wet land as Sarvamanya to Virapurushulu (for conducting worship) by the king's (Kakati Prataparudra-II) officer, Devari Nayanimgaru. This cult of heroes seems to have come into existence towards the end of the Kakatiya rule. This was the age, which produced the popular Telugu ballad, the Heroes of Palanadu. The cult of hero-worship became a major aspect of popular religion during this period.

Temples

All these popular deities had temples in their honour. The temples held a place of supreme importance in the socio-religious life of the people in those days. *Kridabhiramam* mentions several temples and celebrations for the deities. The temple of Mailaradeva was decorated with garlands made of margosa leaves. In the centre of the town they erected a pillar (Simhadhwaja). Elders and children carried the *Poorna Kalasas.* The procession was led by the Madigas, who were intoxicated by liquor. They shouted 'Oyakaro, ammakaro, attattako', and beat the 'tapetlu' and big 'talas' rhythmically. While the musical instruments produced the harmonious sound, 'Jakajum Jamjakjumjum', they passed through the streets very happily. The devotees of Mailaradeva performed feats of self-immolation. A female devotee of Mailaradeva entertained the audience by her physical feats.[23]

The entrance of the temple of Ekavira was decorated with the garlands made of neem leaves. The chief of the Bavani's played on Javanika and sang the stories of Parasurama before the deity. In the afternoon a Mala woman came there, and sang in praise of the Universal Mother, Ekavira. A nicely dressed Kapu woman came to the temple and prostrated before the deity.[24] In another temple dedicated to Palanadu, a woman sang the ballad of Palanati heroes playing on musical instrument 'Viragumbi'. She was accompanied by male dancers, who exhibited their talents in line with the story sung.[25]

Thus, it is clear that the devotees at the temples of village deities exhibited their feelings more through gymnastics and other daring feats than through prayer and penance. The temple dominated the life of even the lowest class of people. The village deities and their worship are widely different from the popular form of Hindu deities, Siva and Vishnu and their worship. The village deities symbolise only the facts of the life of the masses. Thus, it becomes evident that the lower classes were exclusively dependent on gods to get rid of their woes.

They continuously prayed for prosperity. By implication it becomes clear that the state did not make any effort to improve their worldly positions.

Mathas

Along with the temple, Matha was another religious institution which played an important role in diffusing knowledge among the common people. The pontiffs of the Mathas were highly learned in their respective spiritual lore. 'Golaki Matha'[26] was a famous institution that flourished during the Kakatiya period. It had its branches at Mandaram (Guntur district), Tripurantakam (Kurnool district), and Pushpagiri (Cuddapah district). In fact, the Mathas rendered yeoman service to keep up the light of knowledge fully burning. All the contemporary sources refer to their important role in imparting education to the common people.

Tirunallu

Tirunallu (annual festivals for the deities) were extensively conducted in those days. These helped in creating a festival atmosphere and broad mindedness in the people. These functions were largely attended. *Kridabhiramam* refers to the Tirunallu of Andhra Mahavishnu of Srikakulam.[27] During these festivities, for the entertainment of the people, Vidhinatakas were enacted. In the Tirunallu of Srikakulam, kings, ministers and rich people used to throw coins. These were collected by the poor.[28]

In the conclusion, we may observe that the state gave an unquestioned lead to religious activity both directly and indirectly. There were no caste differences, however, either in the choice of god or the form of worship. In the city of Orugallu a Mosque was constructed for Muslims.

The fact that different forms of worship of different deities was not only permitted but also approved and patronized bespeaks of the religious tolerance of the people and their kings.

Notes & References

1. Koravi Goparaju, *Simhasanadvatrimisika,* I, IV, v. 17.
2. Vinukonda Vallabharaya, *Kridabhiramam,* published by V. Prabhakara Sastry, Hyderabad, 1960, v. 145.
3. Srinatha, *Kasikhandam,* I, v. 80.
4. John Dowson, *A Classical Dictionary of Hindu Mythology*, London, 1953, p. 45.
5. Vinukonda Vallabharaya, *Op.Cit.*, v. 151.
6. *Ibid.*, v. 294.
7. An inscription dated S' 1332 (1410 A.D.) states that Madasi Singamu, the Padalu of Velpur, made a gift of a Pandumu of land in Velpur to god Kalabhairava (*South Indian Inscriptions*, Vol. X, No. 576).
8. John Garrett, *A Classical Dictionary of India*, Oriental Publishers, Delhi, 1871, p.713.
9. Vinukonda Vallabharaya, *Op.Cit.*, v. 286.
10. *Ibid.*, v. 149.
11. Ekamranatha, *Pratapa Charitra,* p. 27.
12. Rama Rao, M., *Kakatiya Samchika,* Rajamahendravaram, 1935, p. 252.
13. Koravi Goparaju, *Op.Cit.*, I, VIII, v. 156.
14. Vinukonda Vallabharaya, *Op.Cit.*, v. 127.
15. B. Rama Raju, *Telugu Janapadageya Sahityam,* Hyderabad, 1958, pp. 437 & 438.
16. John Garrett, *A Classical Dictionary of India,* Delhi, 1871, p. 209.
17. P. Thomas, *Hindu Religion Customs and Manners*, Bombay, 1960, p. 26.

18. Vinukonda Vallabharaya, *Op.Cit.*, v.240.
19. Jakkana, *Vikramarka Charitra*, VII, v.15.
20. Koravi Goparaju, *Op.Cit.,* I, IV, v.17.
21. *Annual Report on Indian Epigraphy*, No. 557 of 1909.
22. *Ibid.*, No.586 of 1909.
23. Vinukonda Vallabharaya, *Op.Cit.*, vv.142, 143, 146 & 147.
24. *Ibid.*, vv.126, 130, 131 & 134.
25. *Ibid.*, vv.116 & 117.
26. Golaki Matha was established by Vishvesvara Sivacarya in 1261 A.D. at Mandaram, *Annual Report on Indian Epigraphy*, No. 94 of 1917.
27. Vinukonda Vallabharaya, *Op.Cit.*, vv.204-213.
28. Mancana, *Keyurabahucharitra*, I, v.45.

8

PRIESTLY COMMUNITIES WITH SPECIAL REFERENCE TO THE BAVANIS - A HISTORICAL PERSPECTIVE

Priestly communities occupy an important place in the caste based Hindu society. The Brahmins standing at the top of the Hindu caste society regulated the religious rites and life of the people and enjoyed privileges from the ancient times. But in the medieval Andhra the Sudras emerged as the priest in various temples due to the religious reform movements especially in the Saivaite and Vaisnavite sects. The beginning came from Saivism, a radical religion which undertook social reform. The Vaishnavites also responded to these developments and they also emerged as priestly class of Vaishnavas. Thus, the religious developments consequently brought about a social upliftment in the position of Sudras.

The temple priests are known as Archakas and Pujaris. Infact, certain communities appears to have been specialized in performing some particular temple service. The priestly functions in Hindu temple were performed invariably by the Brahmin community. But during the medieval period in Andhra the Archakas were also from the Sudra caste such as Jangamas, Tamballas, Sattani and Dasari.

Brahmins

The life of a Brahmin was conceptually duty bound towards the society and the god.[1] The Brahmins were well-versed in the Vedas, Vedangas, Agamas, Dharmasastras, Mimamsa, Ayurvedam, Dhanurvedam and poetry in Medieval times.[2] One of the most respected communities in the society was that of the Brahmins. Almost every foreign traveller who visited Andhra during the medieval and later medieval times was struck by the respect that the Brahmins commanded and the simple life they led. The Brahmins were of two main groups, Vaidikis and Niyogis. The former devoted themselves to their religious duties, specializing in the Vedic lore. They were honest, reserved, intelligent and pious. They usually led simple and peaceful lives. The Niyogi Brahmins took interest in material activities like military, trade and agriculture. The Vaidikis do not marry with the Niyogis.

Beside this economic distinction, the Brahmins were divided on various grounds, such as territorial, class-based, Veda-based etc. Territorially there were Velanadus (corresponds to the modern Tenali and Repalli taluqs of Guntur district), Kasalnatis (corresponds to modern Karimnagar and a part of Medak district), Mulkinatis (Pulivendala, Rajampeta, Proddutur taluqs of Cuddapah and northern region of Bellary, Chittoor and Ananthapur belong to Mulkinadu), Venginadus[3] and Telinganas. Another basis of distinction among the Brahmins was the Gotra. The Andhra Brahmins are broken up into 161 Gotras, which are supposed to have branched from the seven sages.[4] They fall into three groups following 3 Vedas, Rig Veda, Sama Veda and Yajur Veda. Another division among the Brahmins was based on religion. The Brahmins following Vaishnavism were known as Smartas and Saivism were known as Aradhyas.

Jangamas

The Jangamas were very important priestly community among the Sudras. It is noted in the Madras Census Report 1901 that "strictly speaking a Jangam is a priest to the religious sect of Lingayats, but the term is frequently loosely applied to any Lingayat....".[5] The word 'Jangam' means 'motion' in Sanskrit and is applied to these priests, who are regarded as being living symbols of the god Siva.[6] In the Census Report 1891 it is further recorded that "the full name is Jangama Lingayat meaning those who always worship a moveable Lingam, in contradiction to the Sthavara (immoveable) Lingam of the temple".[7] In Medieval Andhra Jangamas were highly respected. An undated inscription of the Vijayanagara period refers to a Jangamas priest who worshipped God Sangameshwara.[8] They not only received various land grants but made donations. An inscription dated 1552 A.D. records the gift of income derived from the village Pedakoduru for conducting festivals to the goddess Amkalamma of Pedakoduru by Jangam Sarva.[9] Under the development of the Saiva caste, they called themselves Vira Saiva Brahmins. The Jangamas have four divisions: (1) Mathpati (head of monastery), (2) Sthawara (householders), (3) Ganachari (though householder, but wander from village to village acting as priest to the laity and collecting alms) and (4) Madapati (they officiate at the Lingayat community and lower Hindu castes).[10]

Tamballas

The Tamballas rendered services as priests in the Saivaite temples. C.P. Brown describes them as a class of beggars, who worship Shiva, and who beat drums, secular priest etc. These men are generally the Sudras, but wear the sacred thread.[11] The Tamballas, who officiate as priests in temple of Siva, used to bring leaves for the choultries attached to the temples. It is said that the Tamballas of Rayalseema area bring flowers and betel-leaves on auspicious occasions.[12] They also rendered the service of cooking, keeping lamps, supplying water, flowers etc. It is not known when this custom of supplying all these items to the temple by this community came into existence.[13] Infact, their names were mentioned prior to that of the Brahmin priests in some of the inscriptions of the period under consideration. But the rulers seem to have been not in favour of Tamballas officiating as temple priests.[14] For example, the Kakatiya king Prataparudra under the influence of Brahmin Saivaite priests, removed them from the position and appointed Brahmins in their place.[15] The Vijayanagara ruler, Krishnadevaraya also replaced the Tamballas with Brahmins as temple priests. The *Kaifiyat of Hanumadgundam*[16] gives an interesting account of the wealth and pride of the Tamballas and their consequent removal from priest-hood, when he visited the temple of Pushpagiri. This event reveals that some of the Tamballas acquired greater wealth in medieval times.

Sattani

Another important priestly community was the Sattanis or Satanis. In the Madras Census Report, 1901, the Satanis are summed up as being a Telugu caste of temple servants supposed to have come into existence in the time of the great Vaishnavite reformer Sri Ramanujacharya

(1100 A.D.). In the Census Report, 1871, the Satanis are described as being "frequently religious mendicants, priests of inferior temples, minstrels, sellers of flowers used as offerings, etc., and have probably recruited their numbers by the admission into their ranks of individuals who have been excommunicated from higher castes... ".[17]

As they were priests in Vaishnava temples they imitated the Brahmins in appearance by adorning themselves with the "Tilak" of Vaishnavites known as "*Pattenamalu*".[18] Sattina and Sattani were the two important sects among this priestly class. The former wore 'Jandemu' and did not shave their heads. The latter on the other hand did not wear the 'Jandemu' and shaved their heads. They received considerable donations. The *Choudaladinne Kaifiyat,* records one such land grant to the Sattanis.[19] Sattanis (Sattada Srivaishnavas) were employed for cultivating flower gardens (Nandanavanams) and supplying flowers. They also supplied various items like spices, perfumes and incense for the Tirumanjanam (holy bath) of the Lord at Tirumala Tirupati temple everyday and chanted the Prabhandas of the Alvars in the presence of God.[20] The Satanis play an important role in the social life of the Vaishnavites of the Vizagapatnam district, and are the Gurus of some of the cultivating and other classes. They preside at the final death ceremonies of the non-Brahmin Vaishnavite caste. They burn their dead, and perform the Chinna (little) and Pedda roju (big day) death ceremonies.[21]

Dasari

The Dasaris are also Vaishnavites like Satanis. They are a class of Vaishnava beggars taking their name from the word 'Dasa' or 'servant of God'. Some of them served as priests and some others were mendicant-friars. "The caste, like that of the Satanis, is reinforced by idle members of the lower Sudra classes, who, being branded by the Gurus of Tirupati and other shrines, become Dasaris thereby. They usually wander about, singing hymns to a monotonous accompaniment upon a leather instrument called tappai (tabret)".[22] They wander about to receive alms each wearing as a distinction of garland of beads made of Tulasi wood. They were originally recruited from the Telugu caste and comprise several endogamous groups and the principal among them are: (1)Bukka Dasari (2) Paga Dasari (3) Dande Dasari (4) Bhutte Dasari (5) Telaga Dasari (6) Chinna Dasari (7) Mala Dasari (8) Hole Dasari (9) Chenchu Dasari. Bukka Dasaris also called Kunkum Dasaris, who are perfumers and occupy high rank in the status of that community. The Dasaris were furnished with *talam* (symbols), *tambora* (a sort of Indian violin), *shanka* (conch), *ghanta* (bell) and *diva* (lamp stand).[23]

Dasari girls are married both as infants and as adults. The marriage ceremony is conducted without the assistance of a Brahmin. The bride's parents take some money as a price for their daughter. The '*menarikam* custom' according to which a man should marry his maternal uncle's daughter is followed. The remarriage of widows is permitted but divorce is forbidden. The Dasaris were Vaishnavas by faith. They profess the Tengalai form of Vaishnavism. They were more secular than religious and had liberal religious notions. Animistic deities, such as Pochamma and Ellamma are appeared in the month of Sravana with the offerings of sheep and fowls. Ayyawars or Satanis officiate as their Gurus or spiritual advisers. The dead are buried in a lying posture, with the head to the South. The corpse is borne to the grave in a sitting posture if married and in a lying posture if unmarried.[24] The Chinna (small) and Pedda roju (big day) death ceremonies are observed. Some epigraphs pertaining to medieval Andhra period throw light on the Dasari community. An inscription[25] of 1314 A.D. from Simhachalam refers to these men who supplied garlands to that temple as Tirumala Pettedi Dasarulu. Further, a reference in the Kamalapuram Kaifiyat[26] to Sankirtana Vobala Dasari belonging to a temple Chennakesava, suggests the appointment of Dasari for reciting the sacred names of God. The Dasari collect arms in an alms-basket known as Bura-kaya. Some of them catch fish and pigeons etc. The Vizagapatnam Dasaris are the most popular among ballad singers and sing songs.

Bavanis

Mala and Madiga are the two untouchable castes. Among the Madigas there are 25 sub-castes. The Bavanis are one of them.[27] According to Suryarayandra dictionary, the word Bavana is derived from the Sanskrit term Bhramana, which is changed into Bavana. Bavani + eedu = Bavaneedu, which means a person who sings songs and goes around during the village festivals (Jataras). They were named after the musical instrument called Jamidika, Javanika and Pamba.[28] A Telugu contemporary work, *Kridabhiramam*, mentions that chief of the Bavanis stood before the temple of Goddess Ekavira and sang the stories of Parasurama.[29] They go for begging and reciting the stories of Goddess Ellamma and houses of Goudas after the performance of obsequies.[30] The Bavanis or Bindlawad discharged the functions of priests to the Madiga caste and perform their religious rites to the music of the Jamidika, a musical instrument characteristic of their profession. Occasionally they profess to the possessed and to foretell events and exercise ghosts.[31]

Traditions and Customs

The Bavanis perform birth ceremony on the third day. Later on the 21st day name giving ceremony would be performed. Children are sent to school at the age of five. Most of the parents, due to ignorance, hesitate to send their children to school as they want them to continue in their caste-profession, i.e. folk singing. The children are expected to obtain mastery over their caste occupation and obtain social recognition. This is how since childhood the Bavanis male learn folk singing and get married at the age twenty two.

Bavanis perform marriages according to the Hindu Dharma. The boys are married at the age of twenty five, while the girls get married at the age of thirteen. They follow certain norms before marriage is fixed. There appears to be no practice of dowry (in cash) among the Bavanis. Instead of dowry the cow and caste-musical instruments, like Jamidika, Suti, and Harmonium are accepted. There is also no practice of taking Oli (Kanyasulkum-bride price). Among the families of Bavanis in the place of bride-price, a costly saree is presented to the mother of the bride. Bavanis act as officiating priests for their own marriages by playing their musical instrument. Marriages are performed among the close relations. The Bavanis refuse inter-caste marriages. Whenever such marriages are performed the caste-elders ex-communicate the married couple. It means that the folk-singing communities strictly follow the caste rules.

Caste-Deities and their Worship

The Bavanis are Shaktikeyas. They worship their family deity-The Mother Goddess. In their houses they keep a special place for the deity. They consider it as sacred. The deity is installed on a high pedestal – (Gadde). The

Goddess may be in the form of image or a knife decorated with turmeric. After decorating the deity it is put in a bamboo box and this box is called the Devarabutta. The Bavanis worship the box and organize the festival of the Shakti (Devarakolpulu). They also worship Ellamma and celebrate Ellamma festival. After the installation of the deity (Ellamma) on a Patamu (diagram) she was worshipped. During this festival the Bavanis narrate stories, recite Mantras and sacrifice a goat. In the course of this festival the couple sits on the diagram and the priest narrates the story of Ellamma. Before the commencement of the story the priest sprinkle liquor and drinks it. A hen is also sacrificed. To appease Ellamma he sings and plays the musical instruments such as Jamidika, Suti and Harmonium.[32]

Food Habits

The Bavanis are non-vegetarians. They act as the priest to Madigas. They do not eat the food cooked by the Madigas, at the time of marriages. Rather they collect rice, oil and other provisions and cook the meal by themselves. But in the changed circumstances, inter-dinning is allowed. During village festivals and the worship of village deities the Bavanis are given goat or sheep meat by the villagers. They cook it immediately and eat it. This is practiced at the time of worship of family deity. Whenever village fairs are organized and village-stone (Bodrai) ceremonies are performed, the Bavanis get their share of the sacrificial meat.

Mirasi Rights

The Bavanis are spread across the entire states of Telangana and Andhra Pradesh. However, regional variations in their religious practices and life styles could be found. In the Telangana districts the Bavanis lead life from the gifts they get from the Madigas at the time of marriages. They are experts in charms and demon worship. They act as Magicians and perform magic spells. They ward off ghosts and drive away evil spirits. During village Jataras (fairs) they tour the villages, narrate stories in the night and collect alms in the morning. Therefore, among the Bavanis the names of Biksham, Bikshalu are common. While collecting the donations the Bavanis follow strict norms (Kattadi). They are not supposed to collect alms in the villages, but are allowed to visit only the Mirasi village. Each Bavani Mirasidar is entitled to perform ceremonies and collect donations and presents in their respective villages. There is evidence to the effect in the Telangana districts. The Bavanis are granted Inam (revenue free lands) for their services. For example, they have Inams in the village of Chittalur, Lingotam, Rudra Velli, Brahmanapalli of Nalgonda district. After the crop harvest, the Bavanis beg for the grains. They visit only the Mirasi villages. They also narrate stories in the villages and streets and collect donations from village elders. They normally spend 10-15 days in each village and collect their donations.[33]

Occupation and Rights

The main occupation of the Bavanis is to conduct village festival, to worship the Shakti gods and family deities, to organize village Bonams and village stone (Bodrai) functions. For every ceremonial function they receive donation from the trustees. As per the inscription issued by the trustee of certain temple Bavanis were entitled to receive Serughatam (one bottle of liquor), one-and-half rupees (1-50) and the head of sacrificial animal.[34]

Medical Treatment

The Bavanis act as village doctors. They treat the patients with tree leaves and juices. They are experts in identifying the medicinal plants and treat certain diseases like stomachaches, indigestion etc. They serve the village people health needs by using tree juices for headaches, scorpion bite etc.

Death Ceremony

The Bavanis have no tradition of cremation. The dead body is laid on the floor spread with grass. A lamp is lighted and a portable furnace is put in the courtyard. After bathing the dead body, it is made to sit on a certain diagram known as the Chandrapatam. Later either the husband or the wife, who ever is alive, is made to sit by the dead body and with the magical powers they made the dead person to play their musical instrument Jamidika. This is a unique and peculiar custom that existed among the Bavanis. It indicates the significance of the musical instrument in their lives. The body is laid on the funeral pyre and carried to the graveyard and buried.[35]

Ceremonial Cleanliness

In a general sense uncleanliness means impurity. There is a practice among the village people to perform ceremonial cleanliness at the time of auspicious functions and festivals. This tradition is still alive in the villages. There are two types of ceremonial cleanliness functions. The first one is before performing any auspicious functions and death in the family. The second one is cleanliness ceremony to Mother Goddess during the village festivals.

Village Festival

At the time of the worship of deities, village festivals are organized and a buffalo is sacrificed. The village Bonam festivals are organized once in every year. A sacrificial animal will be killed in the centre of the village. The meat of the animal is divided into two parts. One part will go to the elder of the shepherds; the rest is divided among the Madigas, Bavanis and washermen. The persons who help and assist the Bavanis at the times of village festival are known as "Acharamantalu".[36]

During the worship of the village deities, festivals or Jataras, they play musical instruments which create a terrific situation. After drinking lot of intoxicating drink like toddy and liquor they jump infront of the deity and sacrifice goat and sheep. By biting the throat of the sacrificial animal they kill it, suck its blood wear its intestines around neck, by playing instrument jamidika they go around the streets.[37]

Priesthood of the Bavanis

The Brahmins conduct the marriages and death ceremonies of Vaisyas, Kshatriyas and other upper castes. The Bavanis perform such functions for the Madigas. The Brahmins read Mantras (slokas) in Sanskrit, whereas Bavanis recite them in Telugu. They not only recite Mantras but also play their musical instruments. Thus, it is obvious from the above discussions that the priestly communities played a significant role in the religious and social life of the people.

Notes & References

1. R. Varalakshmi, "Caste System in Medieval Andhra", *Studies in History and Culture*, Journal of Post Graduate Department of History, Berhampur University, Berhampur, 1977, p. 37.

2. Pillalamarri Pinavirabhadra, *Sringara Sakuntalam*, I, v.76.
3. R. Varalakshmi, *Social Life in Medieval Andhra 1300-1500 A.D., as Reflected in Kridabhiramam* (Unpublished) M.Phil. Dissertation, Osmania University, Hyderabad, 1983, pp. 28-31.
4. Syed Siraj-ul-Hassan, *The Castes and Tribes of H.E.H. The Nizam's Dominions*, Madras, 1989, p. 127.
5. Edgar Thurston and K. Rangachari, *Castes and Tribes of Southern India,* New Delhi, 1993, Vol. II, p. 450.
6. Syed Siraj-ul-Hassan, *Op.Cit.,* p. 387.
7. Edgar Thurston and Rangachari, *Op.Cit.,* Vol. II, p. 450.
8. V. Rangachari, *Topographical List of Inscriptions from the Madras Presidency,* Vol. II, p. 620.
9. *Inscriptions of Andhra Pradesh,* Cuddapah, 227, No. 46 of 1968.
10. Syed Siraj-ul-Hassan, *Op.Cit.,* p. 387.
11. Edgar Thurston and K. Rangachari, *Op.Cit.,* Vol. VII, p. 6.
12. S. Pratap Reddy, *Andhrula Sanghika Charitra*, Hyderabad, 1950, p. 207.
13. R. Soma Reddy, *Hindu and Muslim Religious Institutions Andhra Desa 1300-1600,* Madras, 1984, p. 75.
14. N. Vani Sri, *Society in Medieval Andhra,* Ph.D. Thesis, (Unpublished), Osmania University, Hyderabad, 1996, p. 111.
15. *Ibid.*
16. *The Kaifiyat of Hanumadgundam*, L.R. 37, pp. 245-8.
17. Edgar Thurston and K. Rangachari, *Op.Cit.,* Vol. VI, pp. 298-300.
18. Krishnadevaraya, *Amuktamalyada,* II, v. 97.
19. *Chaudaladinne Kaifiyat,* Mackenzie Manuscripts, 142, p. 89.
20. R. Soma Reddy, *Op.Cit.,* p. 75.

21. Edgar Thurston and K. Rangachari, *Op.Cit.,* Vol. VI, p. 304.
22. *Ibid.,* Vol. II, pp. 112-113.
23. Syed Siraj-ul-Hassan, *Op.Cit.,* p. 157.
24. *Ibid.,* p. 160.
25. *South Indian Inscriptions,* VI, No. 938.
26. *Mackenzie Manuscripts,* 127, p. 30.
27. Syed Siraj-ul-Hassan, *Op.Cit.,* p. 411.
28. B. Rama Raju, *Telugu Janapadageya Sahityam,* Hyderabad, 1958, p. 435.
29. Vinukonda Vallabharaya, *Kridabhiramam,* v. 139.
30. B. Rama Raju, *Op.Cit,* p. 707.
31. Syed Siraj-ul-Hassan, *Op.Cit.,* p. 412.
32. Ch. Yadaiah, *Janapada Vignanamlo Bavanilu Oka Parishilana,* Hyderabad, 1990, pp. 26-29.
33. *Ibid.,* pp. 32-35.
34. *Ibid.,* pp. 49-50.
35. *Ibid.,* pp. 39-40.
36. *Ibid.,* p. 49.
37. B. Rama Raju, *Op.Cit,* p. 801.

9

FESTIVALS AND FAIRS – SOME REFLECTIONS

Festivals play an important role in the religious life of people. India is a land of many religions and it might be described as a land of festivals. The word 'festival-day' means feast day. India being a society of many religions there are lots of festivals. Every little occasion from the harvesting of crops, welcoming the spring or rain, seeing the full moon lends itself to joyous celebrations splashed with colours, music, folk dances and songs. Even the birthdays of Divine Beings are celebrated as festive occasions. Most of the festivals are common to the most part of India. There is general uniformity in their observance throughout the country. But the festivals gain various degrees of popularity and are celebrated with certain local variations. On festive occasions homes are beautifully decorated, new dresses are worn and illuminations, fire-works, abundant display of gold, silver, pearls, diamonds and jewels are observed by the people.

During the medieval period, the advent of Islam brought vertical division of the society. The festivals of Muslims varied from those of Hindus as Islam being a developed religion, it had its own days of rejoicing. But still interaction is bound to influence the cultures of one another and eventually it led to their intermingling. This phenomenon is manifest in the aspect of festivals along with other aspects. For example, the Hindu festival of Shivaratri is celebrated by Muslims as Shab-e-Barat by maintaining a holy vigil throughout the night and the Hindus on their turn take part in Muslim Urs.

Though festivals were religious in nature, they had political, social and economic importance in the activities related to their celebrations. Vasantotsava was one festival, which was celebrated by one and all with great jubilation and jocundity and it gained political importance by the participation of the kings. Some festivals had legendary and mythical back-ground like the Deepavali, some others were celebrated while conducting agricultural operations, such as sowing seeds or reaping the crop. The Eruvaka and Sankranti festivals, for instance, were associated with agriculture. The Hindu festivals were thus numerous with atleast one festival being celebrated almost every month.

One of the greatly rejoiced festivals of the period was *Vasantotsava* also known as *Madanotsava*. According to legend in order to disturb Siva from meditation and draw his attention towards *Parvathi*, Gods sent *Madana* and his consort *Rati*. *Madana* fired his arrow of love on *Siva*. Then Siva got angry, opened his third eye and reduced him to ashes. Later, Siva realized his folly and to console lamenting Rati, he gave the boon that Madana would acquire his body once in every year during the spring season. Thus, the name Vasantotsava is derived from the spring season, while the second name *Madanotsava* corresponded to *Madana*, the God of love. This festival was basically a romantic festival, in vogue from the early centuries of the Christian era and received impetus during the reign of the Reddi kings.

The contemporary literary sources like *Bhimeshvara Puranam*, *Kasikhandam* and *Simhasanadvatrimsika*[1] provide us with an embellished account of the celebration of this festival. According to *Simhasanadvatrimsika*, the kings celebrated the festival in a park adjacent to the town, where beautiful pavilions were created with golden arches and the altars decked with precious stones for gods like Kama, Vasanta and others. The floor was decorated with various designs and Purnakalsas. The king used to attend the festival along with his queens, princes, nobles, poets, jesters, common people and army. The festival started with the worship of Madana by the king. After the closing of the worship, the king used to throw camphor, musk, civet, saffron on the people gathered there. Dramas were enacted, dance recitals were given, musicians sang songs, poetic talent and physical feats were exhibited with great gusto. The king rewarded the men of arts and letters and other talented persons.

The Reddi rulers made this festival country-wide popular by giving a political colour with their participation. The Rayas of Vijayanagara also celebrated this festival. This fact is evident from the contemporary Telugu work *Parijatapaharanam*,[2] which mentions that the Raya conducted the festival in great pomp. This significant festival is depicted in the sculptural panels of the Vijayanagara Empire. A few panels are found on the outer walls of Hazara Ramaswami temple at Hampi depicting the celebration of this festival, where men and women are seen spraying water, perhaps coloured water, with sprayers taking it from a tub.[3]

Sankranti is the festival celebrated usually by the agriculturists. This harvest festival marks the commencement of the Sun's journey to the Northern Hemisphere. On this occasion the animals especially the buffaloes were decorated with colourful clothes and floral wreaths.[4] Women made cakes of cow-dung and kept them infront of the houses.[5] Thus, this festival reveals the significance given to the agriculture in the then society. Vittunati Panduga was another festival celebrated exclusively by the agriculturists. The day of sowing seeds in the fields was considered important. On this day the Brahmin priests were invited to perform various simple rituals.[6]

Shivaratri was the important festival to the Saivaites. It was observed by fasting and holy vigil throughout the night as dedication to Lord Shiva. Religious people chanted mantras and anointed Lingams. During medieval period in Telangana and Andhra, the popularity of the festival is known by the fact that books were written describing the greatness of the festival. For example, Srinatha's *Shivaratrimahatyam* is one such work that portrays the efficacy of the festival. Another significant festival was Nagulachavithi. The aim of the festival was to appease the snakes by offering them milk. Srinatha says that this festival was celebrated in winter season in his work entitled *Shivaratrimahatyam*.[7] It is needless to say that the new year day was one of the important festivals of the Andhras, even though it does not find mention in the records of the period under review. *Ramanavami* and *Janmashtami* were the two other important Hindu festivals, which are the birth anniversaries of Lord Rama and Lord Krishna respectively. *Mahanavami* was celebrated in the Vijayanagara Empire. Originally it was a festival for the propitiation of the goddess Durga. But it gained political significance during the Vijayanagara days.[8] Some of the foreign travellers who visited the Vijayanagara kingdom gave vivid account of this festival.

Deepavali is perhaps the happiest of Hindu festivals in India. It is by far the most glamorous and splendid festival of lights symbolizing the victory of righteousness and the lifting of spiritual darkness. Countless number of lamps were lighted at night, giving the impression that the stars have descended on earth. In the medieval Telangana and Andhra, *Deepavali* was celebrated with merry as the festival of Laxmidevi, as today. According to the legend, it was celebrated as a mark of victory of Satyabhama over the demon Narakasura. Koravi Goparaju in his *Simhasanadvatrimshika* describes this festival as *Divvela Panduga* (festival of lights). He further says that the kings rewarded some accomplished persons such as poets, singers and actors etc.,[9] on this occasion. Interestingly, Sarangu Tammayya's work *Vijayanti Vilasam* furnishes us with a graphic account of the festival. He mentions it as Laxmidevi Panduga, which is celebrated in *Sharatrutu* (rainy season), when the sweet smells of camphor and musk coupled with those of sweet dishes made with ghee and oil surrounded the air. The common people cooked the meat of goat and sheep and offered toddy to goddess Parvathi. The king sent various gifts to prostitutes on this day.[10]

Davana Punnama was celebrated in the month of Caitra. A Telugu work *Kridabhiramam* mentions this Davanapunnama (the fullmoon day of the light of the month of Caitra).[11] The annual festival of god Telunguraya of Kakulam (Srikakulam) used to be celebrated on this day. Two inscriptions[12] at Draksharamam dated 1275 A.D. and 1287 A.D. register grants for *havirabalyarcanas* to god Bhimeshvara on the occasion of Dolotsava on Davanapunnama. Another Telugu work *Panditaradhya Charitra*[13] tells us that a certain Vesya paid *katnam* to her guru on this day of *Davanapunnama*. *Nuliponnama* festival was confined to the three upper castes, *Dvijas*, who were only permitted to wear the sacred thread. On this day, the sacred thread (*Yagnopavita* made of *Nulu* or Yarn) was prepared freshly and worn and a feast was arranged to *Balabhaktas* or small boys.[14] *Kartika Purnima* is a sacred day. On this day people worship Lord Siva. We are told in the *Bhimeshvara Puranam* that the Sage, Agastya with his wife entered the fire arch Jvala on the full moon day of the month of Kartika.[15] This act is believed to wash off all sins. There were many other festivals which the Hindus celebrated.

Fairs were conducted during the medieval period in Andhra Desa. Fairs provided an occasion for interaction and intermingling of various communities. Fairs were organized on various important occasions like the marriage festivals or Kalyanotsavas of gods and also annual festivals of gods in different pilgrim centres. A Telugu work *Basavapuranam* refers to *Veerabhadruni Jatara* or the fair of god Veerabhadra.[16] A poet Durjati refers to the fairs conducted by the tribals. He says that the *Katareni jatara* was more popular among the *Kiratas*.[17] Tenali Ramakrishna in his work *Panduranga-mahatyamu* mentions that men and women adorned and decorated themselves and enthusiastically attended the fairs.[18] Animals were slaughtered and offered to the various deities during these fairs. Tenali Ramakrishna says that animal sacrifices were made during feasts and fairs where the blood of animals flew like a stream.[19]

Like the Hindus the Muslims also celebrated their festivals with great gaiety. During the medieval period in Telangana and Andhra, the Qutb Shahi Sultans used these festival occasions to show their might. Muslim festivals were celebrated on a grand scale during the Qutb Shahi reign. These festivals were attended by the Hindus also. The Qutb Shahi Sultans followed benevolent attitude and the festive occasions gave an opportunity to the subjects to be in the company of the rulers.

Muharram was the important festival of the Muslims. It was celebrated by all the sections of the society irrespective of religion. It was celebrated on the tenth day of the month of *Muharram*, to commemorate the great tragedy of *Karbala*, in which Imam Hussain along with 72 of his relatives and friends achieved martyrdom on the battle field. According to Sadiq Naqvi "The Shias are identified by the observance of *Muharram*, as the Qutb Shahis were Shias and therefore *Muharram* was of great importance to them; and they celebrated it with great enthusiasm and devotion".[20] Mirza Nizamuddin's famous work *Hadiquat-us-Salatin*[21] throws a flood of light on the celebration of this festival. It says that the Sultan and his Muslim subjects wore black costumes and observed ten days mourning by avoiding music, dance, drinking liquor, eating meat and pan. Even it was observed by the Hindu subjects also. Every day evening the Sultan used to come to the Ashur Khana. (It is a building which houses the conventional copies of standards carried by Imam Hussain called *Alam*) and offered flowers to the *Alams*. At present in the villages of Telangana State and Andhra Pradesh the Muharram festival is celebrated with great interest. During the festive celebrations the devotees sing songs and dance. They sing:

'aasanna usanna vaarannadammulu
aasanna vusannayi laala
aasamma pattinapu deemi puttennee
aasanna vusannayi laala'

(Hasan and Hussain are brothers; oh God! Bless them. What is that created when Hasan and Hussain are born;

Oh God! Bless them). They lament over the death of these martyrs bidding farewell to them *'alvidaa, alvidda'*.[22]

Idd-ul-Fittr or *Ramzan-ki-Idd* is the most important festival, which is celebrated when the moon of the month of Shawwal is seen. A month long fasting and prayers are followed in this month. It is believed that during this month all prayers and wishes of an individual fulfilled. During the Qutb Shahi period on the *Idd* day the people took bath early in the morning and wore new clothes, took their meals and started for *Idd Gah* (mosque used for *Idd* prayers specially) to offer prayers.[23] The Sultan also went in a procession to *Idd-Gah* sitting on a decorated elephant, accompanied by the commander-in-chief, contingent nobles and jagirdars etc.[24] The *Idd Gah* used to be crowded heavily with people as if they were like incalculable stars in the sky. A great number of Hindus visited their Muslim brothers to greet them on this occasion. *Idd-uz-Zuha (Bakreed)* is another important festival of the Muslim community. On this day a goat is slaughtered as a sacrifice to *Allah*. Sultan Muhammad Quli in his poems[25] wrote that the people were busy in the preparation of the items like *Kabab* etc., and the meat of slaughtered animals was distributed among the relatives and poor. *Milad-un-Nabi* is the festival of the birthday of Prophet Muhammad and the Qutb Shahi rulers celebrated it on a large scale, in their own style of pomp and extravagance. Muhammad Quli describes it in six poems in his *Kuliyat*. When Muhammad Quli Qutb Shah celebrated this festival, the earth got decorated as Heaven.[26]

Muhammad Quli began celebrating the *Basant* festival. On that day piles of flowers were collected inside the palaces and in the gardens. Tanks were filled with colours, and Muhammad Quli along with his harem and band of select girls spent his day celebrating the festival in drinking and dancing.[27] *Shah-e-Barat* festival was celebrated on the night of fourteenth Shaban, on the day when the Muslims go to the graveyards and perform *Fateha* (reciting of the first Sura of the *Holy Quran* in the name of a dead person) over the graves of their departed relatives.[28] The manner in which the Shias performed it resembled the celebrations of the Hindu festival of Deepavali. They decorated their houses with lights, sweets were prepared to offer to guests, children wore new clothes and burned crackers. The Muslims celebrated the death anniversary of the saints and this celebration is called Urs. It was like the Hindu fairs or Tirunallu. A large number of Muslims along with the Hindus participated in the Urs.

Conclusions

Thus, the festivals played a significant role in the political, socio-religious life of the people. They fostered unity, weakening the subversive tendencies of the society, as both the rich and poor celebrated them commonly. They also infused freshness and vigour into life and helped in overcoming the monotony of life. Festive occasions furnished the people with an opportunity of forgetting their differences and enmity as they mixed freely with each other. They brought joy and happiness in the lives of the people. Festivals helped the people to create social harmony by sharing each others joys and tolerating each others religious traditions and customs. Eventually, they spread the message of joy, brotherhood and humanity among one another.

Notes & References

1. Koravi Goparaju, *Simhasanadvatrimsika*, III, v. 172.
2. Nandi Timmana, *Parijatapaharanam*, IV, v. 139.

3. Y. Nirmala Kumari, *Social Life as Reflected in Sculptures and Paintings of Later Vijayanagara Period (A.D.1500-1650) with special Reference to Andhra,* Madras, 1995, p. 90.
4. Srinatha, *Shivaratrimahatyam*, IV, v. 31.
5. Kadiripati, *Shukasaptati*, II, v. 444.
6. N. Vani Sri, *Society in Medieval Andhra (1300-1600 A.D.)*, Ph.D. Thesis (unpublished) Osmania University, Hyderabad, 1996, p. 300.
7. Srinatha, *Op.Cit.*, IV, v. 29.
8. T.V. Mahalingam, *Administration and Social Life under Vijayanagara*, Part-II, p. 238.
9. Koravi Goparaju, *Op.Cit.*, VII, v. 47.
10. Sarangu Tammaya, *Vijayanti Vilasam*, III, vv. 80 & 82.
11. Vinukonda Vallabharaya, *Kridabhiramam*, v. 204.
12. *South Indian Inscriptions*, IV, No. 1368 & 1373.
13. Palkurki Somanatha, *Panditaradhya Charitra,* Puratana Prakaranamu, p. 84.
14. Srinatha, *Palanativira Charitra*, II, p. 361.
15. Srinatha, *Kashikhandam*, III, v. 24.
16. Palkurki Somanatha, *Basavapuranam*, III, v. 71.
17. Durjati, *Kalahasti Mahatyam*, III, v. 36.
18. Tenali Ramakrishna, *Pandurangamahatyam*, III, v. 74.
19. *Ibid*.
20. Sadiq Naqvi, *Muslim Religious Institutions and their Role under the Qutb Shahs*, Hyderabad, 1993, p. 205.
21. Nizamuddin Ahmad Mirzah, *Hadiqat-us-Salatin*, Hyderabad, 1961, p. 53.
22. G. Venkat Rajam, "Moharrum - Fostering Universal Fraternity and National Integration", *The Noor, An Islamic Research Journal,* 1997-98, Hyderabad, p. 39.
23. Dharmender Prasad, *Fairs, Festivals and Social Functions of Hyderabad*, Hyderabad, 1984, p. 78.

24. *Ibid.*
25. Zore Mohiuddin Qadri, (ed.), *Kuliyat-e-Muhammad Quli Qutb Shah*, Hyderabad, 1940, p. 115.
26. *Ibid.*, p. 41.
27. *Ibid.*, p. 206.
28. Sadiq Naqvi, *Op.Cit.*, p. 243.

10

DARGAH – A SYMBOL OF POPULAR CULTURE

The graves of the reputed Sufi saints became the Dargahs. Sufism signifies mysticism in Islam. If Islam had affected Hinduism, the impact of Hinduism on Islam was profound. It gave rise to Sufi Movement in the realm of Islam. However, the original source of Sufism is the Quran. According to some, the word Sufi was derived from *Safa* (pure) because of the purity of their hearts and purity of their thoughts. The Arab word *Suf* means wool, and a Sufi literally means "a man of wool". However, it signifies a man of renunciation devoted to God. Further, it sprang from the doctrine of *Wahdat-u-Wujud,* i.e. "unity of being". Thus, the Islamic mysticism known as Tasawwuf or Sufism was as old as Islam itself. The Sufis of 16th & 17th centuries (Qutb Shahi period) were the torch bearers of the composite culture, resting on communal harmony. Dargahs played a significant role in the lives of the people, irrespective of their caste, creed and community not only in the past but even today. The reason why Dargahs had drawn into their fold all religious sects of people was mainly due to the belief in the supernatural powers of the Peers or Sufi saints, and the liberal and humanistic Sufi preachings based on religious tolerance when compared to those of the Orthodox Ulema.[1] The Dargahs were the tomb-shrines of the Sufi saints built by their disciples. In course of time, these shrines became important centres of worship and pilgrimage, for not only to their spiritual disciples but even to laymen because of the miracles attached to the Peers.

Early Dargahs in Andhra Desa

The Dargah of Baba Sharfuddin situated in Barkas locality of Hyderabad seems to be the earliest Dargah in Andhra Desa. He came from Iraq and carried on his missionary activity in this area. After his death in 1287 A.D., his disciples built a tomb on his relics. The Urs used to attract thousands of people every year in the subsequent period.[2] The Dargah of Kadi Ziauddin Multani and the Dargah of Syed Shah Baghdad Warangal were situated in the village of Urs near modern Warangal, also related to this period. The Dargah of Baba Fakhruddin of Penugonda (Anantapur district) is another one which belonged to the same period.[3] It received the patronage of both Muslims and Hindus. There was another Dargah of Galib Saheb at Rajkonda (Nalgonda district) that had drawn thousands of devotees on the occasion of its Urs.[4]

Dargahs under the Qutb Shahs

The period under study corresponds to the Qutb Shahi rule. The Qutb Shahi administration and society remained under the powerful influence of the Sufis because Qutb Shahis were Shias. Sufis were the Muslim saints preaching a liberal outlook in the folds of Islam rather than the orthodox minded Ulema. The tolerant religious policy adopted by the Qutb Shahi rulers suited them and gave them liberty to preach and practice their ideology. The Sufis of the period belonged to both the sects, Shias and Sunnis. Overlooking the traditions of the times some of the Qutb Shahi Sultans had gone for matrimonial alliances with the Sufis and gave their daughters in marriage to them. Sufis created an atmosphere of brotherhood in and around their Khanqahs. So, they were loved and revered by all people. The people were attracted to Sufis owing to their mystic powers. They sought their blessings to ward off their troubles and get their desires fulfilled. When Sufi saints died, tombs were built over their graves and these buildings came to be known as Dargahs. The doors of the Dargahs like that of the Khanqahs were kept open for all the people to pay their homage in their own way in accordance to their traditions. Thus, Dargahs became Muslim institutions fostering religious harmony. Sultan Quli Qutb Shah, Ibrahim Qutb Shah, Muhammad Quli Qutb Shah, Sultan Muhammad Qutb Shah, Abdullah Qutb Shah and Abul Hasan Tanesha extended their support to Sufi saints and their Khanqahs. Sultans visited Dargahs personally and gave their attendance at Khanqahs.[5] Abul Hasan, the last ruler of Qutb Shahi kingdom lived for fourteen years in the Khanqah of Shah Raju before becoming Sultan.[6]

Some important Dargahs in Hyderabad Area during 16th & 17th Centuries A.D.

Sl. No.	*Name of Dargah*	*Dargah Situated at*
1.	Dargah-e-Hazrat Meer Muhammad Momin	Daira-e-Meer Momin
2.	Dargah-e-Shah Raju	Fateh Darwaza
3.	Dargah-e-Allama Ibn-e-Khatoon	Purani Haveli
4.	Dargah-e-Hazrat Hussain Shah Wali	Toli Chowki
5.	Dargah-e-Hazrat Noorullah Hussaini Chishti	Nampally
6.	Dargah-e-Hazrat Meer Mahmood	Near Meer Alam Tank
7.	Dargah-e-Hazrat Shah Shiblee	Langer Houz
8.	Dargah-e-Hazrat Bodle Shah	Dabirpura

Structure Styles of Some Dargahs

The Dargahs generally developed into simple structures of the Muslims. During the Qutb Shahi period there was tremendous Dargah building activity. The Dargah had a dome typed structure. Many Dargahs fully or partially were built by the Hindus. For instance, the outer *Dalan* (hall) of Meer Momins tomb was built by a Hindu named Kumar Raju.[7] Dargah-e-Hazrat Meer Muhammad Momin is situated in Daira-e-Meer Momin locality of Hyderabad. The tomb is a simple rectangular building. It has a flat roof over which there are four minarets on four sides having *Kalus*. The entrance to the grave chamber is through a wooden door. A number of graves are there inside the shrine. Meer Momin's grave, which is of black basalt rock, is in one corner of the rectangular hall. Dargah-e-Allama Ibn-e-Khatoon is situated at Purani Haveli. It is a very simple structure with a rectangular room. This room has no roof and four stone slabs are placed from wall to wall.

Dargah-e-Shah Raju is situated at Fateh Darwaza in Hyderabad. The grave chamber of the tomb is plastered with power lime over the floor. The entry to this chamber is through a wooden door. The tomb has a large area around it, enclosed with the stone wall. Dargah-e-Hazrat Hussain Shah Wali, which is in Hyderabad, is magnificent in architectural aspect. It has a double arched entrance having two small rooms on either sides. The tomb has a large single dome with a *Kalus* over it. The grave chamber is approached through a wooden door. Inside the grave chamber, there is a wooden carved architecture gracefully built over twelve pillars. The grave of Hussain Shah Wali is built beneath this structure. Dargah-e-Hazrat Bodle Shah in Hyderabad has a huge grave yard, which is a simple rectangular building. Bodle Shah's grave is distinct from the other graves of the period. It is built of red mud and is larger in size.[8] Thus, the construction of the Dargahs of Sufi saints were simple and saintly.

Endowments to Dargahs

The Qutb Shahs and the Hindu rulers of the period liberally granted the lands and gave cash to the Dargahs for their maintenance. During the time of Abdullah Qutb Shah, a Farman was issued on 25th Muharram 1070 A.H. regarding the grant of the village Mallapur as Inam land towards the expenses of a Langar and the maintenance etc. of the Dargah Rojah Munawwar and the Sajjadagi in favour of Shah Muhammad.[9] Another Farman, which was issued on 9th Muhurram 1099 A.H., mentioned the grant of 90 Chawar of land as Inam in favour of the Sufi of the Dargah (un-named).[10] As the Dargah of Baba Fakhruddin of Penugonda was situated in the centre of the Hindu empire, the Vijayanagara kings Vira Narasimha (1505-09 A.D.), Sadasiva Raya (1543-1576 A.D.), Venkata-II (1586-1614 A.D.), and Venkata-III (1630-1642 A.D.) of that empire gave several villages for its maintenance.[11]

Functionaries of Dargah

The information regarding the organization of Dargah in Andhra Desa during this period is meager. It appears that each Dargah had a Mutawalli and generally he was a descendant of the saint to whom the Dargah pertained. In some cases the saints themselves appointed the Mutawallis of their tomb before their death. The Mutawalli was the owner of the properties (lands, buildings etc.) of the Dargah. The other important functionary of the Dargah was the Sajjada (Manager). The functions of the Sajjada were to look after its properties, conduct it's annual festival (Urs) and supervise the work of menial servants. In the small Dargahs with limited income, the Mutawalli himself discharged the duties of the Sajjada. The menial servants of Dargah included the waterman, the sweeper and the lamp-keeper. These functionaries posts were hereditary and they had Inam lands for their maintenance.[12]

My Own Experience with Dargah

A Dargah was situated on the way to my school in Khammam town of Telangana. While going to school, I used to say 'Salam Baba' to the Wali or Muslim Sufi saint, who stayed in a room close to the Dargah. Some times, I used to stand at his door to greet him till he opened his eyes from meditation. After receiving blessings from him my heart used to fill with happiness and contentment. This virtuous act developed a sense of self-discipline in me. In Khammam town we stayed for some years in a small lane (Galli) where there were quite a number of Muslim houses. They were very friendly and affectionate with us. On every Friday, I used to get ready before the Muslim girls to go to Dargah to get blessings and for '*Mitai prasadam*'. It used to bestow on me immense happiness when Mutawalli of the Dargah kept *ud* (ash) on my eyes and blessed on the head with the broom of peacock feathers. Many people from divergent castes and creeds visited the Dargah on Friday and offered valuable things to it. Mingling with different people in the Dargah promoted in me secular outlook. Being a Hindu, on certain occasions, I used to visit temples with my parents. Visiting both a temple and a Dargah inculcated in me the feeling that God is One.

Due to the influence of my association with Dargah in my child-hood, I used to derive delight in participating in the celebrations of Idd. Wearing new clothes and relishing the sweet preparations at my Muslim friends' houses, I used to spend Idd joyfully. The annual festival of Dargah, known as *Urs*, used to be an attraction to me as shops were installed with colourful and beautiful toys and other articles.

Dargah – A Symbol of Popular Culture

The Dargahs of the Sufi saints are the meeting places of the people drawn from different religious sections of people. The devotees visited the Dargahs to pay their respect and ask for their wishes in large numbers with utmost devotion, irrespective of their caste and community, sect and sex. They trusted in the super natural powers of the *Peers*.[13] Because of this reason, that a number of Karamats (miracles) of these Sufi saints are told and recorded. For instance, Abdul Jabbar Malkapuri wrote that a Sufi saint, Meer Mahmood used to light the lamps with water in order to assist the labourers to work at night, as the oil was not sold to him due to the orders of the Sultan.[14] In the similar way Murad Ali Tale writes that when Hussain Shah Wali looked with anger at an attacking eagle, it got burnt and died.[15] But it was not this factor alone which made the Sufis and their Dargahs prominent institutions, but more so it was their preaching's like love, service to the needy and poor, devotion, brotherhood, tolerance, penance, etc. attracted the people to their Dargahs. Their Khanqahs (generally they are the places of Sufi saints that serve as the living quarters of their devotees) promoted the spirit of unity in Deccan where the Amirs and the Faqirs, the Muslims and the Hindus lived and dined together.

A Dargah was a common place of worship for every and any individual. When Shah Charag came and settled down at Chichalam, there was no Muslims, in the village.

The Brahmins of that village looked after him by providing all facilities.[16] Some Dargahs were located in the localities populated by the Hindus. The *Dargah-e-Hazrat Bodle Shah* was situated in a locality named after him in Hyderabad. The locality was dominated by the Hindus and it was constructed in 17th century during Qutb Shahi period.[17] *Dargah-e-Hazrat Shah Shiblee* is situated in a locality where Hindus were in majority. So, the majority of the devotees who came to this Dargah were Hindus. These Dargahs were also provided with all amenities to the devotees. Most of the Muslims and Hindus used to take *Taweez* from the Dargahs in order to protect themselves from sickness and evil spirits. Meer Muhammad Momin, a Sufi saint and also a Peshwa got a stone pillar erected at the entrance arch of Julu Khana on which he inscribed a *Taweez* to remove the evil designs of the enemies of the Sultan when they entered the palace.[18] Urs is the festival of Dargah which is celebrated annually on the death anniversary of a saint. The devotees, more so the poor, attended the Dargahs from far off places. The Hindus participation used to be substantial not only in those days but also even today. Faqirs and poor people were fed during the days of the Urs.

The Sufi saints by their writings in Dakhni Urdu, besides the Persian language, made the Dargah as centres of popular culture. It is interesting to note that some of the titles of their books are the combination of Dakhni Urdu and Persian. For example, *Charka Nama*. In this title, the first word *Charka* is from Dakhni Urdu and the second word Nama is Persian. As the main aim of the Sufi saints was to make the people to understand their preachings, they wrote in the language of the people. One Sufi writer had expressed it in a couplet of his poem in the following manner.

I want to write to fulfill my purpose.

I am not worried which language it is-Dakhni or Persian.[19]

The style of their writings was a reflection of their broadmindedness. Discarding the Persian style of poetry, they followed the styles of the land and some of their poems were written in the style of folk songs. These songs were interestingly sung in the Qutb Shahi kingdom. Further, the characters and themes of the stories were extracted from the traditions of the land, which had Hindu base. Thus, their writings became popular among the people irrespective of religion.

Dargahs not only played an important role during the period under review but also even today they are influencing the lives of people of different communities. In 1998, I visited a popular Dargah known as Dargah-e-Hazrat Jahangir Peeran, which is situated at a distance of 45 kilometres from Hyderabad. It is a popular Dargah that attracts a large number of people everyday. I was moved, looking at the number of Muslims and non-Muslims offering their prayers with utmost devotion. The Dargah had a landed property of 24 acres and 18 Guntas for its maintenance. The annual income of the Dargah is spent for its maintenance and Urs celebrations. There is an Urdu medium Upper Primary school and the salaries of the teachers and attenders are met from the Dargah funds. Among the employees of the Dargah, there are men and women of Muslim and non-Muslim communities.[20]

Most of the Hindu pilgrims come to the Dargah-e-Hazrat Jahangir Peeran for the fulfillment of their desires, such as recovery from sickness, begetting children, for getting marriages, jobs and seat in medicine and engineering etc. Most of the devotees visit the Dargah to get rid of from the family problems. The interesting thing is that a number of politicians of the region both Muslims and non-Muslims visit the Dargah in general and frequently before the elections in particular. It seems that M.L.A.'s became ministers after getting the blessings at Dargah.[21] The non-Muslim devotees, after fulfillment of their vows, offer *Niaz* or *Kanduri* along with their relatives. On this occasion, they offer many goats and feed their relatives, pilgrims and poor people sumptuously. The girls and boys who are born with the blessings of saints of Dargahs are named after them. Yakayya, Yakamma, Usenappa, Usenamma, Laleyya, Lalemma, Mastanaiah, Saidaiah, Saidamma, Jangaiah, Jangamma Ussain Reddy and Saidi Reddy etc. These names indicate the synthesis of Hindu-Muslim sentiments.

Thus, the Dargahs richly contributed to the social and religious harmony during the period under review as they do now. As they are the meeting places of all communities and classes, they promoted friendship, flexibility, understanding, tolerance, solidarity and the spirit of unity etc. They stood as a symbol of popular culture in the annals of history.

Notes & References

1. Sadiq Naqvi, *Muslim Religious Institutions and their Role under the Qutb Shahs*, Hyderabad, 1993, p. 148.
2. Abdul Jabbar Khan Malkapuri, *Mahbubu-I-dhil-manam Tadhkira Auliya-I-Dakhan*, Vol. I, Hyderabad, p. 164.
3. *Annual Report on Indian Epigraphy and South Indian Epigraphy*, 1967, D.n.2.
4. T. Srinivas, "Rajukonda and it Remains", *The Journal of the Hyderabad Archaeological Society*, 1916.
5. Muhmmad Ali Asar, *Dabistan-e-Golkonda*, Hyderabad, 1981, pp. 248-255.
6. Sadiq Naqvi, *Op.Cit.*, p. 257.
7. Record with the Sajjada Nasheen of the Dargah.

8. Sadiq Naqvi, *Op.Cit.*, pp.123 to 142.
9. *Farman*, A.P. State Archives and Research Institute, Tarnaka, Hyderabad.
10. *Ibid.*
11. *Annual Report on Indian Epigraphy and South Indian Epigraphy*, 1911-62, pp. 89-90.
12. R. Soma Reddy, *Hindu and Muslim Religious Institutions, Andhra Desa 1300-1600 A.D.*, Madras, 1984, p. 93.
13. Peer-means a Saint, but generally the term is used for Sufi Saint.
14. Malkapuri Muhammad Abdul Jabbar, *Mahboob-uz-Zaman. Tazkirah-e-Awolia-e-Dakhan*, Vol. II, Hyderabad, p. 326.
15. Syed Murad Ali Tale, *Tazkirah-e-Awolia-e-Hyderabad*, Minar Publishers, Hyderabad, 1984, p.54.
16. Syed Muhammad, "Qutb Shahi Daur Ke Chand Buzurgan-e-Deen", *Dabistan-e-Golkonda* (Ed.), Muhammad Ali Asar, Hyderabad, p. 195.
17. Khaja Gulam Hussain, *Gulzar-e-Asafia*, Hyderabad, 1890, p. 335.
18. Zore Mohiuddin Qadri, *Hayat-e-Meer Momin, Idara-e-Adabiat Urdu*, Hyderabad, 1975, p. 49.
19. Sadiq Naqvi, *Op.Cit.*, p. 149.
20. The then Assistant Secretary of *Dargah-e-Jahangir Peeran* Sadiq Ali Khan furnished this information.
21. This information is from my interview with Mahmood Ali, the then Deputy Superintendent of Dargah-e-Hazrat Jahangir Peeran.

11

SOME ASPECTS OF SOCIAL LIFE IN MEDIEVAL ORUGALLU CITY AS DELINEATED IN KRIDABHIRAMAM

Social history deals with the common habits, customs, beliefs and other creative aspects of life of the people. A good many literary pieces deal with the sunny side of the life of the nobility. Unlike those works, *Kridabhiramam* written by Vinukonda Vallabharaya between 1431-1433[1] A.D. provide the historian with much needed information about the living conditions of the humble and the poor of the city of Orugallu. It is essential to fix the date of *Kridabhiramam* in order to establish the utility of the material taken from this source.

This work is a Telugu Vidhi (street play). It is said to be an adoption of the Sanskrit drama *Premabhiramam,* written by Ravipati Tippana. As the *Premabhiramam* is lost, it is impossible to know whether the author of *Kridabhiramam* closely followed the original text, or followed the text only outline. It was said that Tippana was in the court of Prataparudra-II. In the *'Tirunallu'* (annual festival), which were conducted at holy place, many dramas were enacted for the entertainment of pilgrims. The *Premabhiramam* must have been written to be enacted at the *'Tirunallu'* of Tripurantakesvara. Vallabharaya, the author of *Kridabhiramam* translated this Sanskrit work into Telugu to get it enacted in the festivities of Mopuru Bhairava Swamy.

The introductory verses reveal to us that the *Kridabhiramam* is the work of Vallabharaya and all that we know of him is from this single work, which furnishes some clues to estimate his date. The author's father Tippana served Harihara-II, as the master of elephant of the Governor of the fortress of Vinukonda. It was originally a fort of the Reddi Kings of Kondavidu. Bukka-I of Vijayanagara led a military campaign in north-eastern quarter and occupied Vinukonda about *Saka* 1286 (1364 A.D.). Subsequently, the Reddi King, Anavema recovered his lost possessions from his Vijayanagara contemporary, Harihara-II, in about *Saka* 1299 (1377 A.D.), the date of Anavema's Srisailam record. The Mahanandi inscription, dated *Saka* 1312 (1390 A.D.), record the gift of the village, Vinjanampadu in Vinukonda - *Sima,* by Bukkaraya, son of Harihara-II, for the prosperity of the kingdom. It is clear that Vinukonda was under the rule of Harihara-II, during this period. If Tippana was an officer attached to the fort of Vinukonda, it must be after its re-conquest by the Vijayanagara king Harihara-II. So, it is certain that Tippana flourished in the last decade of the 14th century. His son Vallabharaya must have lived during the first half of the 15th century.

After closely analyzing the poetic style of *Kridabhiramam,* some of the critics opined that it was the work of the great poet Srinatha. Even, we too find a number of similarities in the descriptions and sentences in the *Kridabhiramam*, which clearly betray the hand of the great poet, Srinatha. Srinatha adorned the court of Pedda Komati Vema Reddi of Kondavidu upto 1420 A.D.

Between 1421-25 A.D., the Reddi Kingdom of Kondavidu declined and Srinatha was compelled to migrate to the Reddi Kings of Rajamahendravaram. Local rivalry appears to have forced him to leave the place. At the same time, Srinatha who was equally desirous of fame and recognition decided to take up the challenge offered by Dindima Bhattu, the Court poet of Devaraya-II of Vijayanagara (1424-46 A.D.). In the process of his trial and tribulations to reach Vijayanagara court, he appears to have met on the way Vallabharaya, the governor of Mopur to find opening to the Vijayanagara court.

Probably, Vallabharaya was translating *Kridabhiramam* at this time. Srinatha, who had come seeking the help of Vallabharaya might have helped him in the composition of the work. Srinatha gained access to the court of Devaraya-II and defeated Dindima. Devaraya-II, who honoured Srinatha with the title 'Kavi Sarvabhouma' and had him bathed in a shower of golden Tankas. This event in the life of Srinatha must have occurred before 1434 A.D., for thereafter Devaraya-II was very busy in his military campaign against Gajapathis and Bahmanis. Therefore, the composition of *Kridabhiramam* was definitely before 1434 A.D. Deducting the time-lag for the effort of Srinatha to gain entry into Vijayanagara court, we may fix the date of the composition of *Kridabhiramam* between 1431-33 A.D. So, an attempt is made here to bring into light some social aspects of Medieval Orugallu city as delineated in *Kridabhiramam*. Besides this work, data otherwise available is used for the sake of verification and reconstruction.

Kridabhiramam, the Telugu work is the translation of Premabhiramam, a work in Sanskrit. Unlike many other works in Telugu, this work has an importance of its own. It is one of the most valuable works in Telugu language. One of the principal characteristics of any good and substantial work is to truly reflect the contemporary society. Viewed in this light, *Kridabhiramam*, which faithfully records and preserves the main as well as the subsidiary features of the Andhra society of 14th and 15th centuries is of unique importance as a source material for the history of society in medieval Telangana. This work is a 'Street Drama' (Vidhi Nataka), written by Vinukonda Vallabharaya. The drama was enacted by the actors of Dorasamudram.[2]

Govinda Manchana Sarma and Tittibha Setty are the principal characters of the drama. The former was a cultured and fashionable Brahmin youth, and the latter a shrewd Vaisya youngman. Manchana Sarma, the native of Orugallu, lived outside his state for some time and later returned to Orugallu with his friend Tittibha Setty. The finances for the trip were borne by the rich merchant Tittibha Setty. One day both friends set out at the dawn to see the city of Ekasilanagara otherwise known as Orugallu. The sweet sounds emanating from the city and the beautiful sights of the city are skillfully described by Manchana Sarma to his friend. The two young men saw and enjoyed all the beauties and marvels of the city till at night, and finally reached their scheduled place to spend the rest of night. This, in short, is the theme of the book.

The word 'custom' indicate a habit or practice. The customs are the practices or certain observation in the daily life of man, which are handed over from generation to generation. In fact, these customs regulate the life of the people in society. In medieval times, religious practices were given a new orientation. The performance of Yagas and Yagnas was not considered very necessary. The new tendency was to observe diverse Vratas and innumerable

Danas. The new turn religion removed the divergence between the first three Varnas and knit them more closely. The members of the fourth caste were made to feel that the Hindu religion was as much theirs, as it was that of the higher castes. Panchangam (the Hindu almanac) played an important role in the daily routine of all the people of all communities. Their domestic and social activities were guided by a consideration of the auspicious moment for commencing them in order to achieve success. Though there is no direct reference to the use of Panchangam in *Kridabhiramam,* from all other contemporary sources it is clear that the use of Panchangam was an established habit.

The device to reckon time during this period was called Gadiyaram. They measured the time in Gadiyas. For a day there were sixty Gadiyas and one Gadiya is equal to 24 minutes. *Kridabhiramam* refers to the Gadiyaram in the Mosala (entrance hall) of the Andhra monarch at Orugallu.[3] In *Palanativira Charitra*[4] there is a reference to the Gadiyaram in the entrance hall of the king. Though, it is perfectly clear that the people knew the art of measuring time, it is not very clear whether such devices were in common use and what kinds of Gadiyarams were in existence.

The Brahmins of those days performed 'Sandhyavandanam' thrice daily without fail. Before leaving the house for their work or on journey the men used to complete all their prescribed 'Sandya' and 'Agnihotra' rituals.[5] Self-immolation was a custom of the then society. The devotees of Mailara Deva used to jump down, from a considerable height above, into the pit of sharp iron spikes below, cutting of the cords of the fibrous networking sling, 'utti', as it is called in Telugu, which they held while hanging in the air. They used to light 'aratulu' in their naked palms and wave them before the deity.[6] Fire-walking was another custom of the people of Orugallu. This was also practiced by the servants of god Mailara Deva, who rushed into pits filled with live-embers and walked across them.[7]

Hero-cult was another interesting social custom of Orugallu during this period. The heroes were the Martyrs, who were honoured by the commemoration of their sculptural representations in their act of trying to kill themselves for their religious beliefs, or fighting for their master or country. In Orugallu city there was a temple of Heroes of Palanadu.[8] Before commencing any important act, the people of this age consult omens. It was their belief that a thing could not be achieved without the 'Sakunabala', strength of the omen. *Kridabhiramam* mentioned some auspicious omens, which are conducive to success. The people believed that if they heard the sound of an owl from the left side, it was a good omen. They also believed that the sight of a hen, small jackal or peacock etc, from a branch of a tree is auspicious.[9] While starting on a journey, if the Poornakumba is sighted, it is considered to be a good omen.[10]

Saivism and Vaishnavism provided for many kinds of Vratas in the society. These Vratas served as a means of educating the common man and training him in disciplining his conduct in life. *Kridabhiramam* refers to Ekadasi and Kameshwari Vratams of Vaishnavas and Saivas respectively.[11] Kameshwari Vratam mainly relates to the worship of seven married women, who go by the general name Akkalu. Even to this day, we find this Saivaite Vratas being observed by many families, especially in Brahmin community, on auspicious day like wedding. There are references to festivals like Ugadi, Dipavali, Sankranti and Vasanthotsava etc., in contemporary inscriptions and literature. *Kridabhiramam* mentions the festivals namely Davanapunnama[12] (the full moon day of the night of the month of Chaitra). The annual festival of god Telunguraya of Kakulam (Srikakulam) used to celebrate on this day. Two inscriptions[13] at Draksharamam dated 1275 and 1287 A.D. register the grants to god Bhimesvara on the occasion of Dolotsava on Davanapunnama.

The chief article of food of the people in those days was mainly rice. There were many public-eating houses maintained by widows. They used to provide facilities to the travellers. They charged for these services. These houses used to serve delicious food consisting of the best variety of rice (Kappura Bhogies), preparations made of wheat flour, fresh cow ghee, green gram, four or five varieties of chutnies, savouries, curds and bananas for rupee one.[14] During the winter the rich families of the villages used to take new rice with curry made of mustard leaves, ghee and curds.[15] It appears that green gram was in greater use in those days. Srinatha's works *Sringaranaisadham*[16] and *Haravilasam*[17] refer to its use. Use of turmeric, both in the form of powder and paste by women is noticed, *Kridabhiramam*[18] gives a full length description of a lady grinding turmeric chips.

The habit of taking *tambulam* immediately after meals was quite common in those days. The *tambulam* taken by the commoners consisted of betel leaves, lime and arecanut, where as the *tambulam* consumed by wealthy people consisted of many other ingredients. Adverting to the fact how common became its use, *Kridabhiramam*[19] refers to the woman of Kapu caste who took *tambulam* soon after brushing her teeth. In *Sumati Satakam*, it is stated that taking *tambulam* immediately after brushing teeth is good for health. Even foreigners of those times were very much attracted to the use of *tambulam*. As mentioned already in the preceding pages. Abdul Razzack, who visited Vijayanagara court, says 'it relieves hunger, stimulates the organs of digestion, disinfects the breath and strengthens the teeth'.[20] The common drink that was within the reach of all is water. Some of the drinks were referred to in *Kridabhiramam*. One of these was 'Sidhupanam'[21] prepared out of sugarcane. The contemporary literary work, *Simhasanadvatrimsika*,[22] reveals the use of other liquors known as 'Madavam', 'Ikshavam', 'Goudirasam' and Asavam'.

Chira (saree) and Raika (bodice) was the ordinary dress worn by women. Barbosa was struck by the style of the wearing saree of women and says, "The women wear white garments of very thin cotton or silk of bright colours, five yards long, one part of which is girt round them below, and the other part they throw over one shoulder and across their breasts in such a way that one arm and shoulder remains uncovered, as with a scarf (reguacho)".[23] The number and variety of sarees indicates desire of the ladies of the times to select shades, colours and designs of their choice.

Karnataka woman of Orugallu wore a saree, which had a 'Kongu' with printed flowers.[24] The woman selling 'Sampangi Oil' wore 'Madugu' (silk) saree in a single layer.[25] A 'Kapu' woman wore red saree with cheques and silver lace (jari) border. She converted half of the saree into frills and tucked that portion at the back.[26] To the present day some women are wearing sarees in this fashion in Warangal area. At a function named 'Akkala Aradhana' a woman wore 'Velipattu' (white silk) saree. Men of these days used to wear silk clothes with golden borders.[27] Thus, both men and women were fond of silk garments. Telugu works of this period enumerate a number of cotton and silk cloths which were available in this period. Women mostly stitched their bodices themselves at home. However, tailors (Kutrapuvandru)[28] were there to stitch clothes, though they were patronised by the wealthy and fashionable ladies alone. Batuta says "the women of Hanaur and of all the coastal districts do not wear stitched cloths but only unsewn garments. They tie one end of the cloth round their waist and drap the rest over the head and chest".[29]

'Dovati' and 'Uttariyam' formed the general dress of men. There were many varieties in them in silk and cotton. They had variety of exquisite borders. Manchana Sarma, a Brahmin voluptuary, wore light pink coloured 'nirkavi' Dovati with frills. He draped his upper part of the body with a silk cloth having golden border (Uttariyam). He had the sacred thread made of white silk with golden threads.[30] In the contemporary Telugu work, *Sivaratrimahatyam*,[31] it is stated that the voluptuaries belonging to the Brahmin community wore light pink coloured 'nirkavi' Dovatis. To smear their fore heads with 'Gangamatti' (holy mud) was considered sacred. They applied musk over 'Gangamatti'. It was an age, where the orthodox also had lively sense of enjoyment.

Wool was very little used. Nicolo de Conti says that the people wore a linen cloth round the body; he adds that they could not wear more clothings on account of the great heat.[32] Both men and women wore sandals. They were made of light wood, leather, ivory and metal. Some of the sandals (Cheppulu) produced while walking great creaking sound, while the rest made no noise when in use. 'Malakavalla Kirru Cheppulu', the creaking shoes of the Malakas or Mussalmans, are referred to in *Kridabhiramam.*[33]

Foreign travellers, who visited the country, did not fail to notice the love of the inhabitants of the country for ornaments. Abdur Razzak says 'All the inhabitants of this country, both those of the exalted rank and of an inferior class, down to the artisans of the bazaar, wear pearls or rings adorned with precious stones, in their ear's on their necks, on their arms, on the upper part of the hand, and on the fingers'.[34] Mukkera is the nose ornament.[35] Ear ornaments are known by the names Tatamkas and Kundalas in Sanskrit, and Kammalu in Telugu. In Orugallu city a 'Medara Karana' prostitute wore white Tatamkas.[36] Necklaces are the ornaments worn around the neck. Some of them hung down as far as the chest, and some descended still lower down as far as the navel, and some others were worn round the neck. These ornaments are called Haras in Sanskrit and Perulu in Telugu. The women of Orugallu wore necklaces made in the design of tender leaves of neem. A Karnataka woman of the city had a chain of pearls of three strings known as 'trisaramulu'.[37]

Jewels wore on hands were many and varied. *Kridabhiramam* mentions 'Moravanka Kidiyamulu' which were oval shaped and were worn around the upper arm. They had the images of 'linga' on three sides. Commoners used to wear simple bangles. 'Nupurams' were the ornaments wore around the feet. In those days women wore 'Kanchipura Nupurams'.[38] Growing long hair was the fashion of the day among men and women in Hindu Society. Women had their tresses either plaited or arranged in loops or twisted in knots. Some ladies let their plaits fall in between their breasts,[39] by way of fashion. If small curly locks hang on to the fore-head and move there, it is considered beautiful. Men had their hair arranged in different kinds of knots, tight and loose. Manchana arranged his thick hair into loose knot, known as 'Valudasika'.[40] Warriors dressed up their hair in twisted knots.

The love of scents and perfumes seems to have been only second to that of ornaments. The perfumes used by them varied according to the season. Saffron (a species of crocus with purple flowers) had been applied by the ladies to their chests. In *Kasikhandam*,[41] it is stated that Apsarasas (women of beauty) applied saffron to their breasts. It was used for Rangoli also. Women and men of those days liked sandal wood very much. Sometimes, the solution of sandal paste was sprinkled in front of the mansions to make the atmosphere balmy. Warriors (Virapurushulu) used to apply 'viragandam'[42] (yellow sandal wood) on their foreheads. There were women selling 'sampangi oil' in the city of Ekasilanagara. This oil was used for hair bath. *Haravilasam*[43] of Srinatha mentions that this oil was applied to Parvati, when she was given the holy hair bath.

The people used 'Black Agaru' (Agaru means aloe or scented wood). This Agaru (scented black substance) is applied to protect oneself from cold. During winter the people made use of dried ginger, burnt incense, civet along with this Agaru. In *Madhuravijayam*, there is a reference to the maidens, who exposed their hair to the smokes of Krishna-agaru[44] (black Agaru). It also mentions that in Agaru, the Kalagaru is the most fragrant one.[45] Rose water was distilled from rose leaves. Generally, it was used for bathing. Some Brahmins of those times applied the holy mud (Gangamatti) mixed with rose water.[46]

Notes & References

1. R. Varalakshmi, *Social Life in Medieval Andhra 1300-1500 A.D., as Reflected in Kridabhiramam* (unpublished) M.Phil. Dissertation, Osmania University, Hyderabad, 1983, p.1-8.

2. Vinukonda Vallabharaya, *Kridabhiramam*, published by V. Prabhakara Sastry, Hyderabad, 1960, v.293. Dorasamudram was the Capital City of Hoyasalas.
3. R. Varalakshmi, *Op.Cit.*, p. 50.
4. Srinatha, *Palanativira Charitra*, p. 270.
5. Vinukonda Vallabharaya, *Op.Cit.*, vv. 65, 189 & 273.
6. *Ibid.*, v.142.
7. *Ibid.*
8. *Ibid.*, v.115.
9. *Ibid.*, vv.51 & 52.
10. *Ibid.*, vv.63.
11. *Ibid.*, vv.170 & 139.
12. *Ibid.*, v.204.
13. *South Indian Inscriptions*, No.1373 &1368.
14. Vinukonda Vallabharaya, *Op.Cit.*, v.166.
15. *Ibid.*, v.56.
16. Srinatha, *Srungaranaisadham*, IV, v.120.
17. Srinatha, *Haravilasam*, VI, v.56.
18. Vinukonda Vallabharaya, *Op.Cit.*, v.110.
19. *Ibid.*, v.134.
20. Elliot and Dowson, *History of India as told by its own Historians,* Vol. IV, p.114.
21. Vinukonda Vallabharaya, *Op.Cit.*, v.147.
22. Koravi Goparaju, *Simhasanadvatrimsika*, I, IV, v.256.
23. R. Varalakshmi, *Op.Cit.*, p.56.
24. Vinukonda Vallabharaya, *Op.Cit.*, v.86.
25. *Ibid.*, v.101.
26. *Ibid.*, v.134.
27. *Ibid.*, vv.137 & 42.
28. *Ibid.*, v.106.

29. K.A. Nilakanta Sastry, *Foreign Notices of South India*, University of Madras, 1939, pp.233 & 234.
30. Vinukonda Vallabharaya, *Op.Cit.*, v.42.
31. Srinatha, *Sivaratrimahatyam*, II, v.90.
32. R.H. Major, *India in the Fifteenth Century*, p.22.
33. Vinukonda Vallabharaya, *Op.Cit.*, v.42.
34. Elliot and Dowson, *Op.Cit.*, IV, p.109.
35. Srinatha, *Palanativira Charitra*, p.66.
36. Vinukonda Vallabharaya, *Op.Cit.*, v.68.
37. *Ibid.*, v.86.
38. *Ibid.*, v.258.
39. *Ibid.*, v.101.
40. *Ibid.*, v.42.
41. Srinatha, *Kasikhandam*, Preface, v.14.
42. Vinukonda Vallabharaya, *Op.Cit.*, v.120.
43. Srinatha, *Haravilasam*, IV, v.81.
44. Gangadevi, *Madhuravijayam*, I, v.59.
45. *Ibid.*, v.18.
46. Srinatha, *Kasikhandam*, III, v.119.

12

CONTRIBUTION OF RELIGIOUS INSTITUTIONS FOR URBANISATION

Cities and towns have functioned as focal points in cultural scenario of India from times immemorial. The Indian subcontinent along with the Nile valley and Mesopotamia shares a long history of urbanisation. Modern cities have their roots in the past. In medieval period, towns generally had a temple, market and people following different occupations. In the absence of population figures, the medieval Indian town can be defined as "a compact conglomeration of inhabitants with in delimited area, a centralized governing organism, and industries as the materially productive unit exists".[1]

There was great acceleration to urban growth in medieval Telangana and Andhra. Various factors, such as political, economic, social and religious, contributed to urban growth during the period under review. In fact, urban growth is a complex amalgam of several factors in which no individual factor can be singled out. However, in the present study the contribution of religious institutions in the process of urbanisation is discussed. In medieval Telangana and Andhra the Hindu and Muslim religious institutions like temples, Mathas, pontifical seats, mosques, Dargahs, Ashurkhanas and Khanqahs played an important role in the urban growth. The temple was a powerful social and economic entity and dominated the life of people. Though the religious institutions were present both in the villages and towns, but it was in towns that more significant and large religious establishments could be found.

The temple in medieval times influenced the economic, socio-cultural life of the people. It was considered as an essential ingredient of a city. K.A. Nilakanta Sastri says that the temple was a citadel of economic power enjoying a *status quo* equal to that of the State.[2] Temple developed as a great economic institution. The property of the temple consisted of lands and villages, gold and silver, houses and house sites etc. Temple received innumerable land grants from kings, nobles and private individuals mostly as 'Sarvamanya' or tax free lands. The rulers of the Kakatiya, Velama, Reddi and Vijayanagara donated a large number of villages to all the temples irrespective of their sectarian affiliations. By providing good irrigational facilities, temple promoted agriculture. The enormous yield of agricultural produce from the temple lands not only contributed to the creation of surplus but also to the promotion of trade activity.

Taxes collected from certain communities like tolls and custom duties raised on article of merchandise were also donated to the temples. Various taxes collected from the communities like Viramustis, Vipravinodins and Dommaras were added to the temple economy. The chief of the mercantile corporation of Ayyavole made the gift of toll on different articles of merchandise to God Kalyana Venkateshwara of Narayanapuram.[3] Thus, the income from the taxes made the temple financial position sound and this contributed to the development of urban economy.

The temples received houses and house sites from the kings and other benefactors. It is known from the available sources that the temple employees were furnished with houses for comfortable living and also to enable them to attend their duties on time.[4] These houses contributed for the growth of physical structures in towns. The temple was an institution which had great employment opportunities. As there was an increase in the physical dimensions of temple corresponding to their growth in property and patronage, the administration of the temple became elaborate. The temple staff consisted of the Sthanikas, Senapati, Priests, Pauranikas, reciters of the Prabandhams, temple cooks, car pullers, torch bearers, instrumentalists, needle workers, Panchanamvaru, potters, Sanis, Manis, washermen, the Bhandari, accountants etc. Thus, the temple elaborate administrative staff contributed for the population growth in towns.

Temple was the great consumer of goods. The medieval temple was marked by an elaborate system of rituals and the performance of many festivals required a wide range of articles including luxury items. Consequently, many industries such as textile industry, sugar and oil industries, metal industry, the industry of precious stones, sculpture, woodwork, ivory work, brick laying, masonary, pottery, garland making etc. flourished. This resulted in the promotion of trade and commerce. Hence, this industrial and trade activity helped the growth of towns.

Besides being a centre of economic power, temple served as a potential factor in the social and educational development of a town. Temples received numerous donations for the purpose of fostering education by maintaining teachers and providing free boarding to the students. They imparted education both in religious and secular subjects.[5] It appears that some temples maintained libraries where several manuscripts were preserved.[6] They also became centres of dance and music. They acted as a theatre for the performance of arts. Devadasis (temple girls) fostered and developed dance and music by their excellent performances in the temples. The temple festivals attracted thousands of pilgrims and contributed to the cultural contacts and unity among people.

Besides Vaishnava and Saiva temples, the Jaina temples also played a considerable role in the promotion of urbanisation. The inscriptions at the temples in Tirupathi, Simhachalam and Rayachoti signify that the temple continued to grow with the patronage of individuals despite the frequent political instabilities.[7] In medieval Telangana and Andhra, Srisailam, Ahobilam, Tirupati, Kalahasti, Draksharamam, Kalesvaram, Simhachalam, Srikurman, Alampur, Bhadrachalam, Vemulavada, Vijayawada, Lepakshi, Tripurantakam, Tangeda, Kadiri, Tadipatri etc. flourished with their temples as significant religious urban centres.

The Hindu Mathas or Monasteries played considerable role in the process of urban growth. The Kalamukha and the Pasupatha Saiva teachers first established their Mathas in Andhra country. In medieval period, Srisailam, a reputed Saiva centre became the seat of a number of Saiva Mathas. The Vira Saiva Mathas such as the Basavanna Matha and the Bhikshavritti Matha were founded in Srisailam. The Jiyyangar Matham at Tirupati is believed as founded by Ramanuja, the renowned Srivaishnava Acharya. The Golaki Matha (Pasupata Saiva Matha) of the Kakatiya period had its branches at Mandaram, Bhattiprolu (Guntur district), Tripurantakam (Kurnool district), Pushpagiri (Cuddapah district) and

Gangapuram (Mahboobnagar district). Two Dvaita Mathas, one at Simhachalam and another at Srikurmam were established by Narasimha Bharati, a Madhava teacher in 14th century A.D.[8]

The Mathas were mainly patronized by the kings and rich people. As a result, they became wealthy institutions with a large number of landed estates, buildings and various sources of income. The Mathas had also administrative staff. Mathadhipathi or pontiff was the absolute master of the Mathas. There were junior pontiffs to manage the Mathas in the absence of senior pontiffs. Mostly the Brahmins occupied the pontifical seats in Hindu Mathas, except the Vira Saiva Mathas where the Jangamas became the Mathadipathis. In addition to the pontiffs, there were Karyakarthas and Mudrakarthas (seal-bearer). An epigraph[9] from Tripurantakam mention the Matha-paricharakulu (menial servants), Kavadivaru (men for bringing water), Mathamu-tonta-Chesevaru (gardeners), Math-Satramu-Vantala Vandru (cooks), Mathamuratripagalu Kachikoni Undedi Varu (watchmen) etc. Thus, the Mathas with their rich estates and administrative personnel contributed to the growth of urban centres in medieval Andhra Desa.

A large number of Muslim religious institutions such as the mosques, Khanqahs, Dargahs and Ashurkhanas flourished with the foundation of the Qutb Shahi rule in medieval Andhra Desa. They also become the centres of religious, cultural life of the Muslims and contributed to the process of urbanisation. The mosques or Masjid is an important religious institution for the Muslims. The mosques during the Qutb Shahi times, the other part of India, fulfilled various purposes. They provided a central place for prayers, served as the Sarai and Madrasas. Some mosques such as Jame Masjid provided with bath rooms for the people staying in them. A great number of mosques were built by the Qutb Shahi Sultans, their nobles and traders in Hyderabad, the capital city of the Golconda kingdom. These mosques are both big and small and most of them are ruined. Sultan Quli constructed Masjid-e-Safa (1518 A.D.) near Bala Hissar in Golconda fort. According to tradition Masjid-e-Bala Hissar was built by Ibrahim Qutb Shah in Golconda Fort. Masjid-e- Mulla Khiyali was constructed inside the 'Naya Qila' in 1570 A.D., by the renowned Dakhni poet Mulla Khiyali. Jame-Masjid was constructed near Charminar by Muhammad Quli Qutb Shah to adorn his newly founded capital in 1597 A.D. A school, a guest house and a Turkish bath were attached to this mosque and it represent the Qutb Shahi style of architecture of Indo-Persian style.[10]

Mecca Masjid is a marvellous construction. It lies 100 yards from south-west of the Charminar. The name is derived from Grand Mosque at Mecca on which it is modelled. The construction work started during the time of Muhammad Qutb Shah and nearly 8000 masons and labourers were engaged in its construction.[11] It took 77 years for the completion of the mosque. The following verse was composed by a poet and presented to the king in commemoration of its erection. The verse is translated by Bilgrami thus, "If the pilgrimage of noble Kaaba is not attainable to thee, come and pray in the Kaaba of the Deccan".[12] The Khairatabad mosque was built by Khairat-un-Nissa Begum, the daughter of Sultan Muhammad Qutb Shah.[13] Today Khairatabad locality developed around the mosque. The other mosques such as Toli Masjid (1617 A.D.), Masjid-e-Meerpet (1610 A.D.), Masjid-e-Sayeedabad (1605 A.D.), Masjid-e-Hayatnagar (1612-1626 A.D.), Masjid-e-Rahim Khan (1643 A.D.) and Masjid-e-Mushirabad[14] etc., were some of the religious institutions that adorned the capital city Hyderabad and nearby places.

The religious institutions of Hyderabad city such as the mosque, Dargah, Ashurkhana and Khanqah had their own organisation and functionaries for their administration. As the Hindu temple, the mosque had trustees, which occupied the top position in the hierarchy of its functionaries. A Farman of 1615 A.D.[15] records the grant of trusteeship (Mutawalli) of the mosque, constructed at Hyderabad by Malik Almas, with a Sarai of 83 rooms to a certain Sayyid Muhammad Quadri. The duties and responsibilities of the Mutawalli was to maintain the mosque, look after its affairs conduct its service and supervise the work of the other functionaries. The other important functionary of the mosque was the Imam. He was the leader of the congregational prayers. The other functionaries of the mosque were Maudhain (he calls the people to prayers), Farrash (he spread prayer carpets), Saqqa (water carrier), Diviti (torch bearer) Durban (door-keeper) and Jarubkash (sweeper).[16]

The Dargah was another Muslim religious institution. These were the tomb-shrines of famous Sufi saints. A large number of Dargahs were built in and around Hyderabad and other places during the Qutb Shahi period. Dargah-e-Hazrat Ibn-e-Khatoon, Dargah-e-Shah Raju, Dargah-e-Hazrat Hussain Shah Wali, Dargah-e-Hazrat Shah Charag, Dargah-e-Hazrat Noorullah Hussaini Chishti and Dargah-e-Hazrat Shah Shiblee were some of the important Dargahs of the Qutb Shahi times. It appears that each Dargah had a Mutawalli and generally he was a descendant of the saint to whom the Dargah belonged. In some cases the saints themselves appointed the Mutawalli of their tomb before their death.[17] The Mutawalli was the owner of the properties (building, lands etc.) of the Dargah. The other important functionary of the Dargah was the Sajjada (manager). The duties of the Sajjada were to look after its properties, conduct its annual festival (Urs) and supervise the work of the menial servants. The menial servants of Dargah included the waterman, the sweeper and the lamp-keeper.

The other Muslim religious institution was the Ashur Khana. It was a building which houses the conventional copies of standards carried by Imam Hussain called Alams. Baad Shai Ashur Khana, Ashur Khana-e-Hussaini Alam, Ashur Khana-e-Nal-e- Mubarek, Allava-e-Bibi, Ashur Khana-e-Panj Bhai, Ashur Khana-e-Maki Naal Saheb and Hussaini Alam Golconda were some of the Ashur Khanas of the Qutb Shahi Period.[18] The Ashur Khana also had an organisation and functionaries to conduct its administrative affairs. The chief functionary of the Ashur Khana, appears to have been the trustee, known as Mutawalli.[19] He was the owner of the properties endowed for the maintenances of the Ashur Khana. This institution had a caretaker known as Mujaver to look after its maintenance and to manage its properties.

The Khanqahs were the Muslim monastic institutions. As the Hindu Matha, the Khanqah was organized on the basis of monarchical principles. The pontiff generally known as Shaikh, who was at the apex of the organisation of Khanqah. The spiritual disciples of the pontiff were known as Murid.[20] The Khanqahs must have maintained in their service the teacher, clerks, cooks, sweepers, watchmen and fire-wood supplier's etc.[21] The Muslim institutions played a significant role not in the religious and cultural life of the people but also helped for growth of urban centres during the period under review. Thus, the Hindu and Muslim religious institutions with their magnificent physical structures, sound economic base, a large number of followers and an elaborate organisations and functionaries highly contributed for the process of urbanisation in medieval Andhra.

Notes & References

1. H.K. Naqvi, *Urbanisation and Urban Centres under the Great Mughals*, Simla, 1972, p.3.
2. K.A.N. Sastri, *The Cholas*, Part II, Madras, 1937, p.504.
3. *South Indian Inscriptions,* Vol. XVI, No.314.
4. *Tirumala Tirupati Devasthanam Inscriptions,* Vol. III, No.158.
5. R. Soma Reddy, *Hindu and Muslim Religious Institutions Andhra Desa, 1300-1600 A.D.*, Madras, 1984, p.154.
6. *Ibid.*, p.155-156.
7. K. Srilakshmi, "Temple as a Patron of Industries and Handicrafts in Andhra Desa during the 17th & 18th Centuries", *The Proceedings of the DRS Seminar,* Department of History, Osmania University, Hyderabad, 1995, p.182.
8. R. Soma Reddy, *Op.Cit.,* pp.32-35.
9. *South Indian Inscription*, X, No.388.
10. Raza Ali Khan, *Hyderabad A City in History,* Hyderabad, 1986, pp.25-26.
11. V.V. Krishna Sastri, *Select Monuments of Hyderabad*, 1990, pp.41-43.
12. *Ibid.,* p.44.
13. Raza Ali Khan, *Op.Cit.,* p.26.
14. Sadiq Naqvi, *Muslim Religious Institutions and their Role under the Qutb Shahs*, Hyderabad, 1993, pp.75-77.
15. English Summaries of Farmans and Sanads, *Farmans and Sanads of the Deccan Sultans*, No.4, p.13.
16. A.A. Bilgrami, *Landmarks of the Deccan,* Hyderabad, 1927, pp. 79-84.

17. Sadiq Naqvi, *Op.Cit.,* pp.118-147.
18. *Ibid.*, pp.158-161.
19. Rahat Azmi, "Hyderabad Ke Maqaddas Tabarrukat" (Urdu Article), *Sada-e-Jafariya,* October, 1978, pp.37-56.
20. S. Baba Mala, "The Sufi Convent and Its Social Significance in the Medieval period of Islam", in *Islamic Culture*, Vol. V, 51, January, 1977, pp. 44-42.
21. R. Soma Reddy, *Op.Cit.,* p. 91.

13

BHADRACHALAM: A RELIGIOUS TOWN

My personal miraculous and memorable experience at Bhadrachalam and my affinity and attachment to Khammam district prompted me to take up this topic. In 1974, when I was doing B.A. II year, I visited Bhadrachalam for the first time along with my friend to have Lord Sri Rama's Darshan. Then the Holy River Godavari was flowing with its full bewitching beauty. We craved to travel in the waters and in the evening along with others, we sat in a boat, which was going to sail from the bank of Bhadrachalam to the other bank of Burgampadu. After travelling for sometime due to unfavourable whirl winds, the boat started loosing its balance and the sailors were struggling to restore the same. Meanwhile, the boat crippled and some water entered it. Immediately our co-travellers like women milk-sellers and others began shouting and crying loudly out of dreadful phobia of life. We lost hopes and thought we wouldn't see the next day's sun rising. We offered our heartfelt and humble prayers to Bhadragiri Raghu Rama and completely kept calm. Suddenly, the winds began blowing in a favourable direction and we could reach our destiny safely due to the benign grace of Sri Rama.

Bhadrachalam, a famous Hindu pilgrim center that attracts lakhs of devotees from all over the world, is situated on the left bank of the mighty river Godavari in the Khammam district of Telangana state. It derives the name from the hill called Bhadragiri. Bhadrachalam town is known for the temple of Sri Sitaramachandra Swamy, which is considered to be one of the greatest shrines in South India with rich historical background. It is considered prominently a pious place since Lord Rama is supposed to have sojourned here with his consort Sita and brother Laxmana during his *Vanavasa* (exile). Though there are thousands of temples dedicated to Lord Sri Rama, right from Ayodhya, His birth place, down to Rameshwaram at the southernmost tip of India, it is Bhadrachalam that has acquired great popularity for the sheer beauty of the icon of the Lord. Here, the idol of Sri Rama is captivating, as he is represented as a charming figure with well built physique, wearing in his four divine hands (Chaturbhuja), the Dhanush (bow) and the Bana (arrow), Shanku and Chakra. The uniqueness of the idol is that Sita is seated on Rama's lap. The idol of Laxmana is at Rama's left.

Temple History

According to a legend, there was a sage named Bhadra, an ardent devotee of Lord Rama. He performed frightening penance at the bank of river Godavari in Dandakaranya to get grace of Lord Rama, to obtain the promised Moksha by Him. Pleased by Bhadra's devotion, He appeared in the form of Vaikunta Rama and granted him Moksha. The hillock on which Bhadra Maharishi did penance and attained Moksha, is called Bhadragiri or Bhadrchalam (hill) after the rishi.[1] Another legend associated with the place is that Lord Rama once appeared in the dream of an ardent and an unlettered woman devotee, Pokala Dammakka. She lived in 17th Century and was inhabitant of Bhadrireddypalem, a mile away from this sacred place. She was told by Lord Rama in her dream about the existence of idols on the Bhadragiri. On the next day morning she started searching for the idols and found them hidden in an ant-hill. She poured hundreds of pots of Godavari water on the anti-hill, which tardily dissolved and gave way to appear the hidden deities. Since then, she used to perform Pooja daily and here she got a modest structure built.[2] There is a Shabari Ashram. According to legends, Shabari, a great devotee of Lord Rama was staying at the Ashram longing to see Rama. During His Vanavasa, Lord Rama visited her and thus fulfilled her dream of seeing Lord Rama.

Bhakta Ramadas and Construction of Temple

Bhadrachalam temple was constructed by Kancharla Gopanna popularly known as Bhakta Ramadas in 17th Century A.D. He was a fervent devotee of Lord Rama and was born to Linganna Murthy and Kamamba in Nelakondapalli village of the then Khammamett Taluk. He was the nephew of Madanna, the Prime Minister, under the Sultan Abul Hasan Tanashah of the Qutb Shahi Dynasty. Gopanna was appointed as Tahsildar or revenue officer of Bhadrachalam and was in sole charge of the collection of the revenue of that area.[3] Instead of remitting the amount collected, he constructed a temple with an amount of Rs. 6 lakhs to Sri Rama in Bhadrachalam. Thus, he was also called "Bhadrachala Ramadasu". Soon after the construction his miseries started. He was dismissed from service for the misuse of revenue and kept in jail for 12 long years and was tortured. Unable to withstand the miseries, Ramadas implored Rama to relieve him by singing many praising and emotional songs, which got popularized from the stanzas of Dasaradhi Sathakam and Kirtanas of Ramadasa. Tanashah realized the devotional spirit of Ramadasa towards Rama, when Rama and Laxmana repaid Rs. 6 lakhs Mohurs exposing themselves as the peons of Bhadrachalam circar and obtained a voucher for it from him.[4] There is a variation of the popular tradition that it was in a dream that Abul Hasan received payment from Rama and Laxmana and on awakening he found the money lying by his pillow.[5] The Sultan released Gopanna and reinstalled him as Tahsildar. Further, he endowed the revenue of Bhadrachalam and two other villages as Agraharam[6] for the expenses of the newly constructed temple. The miracle has earned Gopanna the title of Ramadasa.

The Sultan used to offer pearls (Mutyala Talambralu) on the occasion of Kalyana Mahostavam (Sri Rama Navami) to deities on an elephant through a specially sent messenger. Under the Nizam's, the Tahsildar of Burgampad was made responsible for the maintenance of the temple and the preservation of its treasures. Infact, Bhadrachalam had the privilege of Muslim patronage.[7] The procedure of sending pearls to the deities is still followed by successive governments including the present State Government on Sri Rama Navami festival. Thus, the sanctity of Bhadrachalam has increased with the mixture of both tradition and history.

In certain lines of Dasarathi Satakamu, Ramadasa says that it is not worldly pleasures or wealth that he desires but only that his mind be cleansed of dirt.[8] His Kirtanalu or devotional songs are so sweet and melodious that rustic troupes sing them even today, dancing in circles striking brass symbols and leaping forward and backward.[9]

Transport and Accommodation

Bhadrachalam pilgrim centre is well connected with all important places in the state and Jagdalpur in Madhya Pradesh by bus transport. One can reach this place by launch from Rajahmundry, which is 161 kms. distance from here. Communication facilities to this place improved considerably with the construction of a road bridge over the Godvari in 1965.[10] The nearest railway station is at Kothagudem, (Bhadrachalam Road Railway Station) which lies at a distance of 39 kms. from Bhadrachalam. It is situated 325 kms. from Hyderabad and 135 kms. from Khammam. There are quite a number of hotels and inns in Bhadrachalam to accommodate the incoming pilgrims. Among the inns, Devasthanam inn, Gunturuvari Kanyakaparameshwari inn, Tirupati Devasthanam inn, Annavaram Devasthanam inn, Khammamettvari inn and Bhadrachalam Arya Vaishya Sri Kanyakaparameshwari inn are some of the important ones.[11]

Tourist Attractions in Bhadrachalam

It consisted of many places of attractions and interests. Bhadrachala Sri Rama temple has a tall and impressive Gopuram, and it leads to the inner Prakara of the temple. The main shrine houses the idol of Srirama and adjacent to it is the Utsava Vigraham of Rama with Sita and Lakshmana. In 1964 a Kalyana Mantapa was constructed at a cost of four lakhs of rupees with fine sculpture. The main temple was also renovated at a cost of Rs.24 lakhs.[12] The jewels like 'Kalikiturai', 'Pachchala Pathakam' and Chinthaku Pathakam presented to the deities by Gopanna are displayed in the temple museum. To the south-west of this place, there is a spot known as Ushnagundam (hot spring) right in the bed of Godavari. Statues of the epic Ramayana on the Godavari Bund, Park in the entrance of Bhadrachalam, Pushkar Ghat, Anjaneya Statue in the entrance of Bhadrachalam town, Ramadasu Dhyana Mandiram, welcoming Dwara to the temple and greenery around the hill are the places of attractions in the town.

Parnashala

During Vanavasa Rama with his Spouse Sita, Brother Laxmana constructed a hermitage at Parnashala. The picturesque display of some scenes of Vanavasa could be seen at Parnashala like the foot prints of Sita Devi and Mosaic of Surpanaka in the guise of golden deer and Ravana in the guise of Sanyasi for Bhikshatana and the vicinity of the temple, Sita Vaagu, where Sita bathed and collected the turmeric and Kumkum from near by stones. As Ravana kidnapped Sita, the deity at Parnashala is called Sokarama. The tracks of Ravana while kidnapping Sita, is seen on the mountain on the other side of the river Parnashala temple. This stands for the mythological significance of the history. This place lies at a distance about 30 kms. from Bhadrachalam.

Jattayu Paaka (Yetapaka)

This place is situated 2 kms. away from Bhadrachalam. According to Mythology the bird Jattayuvu, a devotee of Rama had obstructed Ravana while he was proceeding in chariot after kidnapping Sita. In the battle between Ravana and Jattayuvu the injured bird had waited at this place in search of Sita.

Dummugudem

Here Rama is called the Atmarama. The story reveals that Rama killed 14,000 demons headed by the brothers Khara and Dushana. As the village was said to be built upon the ashes of these, the place is named as Dummugudem.

Sri Rama Giri

This place is situated on the bank in the down stream of river Godavari, about 32 kms. from Bhadrachalam. The deity of Yoga Rama Temple is on a hill is named as Ramagiri.[13]

Festivals and Fairs

Many festivals are celebrated in the Sitaramaswamy temple of Bhadrachalam. On every Ekadasi the village Mahothsavam will be celebrated. Every month some specified Poojas and celebrations will be conducted. The Srirama Navami festival celebrated here for ten days from Chaitra Suddha Saptami to Bahula Padyami attracts thousands of devotees from all over the country. The government offers Mutyala Talambralu to the deities on this Kalyana Mahothsavam. In the month of Dhanurmasam Vaikunta Dwara Darshanam and Teppothsavam[14] are celebrated. During the festive occasions the temple gets major income. On all the festive occasions the fairs are organized.

Tourist Arrivals in Bhadrachalam During 1987 to 1996 (up to December)

Year	*Indian*	*Foreign*
1987	-	-
1988	5,96,500	-
1989	10,57,650	-
1990	8,52,716	-
1991	8,80,428	-
1992	7,80,950	-
1993	9,59,876	-
1994	13,41,491	179
1995	12,57,115	1,528
1996	10,42,986	38[15]

This table shows the increase and fluctuations in the tourist arrivals to Bhadrachalam.

The Godavari Pushkaram at Bhadrachalam remarkably turned out to be the biggest and memorable event in the history of the temple town. Pushkaram takes place once in 12 years. In 2003 it started from 30th July and ended by 10th August. As Pushkara "Snanam Punya Karyam", about 6.0 crore people had taken a dip in the Godavari across the then state. Over 61 lakhs pilgrims had their dip in the river at Bhadrachalam during the 12 day religious carnival.

The Pushkaram highlighted the living river mother Goddess Godavari, who is with her waters sustaining the lives of human beings, enriching the agricultural yield by promoting green-belt and becoming the adobe of Andhra cultural stream. Pushkaram stood as a splendid tribute to the communal harmony and religious tolerance. It gave an impetus to the economic activities like art handicrafts, shops and stalls, trade and commerce. It yielded major income to the temple and generated employment opportunities. Pushkaram infused awareness about this pilgrim centre to the world and represented cultural development and folk traditions of Bhadrachalam area. The beautification of the temple town and the facilities provided for the devotees helped to boost the image of the town as a tourist centre.

Bhadrachalam has an enchanting tribal belt. Here predominantly the Koya and other tribal cultures flourished. The tribal rites, rituals, customs, deities, festivals and folk dances would certainly become the added attractions to the visitors of Bhadrachalam. As Kothagudem, Palvancha, Kinnersani project, Kunavaram, Bhadra-chalam, Parnashala places imbibed in them the various factors of attractions of tourism, they can be developed and promoted under Rural Tourism by creating fantastic facilities.

Notes & References

1. Andhra Pradesh Tourism Website, Site Map of Temple, p.2.
2. Andhra Pradesh Tourism Website, Temple History, p.1.
3. H.K. Sherwani, *History of the Qutb Shahi Dynasty,* New Delhi, 1974, p.606.
4. S. Krishnaswami Aiyangar, "Abul Hasan Qutb Shah and his Ministers, Madanna and Akkanna", *J.I.H.* 1931, p.125.
5. H.K. Sherwani, *Op.Cit.,* p.607.
6. *Ibid.*
7. R. Parthasarathi, *Places of Interest in Andhra Pradesh,* Vol. I, Hyderabad, 1984, p. 90.
8. H.K. Sherwani, *Op.Cit.,* p. 607.
9. K. Satyanarayana, *A Study of the History and Culture of the Andhras,* New Delhi, 1988, p. 542.
10. R. Parthasarathi, *Op.Cit.,* pp. 88-89.
11. P.B. Veeracharyulu, *Sri Bhadrachala Kshetra Mahatyam,* Rajahmundry, 2002, pp. 75-76.
12. R. Parthasarathi, *Op.Cit.,* p. 91.
13. Andhra Pradesh *Tourism Website,* Godavari Pushkaram, 2003, p.3.
14. P.B. Veeracharyulu, *Op.Cit.,* pp. 81-82.
15. A. Satish Babu, *Tourism Development in India, A Case Study,* Delhi, p. 120.

14

THE CROPPING PATTERN

Agricultural was the main occupation of the people of Medieval Telangana and Andhra as in the rest of the country. The economic life of the people centred round the agriculture. Most of the industries, trade and prosperity of any medieval government largely depended on agricultural development. The surplus in agricultural production promoted the growth of urbanisation during the period under review. The medieval period in the history of Andhra Desa is significant for the agrarian system. This period witnessed the Muslim political power first in Andhra. Like the Kakatiyas, the Qutb Shahi rulers encouraged agriculture by creating wonderful irrigational facilities in the country. Further, the Qutb Shahi period also saw the coming of the Europeans to Coastal Andhra. The establishment of the European trading settlements on the East Coast in the beginning of the 17th century gave fillip to the agricultural sector by giving boost to the cultivation of commercial crop in Andhra country. The present study is based on the contemporary epigraphical and literary sources.

Wet Crops

Land is the basis of agriculture. It was divided into wet, dry and garden based on the means of irrigation and crops cultivated. Wet-land was the land which had either natural or artificial supply of water and paddy was grown in this land. Paddy was the staple crop in all parts of the medieval Andhra as it is today. The lands of Andhra were described as golden in colour with the ripped paddy fields looking like the Meru mount of gold.[1] The term that was used to denote the paddy crop in the contemporary sources is 'Vari'. *Kodrava* and Vrihi are the varieties of paddy referred in the epigraphs of the early dynasties in the Costal Andhra region. 'Adi' was one kind of paddy during the Eastern Chalukyan period. Srinatha in his remarkable work *Haravilasam* and *Bhimakhandam* mention some varieties of paddy such as Kalamasali, Siramukha, Sastika, Patonga and Hayana.[2] Varities of Prasangu (Prasangi) and Rajanam appear to be common. Another good variety of rice was Kappurabogam. The rich people consumed good kind of rice. Low class people generally consumed Ragi and Colam. Regular watchmen called Kavali-kandru[3] were employed to watch and protect the crop. Barbosa says that the people during the Vijayanagara period also mainly used rice. White rice was consumed by rich classes and red rice was used by the poor. He refers to the kinds of rice grown, known as Girasul, Asal, Auvagas and Paccar.[4]

During the Qutb Shahi period rice was produced in abundance. A foreign traveller Tavernier says that even in the smallest village rice was produced in plenty.[5] Another foreign traveller Thevenot says that in the reign of Golconda Qutb Shahis in Golconda, the cultivation of rice was more due to the abundant quantity of water which the farmers had at their disposal.[6] In the contemporary sources we come across some type of wet land, such as Chavuka Bhoomi, Gaddu Nela, Neeru Polamu and Oodupu Bhoomi. Chavuka Bhoomi was the most fertile land. This soil was made up of sand and red earth. The land was used not only for growing wet crops but also for dry crops. Gaddu Nela was also a kind of fertile land. It was also called Madi Nela. Neeru Polamu was a fertile land in which the crops like paddy were grown. Unlike the Chavuka Nela it was cultivated mainly with the supply of water obtained from irrigation tanks. Oodupu Bhoomi was another kind of wet land in which paddy was grown. It was cultivated with the help of water obtained from canals.[7]

Dry Crops

Dry crops may be divided into four classes: (1) Cereals (2) Pulses (3) Oil seeds and (4) Fibres. Wheat, Jonna (Jowar), Ragi, Korralu, Sajja, etc., belong to the first group. The cereals formed important food of people after rice. Wheat was grown on a small scale in Andhra. It was mostly used by the Muslims. Methwold says that good quality of wheat but in small quantities was produced in the interior Andhra country.[8] Jowar was produced in large quantities. Paes calls it as Indian Corn.[9] Srinatha in his Chatu Verses mentions that Millets, Jonna and Sajja were grown in Palanati Seema[10] (modern Guntur District). There are no references to the maize.

Black gram, red gram, green gram, Bengal-gram, horse-gram and beans belong to the category of pulses. Sesamum, Castor and Mustard come under the oilseeds category. Sesamum (*gingili*) which was largely cultivated, was the common edible oil. During the sixteenth and seventeenth centuries the north coast of Andhra along with that of Orissa was known as *gingili* coast for the production of this oil in abundance. Further, it was exported to overseas from here. There are references in the contemporary inscriptions to the tax called Ganugari[11] (a tax on oil mill). The oil mills existed in many villages and towns. There are no references to ground-nut in the contemporary sources. Cotton and hemp may be mentioned under the fourth category. It seems to have been cultivated through out the country in all types of soil. The farmers raised cotton in their own field and their women folk produced cotton yarn. A contemporary Telugu work *Sukasaptati* describes how the women in the Kapu (farmer) houses made yarn.[12] Medieval Andhra Desa must have produced fine cotton which is evident by the fact that some towns in coastal Andhra became famous centres for fine cotton textiles. Indigo was used for dyeing of cotton fabrics. It was cultivated in the coastal regions and also in the interior. Tavernier mentions that Golconda kingdom was one of the producers of the best variety of indigo. It was sold in the form of cakes.[13]

Dry land may be divided into (1) Veli Polamu, (2) Cheluka Bhoomi, (3) Garuvu Bhoomi, (4) Krishna Revadu Bhoomi and (5) Jonna Bhoomi. Veli Polamu was a land that depended mainly on rain water for cultivation. Cheluka Bhoomi was fallow land which was newly brought under cultivation. It was used for growing greens. Garuvu Bhoomi was a type of dry land made up of soil mixed with stones and pebbles. Krishna Revadu Bhoomi was a type of black sandy soil in which coriander (Dhaniyalu) and Komma Senagalu, maize, etc., were grown. In Jonna Bhoomi only maize was cultivated.[14]

In addition to the above mentioned crops, sugarcane was also cultivated wherever water and suitable soil were available.[15] Jaggery was extensively used in preparing various dishes offered to the deities in temples. The spices that were grown during this period were ginger, zeera, etc. Chillis are referred to in an epigraph dated 1516 A.D.[16] It is not known when the crop was introduced in Andhra country. Methwold refers to potatoes. But Moreland says these potatoes were probably some tubers different from those of today's potatoes. A contemporary epigraph mentions garlic (Vellulli) and onions (Neerulli) as items of trading goods.[17] Turmeric was mentioned as one of the articles of merchandise. Methwold, writing about tobacco, states that ".....They have within a few years planted store of tobacco much of it is exported to Mocha and Arrecan..." and further says that "it was not much consumed locally but exported".[18]

Protection of Crops

It was the custom in those days to set up a scare crow to scare away birds and to ward off the evil eye. Kavali Kandru (watchmen) was employed to protect the crops. Vijnanesvara in his work the *Mitakshara* prescribes certain rules pertaining to the punishment of owner of cattle damaging the crops. If the cattle destroyed the crops in the fields, the owner of the cattle had to pay compensation either in kind or in cash to the owner of the land, the equal amount of crop destroyed by them.[19] Further, he says that those who set fire to a field in which the fruits and the crop had ripened should be burnt alive.[20]

Garden Crops

Besides cultivating the above crops, the people were also interested in growing vegetables and fruits. Garden crop may be classified into three categories. (1) Vegetable gardens, (2) Betel leaf gardens and (3) Fruit and flower gardens. The vegetables that were usually grown were Pumpkin (Gummadipandu), Brinjals (Vankayalu),

Onions, Hedge-gourd (Kakarakayalu) and Edible roots (Kanda, Pendalamu, etc.). There are references to these vegetables in the contemporary inscriptions.[21] Various kinds of vegetables were sold in the markets. It reveals the fact that vegetables were grown on a large scale. The chewing of betel leaf was a universal custom among the people. So betel leaf gardens were cultivated in good number. Arecanut were grown in plenty as they were, as it is today, one of the ingredients of *tambulam*. Arecanut gardens were known as Pomka Totalu.[22] In the medieval Andhra Desa Aku-Pemtas a fair of betel leaves were organized. The foreign travellers of this period noticed the extensive use of betel leaf by all classes of people in the society.

Medieval Andhra Desa was noted for its fruit and flower gardens. Many contemporary epigraphical and literary sources refer to the varieties of fruits and flowers that were grown. In the fruit gardens various kinds of fruits such as arecanut, banana, mango, jack, grapes, citron, orange, lime, pomegranate etc. were raised. Paes said that in towns and villages there were mango, jack-fruit and tamarind groves and these trees formed as resting places for merchants to halt with their trading goods.[23] In the Qutb Shahi kingdom the cultivation of fruits such as mangoes, figs, papaya, oranges, grapes, lemons, banana etc., was encouraged notably. Hyderabad was famous for its grapes. They were available in plenty from February to April. The Qutb Shahis must have developed very large kind of grape called *Inab-i-Shahi* or royal grapes.

Many flower gardens were grown during the period under consideration. Roses, Jasmine, and varieties of flower gardens were cultivated. The flowers were cypress, lotus, lily, saffron fragrant yellow flower, roses, etc. The gardens owned by the private individual, government and religious institutions. An inscription from Tirupati dated 1492 A.D. mentions the coconuts ripe and unripe mangoes, plantains, citron and other fruit grown in a grove planted by a donor in the temple of Sri Venkateshwara.[24] The yield from these groves, after meeting the needs of the temple, must have given some income to it.

Agricultural Communities

The agricultural communities of the period were mostly among the Sudras or the fourth caste. They included the Reddi or Kapu, Velama, Kamma etc. All were referred to as 'Kapu' only. The Reddis were the most important among the agricultural castes. The *Mahimalur kaifiyat* refer to thirteen sub-divisions among the Reddis viz., *Desuri, Pakanati, Panta, Pedakanta, Motati, Ari, Palle, Kondi, Balla-Kutti, Erra, Dacha, Velama* and *Neratu*.[25] The Velamas got material boost from the patronage of the Kakatiya queen, Rudrama Devi. They ruled over Telangana as independent ruler from Rachakonda and Devarakonda. Another important agricultural caste was Kamma. They were as distinguished as the Reddis and the Velamas. They served as commanders and generals during this period. The Brahmins and others also took up cultivation. The shepherds, artisans, the Malas, Madigas worked as agricultural labourers in the fields.

Measures and Prices

The contemporary sources contain references to different unit of weights and measures. As regards the volumetric measures of the Kakatiya period *gidda* was the lowest denomination and *putti* the highest. The following tables indicate the relative values of those measures.[26]

Table 1

4	giddas	=	1 sola
2	Solas	=	1 tavva
2	tawas	=	1 manika
2	manikas	=	1 adda
2	addas	=	1 kuncha
2	kunchas	=	1 irasa
2	irasas	=	1 tumu
2	tumus	=	1 iddumu
2	iddumus	=	1 naltumu
5	tumus	=	1 en-dumu
10	tumus	=	1 pandumu
20	tumus	=	1 putti

Table 2

4	Citti	=	1 Sola 70 tola of heaped rice
4	Sola	=	1 munta – 280tolas of 3 ½ pucca seers
4	Munta	=	1 kuncam, 1, 120 tolas or 14 pucca
1	kuncam	=	1 tum, hundred seer weight about
20	tum	=	1 candy or putti or about a ton[27]

The above units were almost in vogue in Andhra till the present metric system was introduced. Sherwani[28] summarized the prices obtaining in the early part of the 17th century in the Golconda Kingdom as shown in the table below:

Rice	40 to 60 seers a rupee
Wheat	20 seers a rupee
Pepper	Rs. 125 for about 240 seers
Cloves	Rs. 25 to 45 for about 240 seers
Sugar	Rs. 14-64 for 17 seers
Sugar candy	Rs. 43-92 for 17 seers.

Conclusion

Thus, the above discussion reveals us that almost all the crops that are now raised were raised in those days. However, now some commercial and plantation crops have been added. The Coromandel Coast was reputed for the large scale rice cultivation due to the abundant water supply. Rice was exported from Andhra coast to various places on the East and West coast of India. Medieval Telangana and Andhra was not merely self-sufficient in the matter of food products but could export the surplus to the neighbouring parts of South India.

Notes & References

1. P.V. Parabrahma Sastry, *The Kakatiyas*, Hyderabad, 1978, pp.210-211.
2. M. Somasekhara Sarma, *History of Reddi Kingdoms,* Waltair, 1948, p.373.
3. Mallana, *Rukmangadacharitra,* III, Vol.10.
4. Barbosa, *An Account of the Countries Bordering on the Indian Ocean and their Inhabitants,* (translated by Longworth Dames), 2 Volumes, 1918, Vol. I, pp.195-196.
5. T. Damodar Reddy, *The Agrarian System in Andhra Desa from A.D. 1300 to 1687,* Ph.D. thesis (unpublished), Department of History, Osmania University, Hyderabad, p.238.
6. Jean De Thevenot, *The Indian Travels of the Thevenot and Careri*, ed. S.N. Sen, New Delhi, 1949, p.144.
7. A. Vaidehi Krishnamurthy, *Social and Economic Conditions in Eastern Deccan, From A.D. 1000 to A.D. 1250,* Secunderabad, 1970, pp.74-75.
8. W.H. Moreland, *Relations of Golconda in the Early Seventeenth Century,* London, 1931, p.8.
9. T.V. Mahalingam, *Economic Life in the Vijayanagara Empire,* p.46.

10. Srinatha, *Chatu Verses.*
11. *South Indian Inscriptions,* Vol.XVI, No.201.
12. T. Damodar Reddy, *Op.Cit.*, p.242.
13. Tavernier, *Travels in India by Jean Baptiste Tavernier, Baron of Aubonne,* Translated by Dr. V. Ball, edited by William Crooke, Vol. II, Oxford University Press, London, 1925, p.7.
14. A. Vaidehi Krishnamurthy, *Op.Cit.*, p.75.
15. Sri Krishnadevaraya, *Amuktamalyada, (Vishnu Chittiyamu)* ed., Vavillas, Madras, 1969, VI, v.70.
16. *Mackenzie Manuscripts,* 106, pp.199-200.
17. N. Venkataramanayya, *Cuddapah Inscriptions,* p.845.
18. W.H. Moreland, *Op.Cit.*, p.36.
19. Vijnanesvara, *The Mitakshara,* ed. Vasudev Laxman, Bombay, 1926, II, 161.
20. *Ibid.,* II, 282.
21. *South Indian Inscriptions,* Vol. V, Nos.66 & 1188; A Corpus of Inscriptions of H.E.H. Nizam's Dominions - *Telangana Inscriptions*, Vol. I, No. 22.
22. A. Vaidehi Krishnamurthy, *Op.Cit.*, p. 76.
23. T.V. Mahalingam, *Op.Cit.*, pp. 47-48.
24. *Tirumala Tirupati Devasthanam Epigraphical Series,* II, No.97.
25. *Mahimalur Kaifiyat,* Vol.40, pp. 104-120.
26. P.V. Parabrahma Sastry, *Op.Cit.*, pp. 266-267.
27. T.V. Mahalingam, *Administration and Social Life under Vijayanagara,* Part-II, Madras, 1975, p. 169.
28. H.K. Sherwani, "The Reigns of Abdullah Qutb Shah (1626-1672), Economic Aspects-I", *Journal of Indian History,* August, 1964, pp. 460-461.

15

TANKS IN GOLCONDA AND HYDERABAD AREAS

Water resources had been the greatest concern of the Indians for domestic and irrigation purpose since the ancient times. The fact that India from prehistoric times attached great importance to water is revealed by an old Indian Folk song which starts with "Mother earth, Father sky, Brother wind, Friends light and Sweet heart water".[1]

Irrigation is of paramount importance to an agriculture-oriented economy like that in the former Hyderabad State or present Telangana State. The arable lands in medieval times were irrigated either by rain water or by rivers, rivulets, tanks, wells and canals. Of all these water source tanks played an important role in the irrigation of the field fostering the growing of gardens, maintaining the cattle and supplying the drinking water. Hence, I made an attempt to describe the multipurpose uses to which tanks were put in Golconda and Hyderabad area, which is situated in Telangana region. A natural question which comes to mind is why tanks are essential in Telangana? The answer is that Telangana landscape possessed of a succession of hills, rocks and valleys there being a large number of isolated boulder-heaps which are barren. The rainfall is very scanty. The soils developed on the old granitic rocks are red Chalka soil, sandy and infertile. So, the numerous seasonal streams have been bounded up to form tanks for irrigation, to mitigate the effects of famine occurring from severe drought conditions and for other purposes. In early medieval period it was the Kakatiya rulers who constructed numerous tanks in Telangana area and provided it with excellent irrigation system. After the Kakatiyas, it was Qutb Shahis of Golconda and Nizams and their ministers constructed many great reservoirs in the State in general and in the vicinity of Hyderabad in particular.

In the construction of a tank, the selection of a site is important. The most suitable site is the slopes of the hill, valley and stream formation. Tank is constructed where narrow site is found and on the availability of material in that region. Generally, clay and stone are used for the construction of the bunds. There was advancement in the construction of the tanks from earlier times to the Qutb Shahi period. It developed from the construction of the mud bunds to the use of mortar. Trapezium of maximum width would be at the foundation, and it became narrow as it goes higher and then the bund was constructed. The present article is based on inscriptions, documentary evidence, survey maps and the scattered information in the manuscripts of the Qutb Shahi period. From among a large number of tanks, I have selected only ten tanks of importance.

Durg Tank

A little distance from the Golconda fort, on the north-western side in the hillocks, is a beautiful tank. Locally, this is known as 'Durg Talab'. It was constructed by Quli Qutb, the founder of the Qutb Shahi Dynasty. In fact, this magnificent tank served as a main source of water to the Golconda fort. The bund of the tank was built of granite stones and painted with lime mortar. The bund was constructed at a narrow place connecting two hill rocks on the east and west flow out through the vent into a channels constructed with granite slabs. The channel is approximately 3 miles long, 2 feet wide and 2 feet deep. It enters the Qutb Shahi tombs after covering a distance of about 2 miles. The main branch directly touches the Golconda fort and small branch diverted to the Qutb Shahi tombs for supplying water to the garden, planned around the tombs. The water was also supplied into the cisterns of the royal hammam, where the dead bodies of the kings were given the ceremonial bath. According to an inscription found during the reign of Sultan Abdullah Qutb Shah the repair of the channels were attended to.[2] From this tank water was supplied for the irrigation of lands just below Jubilee hills, which is now called Dargah area. During 17th and 18th centuries also its water was supplied to Qutb Shahi tombs and gardens through the channel. The tank is capable of irrigating about 180 acres of land.[3]

Ibrahim Bagh Tank

"Ibrahim Qutb Shah was the king of Irrigation" as numerous tanks were constructed during his period. This tank is situated on the western side of Golconda fort. The tank was constructed by Ibrahim Qutb Shah.[4] The tank and gardens there are known as Ibrahim Bagh. The tank is situated on a high altitude. Nekhnampur, Alijapur and Sheikpet villages were its catchment areas. The water of this tank was extensively used for the maintenance of the gardens and also for irrigation. Not only in 17th and 18th centuries but today also the farmers are cultivating paddy under this tank. The present extent of land under cultivation is 60 acres to100 acres.[5]

Shah Hatim Tank

It was constructed during the time of Ibrahim Qutb Shah.[6] It was constructed outside the Golconda fort and situated in the north-east of the fort. The water of the tank was used for irrigation, defence (moat) and drinking purpose. Its water was let off into the moat of the Golconda fort. The tank was capable of irrigating 76 acres and 30 guntas of land. But the land under cultivation at present is only 22 acres, since three hundred dwelling units have come up in the tank area.[7]

Langar House Tank

This tank was also constructed by Ibrahim Qutb Shah[8] for irrigation of land, for cattle rearing and for defence purposes. It is situated near Fatedarwaja. This tank received its water for the present Apollo hospital hills area and Hakimpet. This tank's water was used to fill the moat of the Golconda Fort. About 5 years back the Ayacut under this tank was 33 acres and 11 guntas. Now, cultivation has been banned as it came under the control of the Municipality.[9]

Hussain Sagar Tank

It was a large sheet of water, extended over an area of 8 square miles between Secunderabad on the North and Saifabad, a portion of Hyderabad on the South. It was constructed by Ibrahim Qutb Shah in about 1575 A.D. at a cost of 2.5 lakhs.[10] It was the largest body of water sheet near Hyderabad. It was the main source of water supply for the Residency and Suburbs north of the Musi River. The ground below on the east of the bund was irrigated and cultivated. The lake is principally fed by a canal about 36 miles in length which runs from the Musi river.[11]

The following story regarding the construction of the bund which is given in the appendices to *Our Faithful Ally* - "His Highness, having been disappointed and his expectations unrealized, with respect to the filling of the tank, directed a nobleman of his court of the name of Khaja Nek Nam Khan to cause a channel to be made from the river Musi, to the Hussain Sagar, in order to fill it. Nek Nam Khan accordingly cut a small channel paying the expenses out of his own private funds, and succeeded in bringing the water into the Hussain Sagar Lake intending to enlarge the channel, and make it a complete work, but unfortunately before its completion he died. One day His Highness went on a pleasure excursion to the Hussain Sagar Lake and enquired the spectators about its name. They replied that it is called 'Hussain Sahib Cherroo'. His Highness, indignant that his own name was not given to the tank, resolved that another tank should be sunk. Accordingly, he on leaving, proceeded to Ibrahimpatnam, where he marked out the outlines of a tank in order that it should bear his own name.[12] Hussain Shah Wali, a famous Sufi saint, the son-in-law and the Superintendent of Public works of Ibrahim Qutb Shah looked after the construction of this Hussain Sagar tank.

Ibrahimpatnam Tank

Ibrahim Qutb Shah constructed this tank.[13] This bund was constructed by mud in haste as the Sultan ordered to complete it soon. The bund of this tank is equal to the size of the bund of Hussain Sagar in Hyderabad, but its storage capacity is only half of that of Hussain Sagar. The area below the tank is even today irrigated and paddy is grown in abundance. The tank is capable of irrigating 1,209 acres of land. The extent of land under irrigation is about 950 acres.[14]

Maa-Saheba Tank in Hyderabad

There was a tank in Hyderabad which was generally known as 'Masab Tank'. The tank bund is completely dry and converted into a public park now. Many people believe that this tank was built by Hayat Bakshi Begum, as she was called '*Maa Sahiba*'. But it was not built by Hayat Bakshi Begum but by Khanum Agha, the daughter of Mir Maqsood Ali Tabataba. Khanum Agha was the wife of Mirza Muhammad Amin and mother of Muhammad Qutb Shah. We know this fact by the epigraphs that were carved out on the two towers of both sides of the bund. They were in 18 x 26½ size in Naskh script.[15] A mud Bund was constructed over it to stop the water. Banjara hills and Jubilee hills areas were its catchment areas.

Maa-Saheba Tank near Hayatnagar

This tank was built on the highway of Nagarjuna Sagar, at a distance of 8 miles from Hayatnagar and 15 kms. from Hyderabad city. Gulam Hussain Khan in *Gulzar-e-Asafia* (Persian) clearly writes that Hayat Maa Sahiba had built a tank near Hayatnagar.[16] Syed Khaja in his book which is also named as *Gulzar-e-Asafia*' wrote that Baksh Begum built a tank eight miles away Hayatnagar in 1642 A.D.[17] There are other sources which are also furnishing the same information. So, basing on these authentic sources we can conclude that Maa Sahiba tank near Hayatnagar was built by Hayat Baksh Begum. The tank is still in good condition and its capacity is 140-10 Mcft, the available yield is 108.26 Mcft, top width 8 ft., length of the bund is 50 chains, and catchment area is 11.64 sq.miles.[18]

Mir Jumla Tank

It was constructed in 1625 A.D. by the celebrated Qutb Shahi officer Mir Jumla.[19] It was situated to the east of the city in the Yakutpura suburb. Most of the water used in the city was supplied from this tank in those days. But, now it is in a very in-sanitary condition. The tank used to get its water resources from Falaknuma hill, Chandrayanagutta, Bandla Guda and Uppuguda areas. Now houses have been built in the bed of the tank.

Mir Alam Tank

It lies on one side of the Nehru Zoological Park, i.e., South West of the city and it is a piece of engineering skill. It was built by Mir Alam who led the Contingent forces of Nawab Ali Khan Bahadur Asaf Jah-II, during the war with Tipu Sultan in 1799 A.D. He was the great-grand father of Salarjung-I. He commissioned the army to build it from the handsome reward he received from Nizam for winning fourth Mysore war against Tipu Sultan in 1799 A.D. The construction of the tank started in 1804 A.D. and the tank came into being in the year 1806 A.D. Its construction was supervised by Mr. Russel, an Englishman of the Royal Engineers, Madras Regiment. Its bund was constructed by French Engineers. The tank was 8 miles in circumference and dam alone cost 8 lakhs. The bund is 1,120 yards in length and consists of 21 large granite arches laid on their sides with the semi- circular projection opposed to the body of water. The miles long bund with 21 Granite arches earned for it the title of "Queen's Necklace". The tank is still in existence with good water-sheet and supplying water to city and suburbs.[20]

Notes & References

1. Naram Krishna Rao, "Water Supply in Hyderabad (past, present and future)", *History of Hyderabad District 1879-1950 A.D.*, Vol. I, p.116.
2. Extract from the research work done by M.A. Qaiyum, Asst. Director, Department of Archaeology and Museums, A.P., Hyderabad. On "*Golconda Fort*" (Unpublished).
3. Statement showing the Ayacut under Existing and completed Minor Irrigation Sources, I.B. Division, Ranga Reddy District: Hyderabad, available as on 1-4-1992.
4. *Ibid.*
5. *Pahani Records*, M.R.O. Officer, Golconda Mandal, Hyderabad.
6. Extract from the research work done by M.A. Qaiyum on "*Golconda Fort*" (Unpublished).
7. *Pahani Records*, M.R.O. Officer, Golconda Mandal, Hyderabad.
8. Extract from the research work done by M.A. Qaiyum on "*Golconda Fort*" (Unpublished).
9. *Pahani Records*, M.R.O. Officer, Golconda Mandal, Hyderabad.
10. *Imperial Gazetteer of India*, Provincial series, Hyderabad State p.118.
11. *Glimpses of Nizam's Dominions*, p.199.
12. *Ibid.*
13. *Ibid.*
14. As per *Agricultural Census*, C.P.O., R.R. District, Nampally.
15. Afzal Begum, "*Hayat Baksh Begum*", M.Phil. dissertation (Unpublished), Osmania University, Hyderabad, p.136.
16. Gulam Hussain Khan, *Gulzar-e-Asafia*, MSS No. 2547. *Oriental Manuscript*, Library and Research Institute, Hyderabad, p.66.
17. Syed Khaja, *Gulzar-e-Asafia*, Hyderabad, p.1916, p.184.

18. Afzal Begum, *Op. Cit.*, p.136.
19. Bilgrami and Willmott, *Historical and Descriptive Sketch of H.E.H. The Nizam's Dominion*, Vol. II, p.609.
20. Bilgrami and Willmott, *Op.Cit*, pp.608-609; and G. Yazdani & H.K. Sherwani, *A Guide to Hyderabad*, 1937, p.63.

16

WATERWAYS AND COMMERCE

Water ways play a prominent role in the trade and commerce of India in general and Andhra Pradesh in particular. As the cost of water transport was relatively low, a substantial part of the inter-regional trade in cheap bulk commodities such as food-grains, salt and saltpetre were carried along the coast in the inland waterways. Due to the same reason even the cross country merchants followed the water routes whenever necessary in the trade of more expensive items.[1] The Godavari and the Krishna are the two big rivers in Andhra Desa. They do not dry up even in summer. They are navigable through Tilang-Andhra. As there were no bridges over the rivers, it affected the navigation when they were fresh. The only exception was the bridge now called the Puranapul over the river Musi. It was constructed by Ibrahim Qutb Shah in 1578 A.D. The rivers were crossed by means of a kind of circular basket boat called Putti or Putika in Telugu. This kind of basket boat was extensively used in Andhra Desa during this period.

Navigation

Navigation plays an important role in the successful voyages of ships. A number of factors such as the monsoons, the nature of the sea, the winds etc. would influence highly the course of navigation. In the eastern waters the sailors could navigate eight months in the year that is from September to April. The sea would be stormy from May to August. The ships usually depended on taking the advantage of the prevailing winds of the monsoons and avoid the risks or losses of storms during the voyage or at ports. The navigators were highly afraid of the rough sea and storms. Some contemporary works dealing with the sea-borne trade and navigation warned sailors to avoid storms and whirlpools which were dangerous to the movement of the ships. Among such works, The *Mohit*, which means Ocean, throws a flood of light on the navigation. It suggested fifty dates for leaving and entering the ports on Indian coasts as delay might result in loss of life and property.[2] So, it is obvious that in addition to the knowledge of the winds, the mariners must be well acquainted with the dates of monsoons of each country. While the small ships dreaded the storms, big ships like Chinese junks did not invite a calm sea.

In the navigation more than the winds and the waves, the shallow water posed greater danger to sailors as the ships ran around in shallow water. Further, rugged rocks caused wreckage.[3] The sailors had to face the sorrows and sufferings of the strong currents, dangerous fish and menacing snakes. When the sailors see a sea-serpent (the dragon-monster) they cut off their hair, take fish scales and bones and burn them, upon which it will generally disappear in the water.[4] The time for navigation plays an important role in the maritime trade. The sailors have to be careful and cautious about it. Usually the ships used to leave the shores of India in summer and return in winter, as these months are supposed to by ideal for voyages. The Chinese authority Ping-Chou-Ko-tan says

"Ships sail in the eleventh or twelfth moons to avail themselves of the north wind (the north-east monsoon) and come back in the fifth or sixth moon to avail themselves of the south wind (the south-west monsoon)".[5]

The mariners were fully equipped with masts, rudder, anchor along with nautical instruments to face the risks on the sea. The huge wooden anchors were very useful in the ports at the time of steering through the river mouths and sand banks. Gods were appeased to activate the sea and holy water was sprinkled to becalm the waves and wind.[6] The sailors were guided by the stars. The work *Mohit* says "when sailing out of sight of land the skippers steered by the Sun, Moon and Stars".[7] It is confirmed by the Ping-Chou-Ko-tan, according to which "The ship masters know the configuration of the coasts; at night they steer by the stars and in the day time by the Sun".[8] The mariners compass came into use.

Seaports

The ports played an important role in the water transport sector. They facilitated the coastal and overseas trade. The port *Ganjam* is situated at the mouth of the river Rusikulya. It is a river mouth port with shifting sand banks and narrow channels. Local boats carried articles to the large vessels. *Kalingapatnam* is located at the mouth of the river Vamsadhara. It was an open roadstead and provided safe anchorage to vessels. *Bhimilipatnam* was an important centre of trade during this period. The coastline between Bhimilipatnam and Kalingapatnam is inhospitable with ridge of rocks within six miles of the shore. Though it was not so congenial for trade, it however provided safe anchorage with its headlands to vessels in South-West and North-East monsoons. From this port rice was exported to other places and it was called the "rice bowl" for Ceylon by Dutch travellers.[9] *Visakhapatnam* was situated to the south of Bhimilipatnam. It has some natural advantages. In this port dockyards were constructed for the repairs of ships. It became an important centre of trade in 18th century due to the dockyard and other facilities. *Coringa Bay* is situated to the south of Visakhapatnam. It contained a number of ports such as *Coringa*, Kakinada, Yanam, *Bandaramlanka*, *Ingeram* and *Jagannathapuram*. These ports might have promoted indigenous trade in 17th century. During the 18th century the English shipped goods from Ingeram, the French from Yanam and the Dutch from Jagannathapuram. Another port *Narsapur* is situated with its ports and docks on the west branch of the river Vasista Godavari. Narsapur and its adjoining town of Madapallam were important ship building centres. The timber, iron and steel were available in this region for the building of ships. Hence, the Dutch and the English established their own dockyards with their officers.[10] The port lost its importance due to several factors. Among them mention must be made of the encroachment of the Godavari river.

Masulipatnam situated on latitude 16° 9' N, longitude 81° 10' E was a leading port during the period under review. The European companies operated from this port with their officers and personnel from the beginning of the 17th century. But the port was not endowed with natural advantages. It suffered from the shortcomings like an open and unprotected roadstead and a heavy grounds-well at the time of north-east monsoon. It was situated at the mouth of one of the branches of the Krishna river that joined the sea in Masulipatnam. Consequently, the sand banks and shoals posed a serious problem for the ships. Fortunately, the river was free of silting that could make the boats smooth passage upstream.[11] From this port the ships sailed directly to the Red sea port of Mocha, the South Arabian port of Muskat and Basra and Bandar Abbas the Persian Gulf ports.[12] The Dutch and the English Companies entered the trade in Masulipatnam from 17th century A.D. The decline of the port appears to have set in with the setting up of the Mughal administration in Andhra. Infact, the major strength of Masulipatnam was its political links with the Qutb Shahi kingdom. Divy Island is situated at 12 miles south of Masulipatnam. This area was highly fertile on account of the Krishna River. A promontory is formed in the place where this river flows into Bay of Bengal. It was not a harbour but was exceedingly fertile on account of the alluvial deposits of the Krishna River. There was great availability of provisions and constant supply of food from this region. So, it attracted the Europeans.[13] Another port *Pulicat* is situated about 35 miles south of Armugam. It was not conducive for the entry of large ships as the coast was shallow. It functioned as the port of outlet for handloom goods for there were many weaving villages in its hinterland. The Dutch developed it into a substantial port town in the later part of the 17th century.[14] The port disappeared by 19th century for natural reasons like the shifting of the river estuary, the sand banks and coastal erosion. *Madras* is situated 25 miles from south of Pulicat. Madras remained as an unimportant port with few fishing settlements till the English Company founded a factory there. It was a bad port with open roadstead, ground swell, dangerous surf and dangerous to large vessels and country boats that linked the ship and the shore. The goods were carried on by the masoola boats and they proved to be hazardous in bad weather. During the period from October to December the ships didn't sail from the port.[15] Near the fort of St. George there was a river Cooum that flowed into the sea. As the river was barren for most of the year, it didn't favour the trade with the interior places.[16] From this port ships sailed regularly to the West Coast ports of Malabar, Bombay, Surat, Red Sea and Persian Gulf and eastwards to the Achch, Bantam, Manila and Canton.

The above discussion suggests that the coast of Andhra was not furnished with havens of shipping. The ports suffered from some defects such as roadsteads open to the sea, silting of rivers and shifting of sand banks effecting in the decline of some ports and rise of other ports. The coastline was interspersed with rivers. The rivers were shallow. At the time of monsoon rains, large quantities of soil were deposited at the points where the rivers joined the sea. The sand banks of shallow depth blocked the large rivers like the Godavari and the Krishna. Further, the large ships had to remain in the open as the ports had roadsteads open. In such conditions a number of flat-bottomed boats suitable to withstand the surf were used for loading and unloading the commodities. Though the coastline of Andhra was interspersed with a number of perennial rivers they dried up totally in the dry months. Generally, the high flow and low flow of the rivers affected the trade and commerce adversely.

Sea Routes

The Qutb Shahi rulers maintained good commercial relations with South Asian and West Asian countries during the period under review. The sea-routes used by the traders from the ports of Andhra to other countries may be classified as follows:-

1. Sea Route to Africa and Europe
2. Sea Route to Persia and Arabia (West Asia)
3. Sea Route to Far East or South East Asia

From the port of Masulipatnam, the sea route to Africa and Europe was either through the Persian Gulf route or by the Red Sea route. The Red Sea route was hazardous due to the prevalence of a number of rocks, violent gales of wind and thick fog. So, the sailors used mostly the Persian Gulf route. From the port of Masulipatnam the Indian goods were carried to Damascus and Alexandria, to the coast of Africa and then to various countries of Europe. In other words commodities transshipped to Europe would be taken first to Aden or Mocha, then unloaded in the Gulf of Suez carried by land and water to the Mediterranean coast, paying very heavy duties for the passage across Egypt. The sea route to Persia and Arabia from Masulipatnam and other ports went to Hormuz and Bandar Abbas. The articles were then transferred in smaller vessels for voyage upto the Persian Gulf till it touched Basra and then taken inland upto Baghdad. It would also go through the Red Sea, where the important ports Aden, Mocha and Jidda were situated. The sea route to the Far East from Masulipatnam, across the Bay of Bengal followed the usual line to Achin (in Sumatra) and then to Bantam, Batavia (in Java) from there to Bornea, and to China and Japan. Another route was from the port of Masulipatnam to Calcutta (Bengal) and then to Arakan, where it touched Pegu and then Tenasserim in the kingdom of Siam or Ayuthya.[17]

Commerce on Waterways

The advent of the Europeans gave fillip to expansion of trade in Andhra Desa. There was active coastal trade and commerce. Madras transported salt to other coastal towns. The minor ports like Kothapatnam and Ramapatnam near Nizampatnam transported in small vessels the piece goods to the north and the south coasts.[18] From the port

Bimilipatnam a large number of native ships sailed to Bengal. Rice was exported from here to South Coromandel and the Malabar Coast. From the port of Ganjam rice was exported to Madras, Pulicat and other places, where it was in demand. It was estimated that about 4000 garce of rice costing 300,000 to 3, 20,000 Pagodas was exported to Madras from Andhra.[19]

During the 17th century, a brisk overseas trade was carried from Andhra Desa to Western Europe. A cargo dispatched to Europe via Batavia in 1642 A.D. will give us an idea of the quantity of goods sent to Europe. This cargo was dispatched from the port of Masulipatnam for Batavia in November, 1642 A.D. It consisted of 597 bales of cotton goods, 297 bales of indigo, 498 bales of crude and 538 sacks of refined saltpetre with some yarn. These figures furnish us with an idea of the quantities of various commodities that were exported.[20] The Dutch Company exported indigo to Europe wherever they obtained it in large quantities. Shortly after their settlement on the Coromandel Coast, the Dutch exported substantial quantity of indigo to Holland. The Commissioners of the English navy urged that Saltpetre should be imported from India following the Dutch pattern of trade. There was substantial increase in the exports of cotton goods from Andhra. In 17th Century there was a remarkable change in the fashions of clothes in England. The higher classes and the common classes of the society chose the light and elegant clothing. So, the Calicoes and Chintzes of Andhra were favoured. Animal skins were exported to Batavia and Japan. Iron and steel were exported to Pegu, Arakan, Tenasserim, Arabia and Persia. Golkonda was called a "country of Diamonds".[21] From Andhra, diamonds were sent to South East Asia and Europe. Tobacco, redwood, lack, and drugs were exported to other countries.

Though slave trade was not a regular one, there was a market for them in South East Asia and Ceylon.

There was extensive demand for foreign goods in Andhra among the rulers, ministers, officials, feudal lords and the upper classes of the society. Among the imported articles, the spices[22] came from Sumatra, Malacca and Ceylon. Precious metals formed as a largest item of imports and gold was brought from Europe, Persia and Burma.[23] The Andhra merchants procured copper from South East Asian ports. Burma supplied the same to Andhra. The other imported articles like perfumes, coconuts and coir, porcelain and natural gum were imported from West Asia, Ceylon, China and South East Asia respectively.

The European Companies organised courts and judicial officers in the ports to protect their commercial privileges. Streynsham Master, the Governor of Madras reorganised the choultry court which was conducted in the choultry or Town House presided by Indians or Europeans appointed by the Governor. Master increased the number of Justices to three to deal with the cases pertaining to the sale of property including land. Streynsham Master founded a superior court for the trial of civil and criminal cases. The Governor and Council tried cases in the Chapel in Fort St. George every Wednesday and Saturday according to English laws. The superior court was assisted by a clerk, an officer and a marshall. This court was specially founded to deal with the criminal cases like murder committed by the Portuguese and British residents, who could not be tried according to Indian laws.[24]

Taxes on imports and exports were collected at the seaports. Tax on imports was generally fixed at 2 ½ to 3 per cent ad valorem in all the ports of the coast. A stamping and brokerage duty of 12 per cent was imposed on textiles exported from Masulipatnam. Anchorage duty was charged on all ships in the ports of Andhra. Measuring and weighing duties were also levied. In Masulipatnam there was a weighing duty of 1/6 pagoda on 480 Dutch pounds of copper brought into the customs house.[25] Sunkam duties were levied. In Masulipatnam the duty was 6 pagodas per candy of 500 pounds on goods that were weighed.[26] There were other taxes which were imposed on the merchants. The port revenue was more than other sources of revenue.[27] The trade and commerce was carried on by Komatis, Baniya, Beri merchants of Tamil districts, Balijas, Telikis, Perikes, the Golconda Muslim merchants (mainly Persians) the Dutch, the English and the French during the period under review.

Conclusion

The above discussion reveals us that waterways played a significant role in the coastal and oceanic trade in Andhra Desa during this period. Inspite of certain physical disadvantages lakes and banks, open roadsteads, silting of rivers, shifting of sand banks and intensive cyclones, the waterways highly contributed to extensive indigenous and foreign trade of Andhra. Cyclones caused great ravage to the ports and shipping. In 1679 A.D., the buildings of wood and the bridge linking the port and the main road of Masulipatnam town were totally ruined due to a storm.[28] A Dutch ship was buried under seven feet of sand due to the adverse effect of hurricane in Narsapur.[29] The impact of these natural calamities led to the decline of some old ports and rise of new ports and also the trade and commerce on waterways.

Notes & References

1. Jean Baptiste Tavernier, *Tavernier's Travels in India*, 1540-67, II, London, 1925, p.35.
2. Sidi Ali, *The Mohit*, J.A.S.B., III, p.547.
3. *Ibid.*, V, p.453.
4. *Ibid.*, pp.456, 463.
5. Chau-Ju-Kua, *Chu-fan-Chi*, p.30.
6. Saroj Cherian, *Seaports in Andhra with Reference to Later Medieval Period (17th & 18th century)*, Ph.D. thesis (unpublished), Osmania University, Hyderabad, 1993, p.69.
7. Sidi Ali, *Op.Cit.*, Ch.III, IV.
8. Saroja Cherian, *Op.Cit.*, p.68.
9. Daniel Havart, *Open Ondergang Van Coromandel* (Amsterdam), 1693, 1, p.75.
10. Bay of Bengal Pilot, S.V. Narsapur, Point, London, 1901, pp.120-121.
11. Bay of Bengal Pilot, S.V. Masulipatnam, London, 1901, pp.168-169.
12. *Islamic Culture*, XXXII, 3, (1959), pp.174-178.
13. I.O.L., *Factory Records*, Miscellaneous, G/40/26.
14. Thomas Bowrey, *A Geographical Account of the Countries Round the Bay of Bengal 1669-1679*, ed., R.C. Temple, Hakluyt Society, 1905, p.53.
15. Saroja Cherian, *Op.Cit.*, p.47.
16. C.S. Srinivasachari, *History of the City of Madras*, Madras, 1939, p.1.
17. Saroja Cherian, *Op.Cit.*, pp.175-178.
18. W.H. Moreland (ed.), *Relations of Golkonda in the Early Seventeenth Century*, Hakluyt Society, 1931, pp.67-68.
19. *Despatches to England*, 15th January, 1719, p.1.
20. W.H. Moreland, *From Akbar to Aurangzeb*, London, 1923, p.97.

21. Jean Baptiste Tavernier, *Op.Cit.*, pp.328-332.
22. S. Arasaratnam, *Merchants, Companies and Commerce on the Coromandel Coast*, Oxford, 1986, p.107.
23. *Ibid.*, pp.110 & 136.
24. Saroja Cherian, *Op.Cit.,* pp.274-276.
25. Havart, 1, p.141.
26. Consultations, 7th January, 1679, *Factory Records, Madapollam*, I.O.L., G/26/2.
27. J.F. Richards, *Mughal Administration in Golconda*, Oxford, 1975, p.159.
28. *Van Dam*, 11, 2, pp.145-146.
29. Love, *Vestiges of Old Madras*, I, p.179.

17

MEANS OF TRANSPORT AND COMMUNICATION

Transport and communication facilities played an important role in the development of trade. The account of the foreign travellers like Tavernier, Bernier and Thevenot throw a flood of light on this subject. Their accounts may be corroborated by journals and letters of the European factory officials on the east coast. It is evident from the contemporary accounts that there was a fairly good network of roads connecting the different industrial centres, the markets and the ports. The royal capital Hyderabad was connected by an excellent network of roads with Surat, the chief Mughal port, Bijapur, the Adil Shahi capital, Goa and Masulipatnam by covering all the commercial centres and important towns. These trunk roads enabled the speedy movement of goods as well as human locomotion.

The road from Surat to Hyderabad was one of the principal roads, on which traffic from Surat passed on to Qutb Shahi territories. The road led from Surat to Daulatabad and Aurangabad, and from there it followed more or less the line of the South Central Railway passing Parbhani and Nander right upto Indur (Nizamabad), it followed the modern road to Indalwai and a few miles from there entered Qutb Shahi territories near Kalvarel and passed Biknur, Medchal, Maula ka Pahar, from there crossing Hussain Sagar and Puranapul reached Charminar.[1] There was another trunk road from Surat to Hyderabad via Burhanpur.

Road from Hyderabad to Masulipatnam was the most important trunk road, as they connected the capital and the port. There were two main roads to Masulipatnam via Vijayawada. The direct road was not in good condition, as most of the traffic from the capital to East coast passed along this section. The direct road ran from Hyderabad to Kollur mines, passed by Tenara and Jatenagar. The other road leading to Pantangi and to Panagal went direct to Nagalpad and Kulur. The distance between Hyderabad and Masulipatnam was 11 to 14 "costes" and between Vijayawada and Masulipatnam was 4 to 6 "costes" only.[2]

There was another road from Hyderabad to Madras via Gandikota. Tenara or Hayatnagar was its junction. The road may conveniently be dealt with according to the three sectors, into which it was divided. (1) Sector from Hayatnagar to Kumbum via Devarakonda, Merrivamula and Tripurantakam to Kumbum,[3] (2) From Kumbum to Gandikota, the headquarters of Mir Jumla, (3) The sector from Gandikota to Madras runs from Guntakal to Renugunta and Madras. There was road from Vijayawada to Madras, more or less followed the modern railway line, though it took detours at important places such as Kondavidu, Kondukur and Pulicat and reached Madras.[4] The road from Masulipatnam to Srikakulam ran along the coast to Palakollu, connecting Draksavaram, Bimilipatnam, and finally Srikakulam. Another road from Hyderabad to Ramallakota passed through Golconda, Kovikonda, Jatpol and Alampur on the Krishna. The road then marched to Kurnool and Ramallakota.[5] There was a road from Vijayanagara to Udayagiri, Kondavidu, Kondapalli and along the coast to Simhachalam and Srikurmam.[6]

Condition of Roads

The account of Tavernier and Thevenot reveal the fact that the condition of the roads in Golconda was bad. There were no bridges over the river which flowed the country, except Puranapul over Musi river. Tavernier said that wheel carriages did not travel between Golconda and Masulipatnam, the roads being too much interrupted by high mountains, tanks and rivers, and because there were many narrow and difficult passes. It was with the greatest trouble that even a small cart could be taken. He had taken one to the diamond mines, but he was obliged to take it to pieces frequently in order to pass bad places. It was the same between Golconda and Cape Comorin. There were no wagons in all these territories, and one could only find there oxen and pack-horses for conveyance of men, and for the transport of goods and merchandise.[7]

Safety of the Roads

Tavernier says that "He who desires to travel with honour in India, whether by carriage or Palankin, ought to take with him 20 or 30 armed men, some with bows and arrows and others with muskets, and you pay them as much per month as those who carry the Palankeen. These attendants not only conduce to your honour, but watch also for your protection, and act as sentinels at night, relieving one another, and striving to give you no cause of complaint against them. For it should be mentioned that in the towns where you hire them they have a head man who answers for their honesty, and when you employ them, each one gives him a rupee".[8]

Thevenot said that Hindu guards were better than Muslim guards. He hired two chariots and two peons for protection and he was accompanied by a French merchant Monsieur Bazon, who had with him 10 chariots and 14 peons. This party totally consisted of 45 men including 8 Europeans.[9] Tavernier also said that the Governor of Ramallakota mines provided him with horsemen who escorted him up to the Krishna river for greater security.[10]

Tavernier reports an excellent security arrangements made in the route from Madras to Gazulamandyam. He says: "Throughout all this country at every league the road is closed by gates and barricades, where a strict watch is kept, and all passersby are questioned whence they are going, so that a traveller can without danger and in perfect safety carry his gold in his hand. In all these places rice can be bought".[11] Travellers were also provided with the amusement of watching monkey-fights.[12] In the region of Utukuru Tavernier encountered some women who, having taken a vow to help the travellers for seven or eight years, served the travellers with cooked rice, beans, "Quichery", rice-water and bean-water. They also kept fire always ready to light the tobacco of the travellers.[13]

It was not necessary that those who travel in India should provide themselves with food beforehand – because even in the smallest villages rice, flour, butter, milk, beans, and other vegetables, sugar and other sweetmeats, dry and liquid, could be procured in abundance.[14] The sides of most of the roads were planted with avenues of trees, and where there were no trees planted, at every 500 paces small pieces of stones were fixed, which the inhabitants of the nearest villages were bound to whiten from time to time so that the letter carriers could distinguish the road on dark and rainy nights.[15] During the reign of Abdullah Qutb Shah, "Kos-minars" or mile-posts were erected along some important roads. One did find many of them still along the Hyderabad-Masulipatnam road up to the village of Chautuppal, though they were being removed for widening the existing road. These "Kos-minars" were in pairs, erected on either side of the then-existing road.

The guilds maintained either mercenary troops or had martial exploits for their credit. The Mummuri-dandas that are referred in the epigraphs of Andhra and Karnataka, prior to 17th century A.D., must have been either the regular or advanced guard soldiers of the Vira-Balanja merchants.[16] An epigraph of the year 1521 A.D. refers to the death of some men of the Reddi community while defending the goods of Balanja merchants from the thieves.[17] From the above discussion it is clear that the travellers and merchants were moving in large groups.

There were many caravansarais in and around Hyderabad. Tavernier says that in Karwan there were two or three mosques which served as caravansarais for strangers.[18] A caravansarai was attached to Kulthum Begam's Mosque in Karwan. It still retains its beauty and gives information as to how lodging facilities were provided to strangers.[19] In the city itself there were four or five caravansarais, having two stories, where there were large halls and chambers which were cool.[20] Thevenot says that the caravanseras in Hyderabad were all beautiful, and the most esteemed one was the "Nimet-ulla" serai.[21] He stayed in that place paying two rupees a month for two chambers. It had a "spacious square, and the court of it is adorned with several trees of different kinds, and a large bason where the Mahometans perform their ablutions".[22] Generally in the Deccan, mosques and temples often offered shelter to the passing strangers.

Mode of Transport

The bullock-cart constituted as the most important conveyance for men and goods. Articles of internal trade were transported from one place to another in carts, Kavadis, on pack animals and by means of headloads on land routes and in boats across rivers and lakes. Oxen and bullocks were important conveyers of goods. They drew carts and carried bags containing Perikes or goods on their backs.[23]

Another method of transport was Kavadis. *Simhasanadvatrimsika* mentions that goods were carried through Kavadis in Andhra.[24] By head-loads also articles were transported from place to place. Thevenot says that "Indians used oxen in travelling and ride them like horse, though commonly they go but at a very slow pace. They saddle him (ox) as they do a horse.... There beasts are made use of generally all over the Indians; and with them only drawn wagons, coaches allowing more or fewer, according as to the load is heavier or lighter".[25]

Tavernier states that oxen were ridden as horses and they could be bridled.[26] He further says that an ox could carry a weight of 300 to 350 French livres (4 to 5 *maunds*).[27] Some oxen were very healthy and a pair of such oxen cost 600 rupees.[28] According to a letter of the Dutch factors drafted in 1615 A.D. goods from Masulipatnam to Pulicat were transported by 900 oxen and 900 coolies.[29] The average hire money for an ox-cart was one rupee per day, including a fully equipped cart, food for the driver and oxen and the wages of the driver himself.

Light carriages or coaches drawn by oxen were also available for travel and a carriage could carry two persons.[30] Tavernier says that some carriages were made in such a way that they could be broken while going on bad roads. He met with this sort of experience, while travelling from Lakkavaram to Kollur, as the road was very rocky and in two or three places the carriage was dismantled.[31] Camels were rarely used for caravans, as they were particularly reserved to carry the baggage of the nobles.

Palanquins were also used. Normally six members were required to carry a palanquin, each was paid 4 rupees a month for short journey and 5 rupees for journey lasted for more than[32] 60 days. The rich used decorated palanquins, though they were costly but porters were available at a easy rate.[33] Tavernier observes that in Golconda kingdom there was "the convenience of much larger Pallankeens than in the rest of India, for one is carried much more easily, more quickly and a less cost."[34] Toll taxes were collected near Kanumalu, mountain passes.

The cost of water transport was relatively low; a substantial part of the inter-regional trade was carried by it. The rivers were crossed by means of a kind of circular basket boats called Puttis or Putikas in Telugu. These ferries were large wicker boats covered with oxhide at the bottom and outside, and spread over with some kind of carpets and were propelled by four corners. Paes, who visited Vijayanagara in the reign of Krishnadevaraya provide us with information about the basket boats that used in crossing Tungabhadra.[35]

The Godavari and Krishna were the two big rivers and the cheap bulk goods like food-grains, salt and salt-petre were carried along the coast in the inland water ways. But some times for more expensive items also traders used the water routes, whenever necessary. Krishna river (near Alampur) then served as the boundary of Golconda and Bijapur kingdoms. Tavernier provide us with an account of how this river was guarded. He says that "Good boats or a bridge over this river might be provided, but the kings of Golconda and Bijapur do not allow this, because the river serves to separate the two kingdoms. Every evening the boatsmen on both banks are obliged to report to the two sub-governors, who reside on either side, at about a quarter of a league from the river, an exact statement of the people, beasts of burden, and merchandise which have crossed during the day".[36]

The Postal System

No postal system in the modern sense existed during this period. But, Ibrahim Qutb Shah (1550-1580 A.D.) introduced a new intelligence service in order to keep the king in touch with the subjects and officers. A great number of reporters were posted in different parts of the country for conveying local news to the capital, Golconda. Tavernier, who came to Golconda in the Seventeenth century, gives interesting account of the postal system in the Qutb Shahi kingdom. He stated that all those letters which were sent by foot-post all over India, go with more speed than those letters which were carried by horsemen, as at the end of every two leagues there were little huts where, there were men always ready, who were engaged to carry the letters, came to one of these huts, he threw the letters into the hut and then he who was appointed ran with them to give letters into the messenger's hands but they must be thrown at his feet and he must gather them up. He also wrote about the postal system between Golconda and Gandikota, founded immediately after it was conquered by Mir Jumla and for facility in transmission of news, Mir Jumla set up *dak chaukis* from Hyderabad to Karnataka.[37]

In 1724 A.D. Nizam-ul-Mulk Asaf Jah-I, the Mughal Viceroy of the six Subhas of the Deccan – Aurangabad,

Berar, Bidar, Bijapur, Hyderabad and Khandesh, adopted and continued to follow the pattern of postal system, that prevailed in the Deccan Provinces, in the Mughal Empire. Dargah Quli Khan was the head of the postal organization (Derogha-i-Harkara) under Nizam-ul-Mulk. The postal system which was established by Nizam-ul-Mulk in the state that extended from Narmada to Cauvery and from Masulipatnam to Bijapur was adopted by Nazir Jung (1748-1750 A.D.) and Salabat Jung (1750-1761 A.D.). Later Nizam Ali Khan improved the postal system in the kingdom.

Thus, the foregoing discussion makes it clear that there was a fairly improved means of transport and communication system in Telangana and Andhra during 17th and 18th centuries, which gave great fillip to trade and commerce.

Notes & References

1. H.K. Sherwani, *History of the Qutb Shahi Dynasty*, New Delhi, 1974, pp.493-494.
2. *Ibid.*, pp.494-497.
3. *Ibid.*, pp.497-498.
4. *Ibid.*, p.498.
5. *Ibid.,* p.499.
6. Robert Sewell, *A Forgotten Empire*, Delhi, 1984, p.307.
7. Tavernier, *Travels in India by Jean-Baptiste Tavernier, Baron of Aubonne,* translated by Dr. V. Ball, edited by William Crooke, Vol. I, Oxford University Press, London, 1925, p.142.
8. *Ibid.*, p.38.
9. Thevenot, *Indian Travels of Thevenot and Careri,* edited by Dr. Surendranath Sen, National Archives of India, New Delhi, 1949, pp.101-102.

10. Tavernier, *Op.Cit.*, Vol. II, p.54.
11. *Ibid.*
12. *Ibid.*, p.217.
13. *Ibid.*, p.225.
14. *Ibid.*, p.238.
15. *Ibid.*, pp.233-234.
16. *"Journal of Oriental Research"*, XXX, p.26.
17. K. Sundaram, *Studies in Economic and Social Conditions in Medieval Andhra (A.D.1000-1600)*, 1968, p.182.
18. Tavernier, *Op.Cit.*, Vol. I, p.123.
19. H.K. Sherwani, *Op.Cit.,* p.547.
20. Tavernier, *Op.Cit.*, p.123.
21. Thevenot, *Op.Cit.*, p.133.
22. *Ibid.*, pp.132-133.
23. *South Indian Inscriptions*, Vol. X, No.304.
24. Radha Krishna Murthy, *Economic Conditions in Medieval Andhra*, p.270.
25. Thevenot, *Op.Cit.*, p.73.
26. Tavernier, *Op.Cit.*, Vol. I, p.36.
27. *Ibid.,* p.32.
28. *Ibid.,* p.37.
29. K.A. Letters, LXXIX, 28th November, 1615.
30. Tavernier, *Op.Cit.*, Vol. I, p.36.
31. *Ibid.,* p.141.
32. *Ibid.,* p.38.
33. Thevenot, *Op.Cit.,* p.76.
34. Tavernier, *Op.Cit.*, Vol. I, p.142.
35. Robert Sewell, *Op.Cit.,* p.259.
36. Tavernier, *Op.Cit.,* Vol. II, p.54.
37. Chandraiah, K., *Hyderabad 400 Glorious Years*, Hyderabad, 1996, pp. 108-110.

18

CHANGING PROFILE OF THE TRADING COMMUNITIES

The trading communities played a vital role in the commercial activities of medieval Andhra. Trade both internal and external was in a flourishing condition during the period under review. The trade of the country was practically in the hands of some commercial communities both indigenous and foreign.

Indigenous Trading Communities

The Vaisyas constituted as the main trading community throughout the history of Telangana and Andhra areas. It seems that Komatis claimed to be Vaisyas. They dominated coastal trade, wholesaling and retailing and banking activities. However, in overseas trade they had to compete with the Muslims. They had to carry on business in the opposition from the Beri merchants of the Tamil districts who also claimed to be Vaisyas.[1] But the Komatis would not recognize them as Vaisyas. As a result there arose bitter quarrels between these two castes. The Beris were skillful traders and dominated all along the coast right up to the port of Nagapatnam.[2] They distinguished themselves as suppliers of textiles from the centres of production to the ports on the coast. They built ships and exported goods to other countries. They also carried on trade in foodstuffs. They became great influenced people in Godavari delta. They accumulated great wealth and enjoyed respectability in the society. On account of this they became leaders of the Valangai or right hand faction.

The Chettis or Settis were another trading community in these regions. It is evident that the ancestors of the Chettis constituted the Vaisya caste of ancient Indian society. Trade and banking were their allotted functions. During the middle Ages, the Chettis were the principal merchants throughout the country. Mahuan said that all trading transactions were carried on by the Chettis, who bought the pepper from the farmers when it was ripe, and sold it to foreign ships when they passed by. They also bought and collected precious stones and other costly wares. The Settis exercised a remarkable influence in Vijayanagara times. They had their own head of caste.

The Beri Chettis were wealthy merchants, brokers, wholesale dealers and ship owners during the period under review. As stated earlier they were great rivals of the Komatis in trade and became the leaders of the Idangai or left hand faction.[3] It is to be noted in this connection that the indigenous merchants were described as pirates by the Dutch. Particularly they seem to have developed some hatred for the Beri Chettis. For example, the Dutch accused the Portuguese of conspiring with "that pirate Beri Rama Chetti" to capture Dutch ships in the Gulf of Sind.[4] Astrappa Chetti belonging to Pulicat was a prominent merchant who owned ships and carried on trade with South East Asian countries and Ceylon.

The Balinjas or Banajigas played an important role as merchant community during the period under consideration. They established their hegemony in trade and attained a position of importance and supremacy among the various sub-castes that constituted the Sudra Varna. They were referred to as "Settis", a suffix, which is usually attached to the names of Vaisyas indicating their supremacy. They were also known as Vira Balijas, the term "Vira" indicating either their religious leanings, as they were the followers of Virasaivism or their heroic spirit, which must have been a pre-requisite to face the dangerous and perils associated with their profession. The inscriptions of the period also highlight the origin of the Balijas. They seem to have emigrated from North India, where they lived at Ahichchatrapura, and settled at Ayyavolu or Aihole, grew prosperous through the trading activities and spread throughout the South India. Among the merchant communities the Balijas played an effective role in the distribution of goods. There were many sub-castes among the Banajigas who specialized in different articles. They are:

1. Dasa banajigas or Tota banajigas (betel growers)
2. Dudi banajigas (cotton traders)
3. Gazula banajigas (glass bangle traders)
4. Puvvula banajigas (flower sellers)
5. Nayudu balija
6. Jidipalli balija
7. Rajamahendra balija (belonging to Nellore, Cuddapah and Anantapur).[5]

The Vira Balija traders of medieval Andhra Desa were highly organized with headquarters at Ayyavole or Aihole in the Bijapur district. They exhibited heroic spirit, to face perils associated with their profession, as well as defended themselves from the competition of the Vaisyas. They were experts in business in a wide variety of articles like elephants, horses, oxen, buffaloes, cows, carts, rubies, pearls, coral, emeralds, topazes, sapphires, agates, civet, camphor, musk, saffron, perfumes, drugs, arecanuts, salt, grain, flowers, pepper etc. They also possessed great expertise in the testing of the diamonds, selecting horses and elephants. They carried the articles on oxen, asses or buffaloes adorned with red trapping and tinkling bells. They sold them either wholesale or hawked them about on their shoulders. They were credited with conducting trade in thirty two seaports and eighteen cities. The corporation of Ayyavole merchants consists of Salu-mules, Svadesis, Paradesis, Nana-desis and Settis hailing from fifty six countries which suggest the diverse character of the guild. The Ayyavole merchants were highly organized with branches in fifty six countries.[6] Among the Balija Chettis, Astrappa Chetti was a prominent merchant. He carried on business operations extending from Masulipatnam to Nagapatnam. His brother Chinnanna was also a reputed merchant, who developed inland and foreign trade. He entered into partnership with the king of Arakan in his oceanic trade. He enjoyed the support of Sriranga, the king of Chandragiri.

The *Perikes* were another important Sudra trading class. The term "Perike Setlu" shows that trade was their main occupation and assuming the suffix "Setlu" which is usually attached to the names of Vaisyas and later Balijas and Telikas, all of whom were economically powerful, shows that Perikes too were a caste of significance. The caste attained its name "Perike" from the bag or sack which was known as Perikelu. These bags were transported on donkeys or bullocks and contained grain, vegetables etc. They were put on the back of the animals, with an opening in the middle and both the ends carrying commodities on either side. The word "Perike" is defined in the Madras Census Report, 1901 as meaning literally a gunny bag. Gunny bag is the popular and trading name of the coarse sacking and sacks made from the fibre of jute, much used in Indian trade. It is noted in the Census Report, 1891 that "the Perikes claim to be a separate caste, but they seem to be in a reality a sub-division, and not a very exalted sub-division, of Balijas, being infact identical with Uppu Balijas. Their hereditary occupation is carrying salt, grain etc., on bullocks and donkeys in Perikes or packs".[7] The Perikes worshipped Lord Shiva and while organizing their trade journey they offered prayers to Lord Siva.

The *Telikis* were the oil-mongers. They are said in the Madras Census Report, 1901 as "Telugu oil-presser caste, which should not be confused with Tellakula, a synonym for Tsakala, or with Telli, a caste of Oriya oil-pressers".[8] Telikula is a synonym for the Ganiga or Gandla caste of oil-pressers, derived from the oil, whereas the names Ganiga and Gandla refer to the oil-mill. In the Northern Circars the name Telikula is used in preference to Ganiga or Gandla and the oil-pressers in that part of the country are known as Telikula-Vandlu. The Telikulas are Onteddu that is use of a single bullock for working the oil-mill, whereas among the Ganigas, there are both Onteddu and Rendeddu sections, which employ one and two bullocks respectively. The Telikis seems to have been highly organized and formed themselves into a powerful corporate body. This body regulated the life of its members. Like the other communities of a same nature, Telikis carried their own distinct number-Thousand with the name of the community. But it may be assumed that the guild of Telikis, at the time of its formation, must have been represented by members of one thousand families, and hence attained the name Teliki Vevuru or Teliki one thousand. The principal seat of Telikis was Bezawada, the modern Vijayawada on the bank of the river Krishna. They were the followers of Saivism and worshipped particularly Malleshwara of Bezawada. It appears as if there exists a greater unity among the Tilikis. They made donations to temples in the name of Teliki Vevuru or Teliki-one thousand castes. While making individual donations, they eulogized their caste and mentioned their name prefixing with that of their caste.

The Muslim Traders

The Muslim merchants of the Andhra coast were mentioned in the European records as "Coromandel Moors". They were also like the Hindus a diverse group. The merchants of the Golconda kingdom called as Golconda Muslims. They were predominantly Persian in character with an intermingling of Arabs, Turks and Pathans. The Golconda Muslims were prominent overseas traders and active participants in coastal and oceanic trade. They were urban communities operating mainly from Masulipatnam and other ports such as Nizampatnam, Vizagapatnam and Bimilipatnam. They maintained good relations with administrative nobility and royalty of Golconda. They enjoyed political connections and influenced the diplomatic relations between the rulers of Golconda and the rulers of the trading states of Asia.[9] In a letter written by the Dutch agent at Masulipatnam to his Company some names of the chief Muslim merchants of that region were furnished. They were Khwaja Nizam, Khwaja Hassan Ali, Khwaja Araby, etc.[10] Muslim merchants were so powerful that they mediated between the merchants and the Companies when problems arose. For example, an eminent merchant by name Mir Kamaluddin negotiated with the Dutch on behalf of the Sultan of Golconda at Masulipatnam in 1629 A.D. and helped a trader Raghava Chetti. The Golconda Muslim merchants, who were great overseas traders, became most influential in medieval coastal Andhra area. Mir Jumla was an outstanding merchant and amassed enormous wealth.

Foreign Commercial Communities

The Persian merchants occupy a significant place among the foreign trading classes. As the Qutb Shahis belonged to the Shia sect, many Persian traders and adventurers came to Andhra Desa. In the early years of the 17th Century, there existed a market for north Coromandel textiles in Persia. Masulipatnam shipping was owned largely by Persians. They included traders like Mir Qasim and Mir Muhammad Murad, also Mir Kamaluddin Haji Jamal, and Mulla Muhammad Taqi Taqrishi, governor of Masulipatnam in 1627-1628 A.D. These Persians, who were as politically powerful, were intensely disliked by the European factors at Masulipatnam.

Of all the important ship-owners, Mir Kamaluddin might be described as fairly close to the Dutch and English factors at any time. References to him occur as an overland trader's courtier, ship owning merchant and sometimes administrator of parts of the Krishna and Godavari delta areas. The most powerful figures at Golconda for almost two decades was the Mir Jumla, Nawab Allam Fatimi, Mir Muhammad Mumin. The trade between Masulipatnam and Persia was in flourishing condition and further the Persian merchants in Masulipatnam and other sea ports of Andhra played an active role in the commercial activities. The Armenians established themselves as traders, concentrating their commercial activities at Masulipatnam by eighteenth Century A.D.

They dominated shipping and oceanic trade as far as Manila in the East and Persian Gulf and the Red Sea in the West. An Armenian merchant Coja Panous Calender a merchant entered into a contact with the English at Madras in 1688 A.D. By this the Armenians were given freedom to travel in the ships belonging to the Company, to live in the Company's settlements in India and to enjoy all civil rights "in the same manner as if they were Englishmen born", and also to have "the free and undisturbed liberty of the exercise of their own religion".[11]

Among the foreign trading classes the Europeans predominated the trade in Coromandel Coast during the period under review. The Dutch, the English and the French established their settlements and factories on the East Coast. The rulers of medieval Andhra Desa, specially the Qutb Shahis of Golconda realized that the Europeans were likely to promote trade in the areas where they settled and thus to bring about prosperity of the kingdom. The Dutch Company was established in 1602 A.D. under the name of Vereenigde Oostindische Compagnie (United East India Company of the Netherlands) popularly known as V.O.C. The first fleet of the new chartered company which sailed in 1602 A.D. consisted of 15 ships. In the beginning the Dutch interest was not in India but in the Indonesian Islands of Java, Sumatra and the Spice Islands wherein spices were produced. But after gaining control of the most important profitable part of Asian trade, they concentrated on Indian trade. In India they established factories at Surat, Masulipatnam, Bheemunipatnam, Narasapur and Nagapatnam. The Dutch East India Company was incorporated in 1602 A.D. and in 1606 A.D. an agreement was signed between the Dutch and the Qutb Shahi officers under which the former established their factories at Masulipatnam and Nizampatnam and this was followed by the Pulicat factory in 1610 A.D.[12] The Dutch got some important trading concessions from the Qutb Shahis who were the most powerful rulers in the 17th Century. They entered into an agreement with Muhammad Quli Qutb Shah (1580-1612 A.D.) and succeeded in obtaining permission for the establishment of factories at Masulipatnam and Nizampatnam in 1606 A.D. The painted Chintz were in great demand in Molucca islands. The Dutch came to know that the Krishna Delta did not supply the same. These painted Chintz were available in the vicinity of Pulicat and San Thome. Very soon the Dutch founded factories at Tengapatnam or fort St. David.

The Dutch obtained a site in Pulicat from the ruler of Chandragiri. In 1639 A.D. during the reign of Abdullah Qutb Shah, they were exempted from a number of duties in Masulipatnam, embarkation and disembarkation duties, weighing duty, town duty and transit duties. Again in 1647 A.D., the same Sultan granted a Cowle exempting the Dutch from disembarkation and embarkation duties on their goods in the port of Pulicat. The Dutch were allowed to share the duty with the Sultan, the share of the Dutch being 25% to 50% on different categories of imported and exported goods. In 1653 A.D. the Dutch acquired permission from the Qutb Shahi government to build a factory at Masulipatnam. In 1674 A.D. Abul Hasan Tanashah exempted the Dutch from all customs duties in ports north of Masulipatnam. Another Farman gave the Dutch complete freedom from tariff in the Golconda dominions. In 1675 A.D. Abul Hasan granted the Dutch a piece of land in Narasapur where they built a house, a carpentry workshop and an iron smithy. When the kingdom of Golconda was overrun by the Mughals in 1687 A.D., the Dutch had to negotiate afresh with the Mughal administrators for trade concessions. Joanna Bacherus, a senior officer of the Dutch Company, was sent as Ambassador to the court of Aurangzeb in 1689 A.D. He presented elephants, Persian horses, a gold lamp stand, gold and silver ornaments etc., to the Emperor. Pleased with this gesture, Aurangzeb confirmed all the grants and concessions given to the Dutch from their establishment in Andhra now conquered by the Mughals.

The Dutch were further exempted from the following duties - the tax on boats, the road duties of Ellur, Rajahmundry, Draksavaram, Palakollu and Narsapore, Masulipatnam, the duties on provisions for the consumption of the Dutch etc. The extensive customs exemption given to the Dutch were not recognized by the Hindu Zamindars. The Hindu Rajas of the Godavari area opposed the trading privileges of the Dutch given by the Mughals.[13] As a result of it, by the early eighteenth century A.D., the Dutch lost control of Srikakulam, Draksavaram, Narsapur and Bhimilipatnam. They were compelled to confine to Nagapatnam, the centre of Dutch power.

The English were also interested in Asian trade. The East India Company established in 1600 A.D. with the exclusive privilege to trade in the East decided to open a factory at Surat on the West Coast of India. Factory was the name given to a trading depo. The Company understood that the British woollens were not in demand in South East Asia but there was a great demand for Indian textiles, particularly the Andhra textiles. Hence, the Company decided to force its way into the textile trade of India. The English Company dispatched a ship called Globe under the command of Hippon to open trade in the Bay of Bengal which arrived in Masulipatnam in January, 1611 A.D. The English opened negotiations with the ruler of Golconda Muhammad Quli Qutb Shah for trading facilities on the coast of Andhra. The English Company was permitted to establish factories at Masulipatnam, Nagapatnam and Pulicat in 1611 A.D. But the English lacked some of the facilities obtained by the Dutch.

The English felt strongly that Masulipatnam, which they made headquarters on the North Coromandel Coast, was not a heaven for their commercial activities due to the Dutch rivalry. They determined to find a new factory at Armagoan near Pulicat in Nellore district in 1626 A.D. Very soon the English found that superior quality of textiles not available in the hinterland of Armagoan and the political conditions of Karnataka in which it was situated were very disturbing.[14] In 1639 A.D. the English received a grant from the Damerla brothers according to which they were allowed to receive half of the customs and revenues of Madraspatnam port. Thus, the English took possession of Madraspatnam on 20th February, 1640 A.D. and started the construction of Fort St. George. The place which became a settlement of weavers came to be called Chennapatnam after Damerla Chennapa father of Damerla Venkatadri.[15] The English were granted a Farman known as the golden Farman by Abdullah Qutb Shah in 1636 A.D. By virtue of this Farman, the English were freed from the port and town duties in all port towns within the Qutb Shahi dominions. The English faced some opposition from the Qutb Shahi governors like Neknam Khan and Podili Lingappa, who strongly felt that the concessions given to the English cause loss of revenue to the state.

After the Mughal conquest of Andhra, the English thought of acquiring political power there to get free hand in trade. But the English underestimated the Mughal strength as Aurangzeb was more powerful than East India

Company. In accordance to the imperial orders the Mughal faujdars in Andhra by force seized the British trading settlements at Masulipatnam, Madapollam and Visakhapatnam in 1689 A.D. The British Mughal relations improved when the English agreed to pay an indemnity of 1,50,000 rupees. The English helped the Mughals in suppressing the revolts of Telugu Zamindars in Karnataka. Asad Khan, the Wazir of Aurangazeb promised many trading privileges to the English but they did not materialize in the form of a Farman. Moreover, the Mughals became aggressive towards the English after they enforced imperial authority effectively in Andhra. Unable to withstand the Mughal pressure in the area around Masulipatnam the English started concentrating on Madras and developed it as important trading centre in South India by investing enormous funds. Mughals realized that the Madras administration posed a threat to the Mughal power in Karnataka and so the faujdar of Hyderabad Karnatak was instructed to leave the English at Madras undisturbed.

Sadutullah Khan became the independent Nawab of the Karnataka in 1710 A.D. and he only accepted the status quo. The English on the other hand strengthened their base at Madras and from there they operated their two important coastal establishments namely Fort St. David and Visakhapatnam. Visakhapatnam became the most important trading centre on the northern coast with the decline of Masulipatnam. Simon Holcombe was mainly responsible for building and fortifying the town of Visakhapatnam from 1692 A.D. to 1705 A.D. He was friendly with the insurgent Rajas like Pusapati Anandaraju with the English Company as they controlled the hinterland producing cloth. The Rajas were also content that the English purchased cloth for export from their territories.

But after the death of Holcombe, Visakhapatnam faced serious confrontation from the Mughal faujdar Fakrullah Khan of Visakhapatnam. After some years Fakrullah Khan laid seize to Visakhapatnam. The seize was finally lifted when the English accepted to pay more than 20,000 gold Hunns to the faujdar.[16] By 1710 A.D. the British gained the confidence of Ananda Raju, son of Sitaram Pusapati and also fortified Visakhapatnam on the model of Madras. When the Mughal administration became weak in Andhra, the English strengthened their trading settlements and transformed them as coastal city states.

The French also appeared on the scene with their 'Company La Compagnie India'. The Company established trading settlements at Masulipatnam (1669 A.D.), Pondicherry (1673 A.D.) and Chandranagore (1690 A.D.). The settlements at Mahe, Karaikal and Yanam were established at a later date. The French encountered the problem of securing proper trade concessions and privileges from the native rulers and the antagonism of the fellow Europeans those who were already well established in the sub-continent. From 1647 A.D. to 1687 A.D. the French trade began to grow in India from the port of Masulipatnam. After the Mughal conquest of Golconda in 1687 A.D., the French obtained trading rights from Emperor Aurangzeb. Aurangzeb issued a Farman allowing the French to carry on duty free trade at Masulipatnam only after the French paid 10,000 rupees to the Emperor.[17]

In 1693 A.D. the Dutch seized Pondicherry and expelled the French garrison and the merchants. The Dutch occupation of Pondicherry gave a serious blow to French trade in Masulipatnam. It was only after the peace of Ryswick which was concluded in Europe that the French governor Francois Martin occupied Pondicherry in 1699 A.D. in accordance with the provisions of the treaty.

Francois Martin maintained friendly relations with the Mughals and obtained some more trade concessions in 1703-1706 A.D. Martin revived and reorganized French trade particularly the production of cloth for export. As many as 500 weavers were employed in Pondicherry during 1700-1706 A.D.[18] Martin's remarkable contribution was to fortify Pondicherry with full fledged brick bastions around the fortress. By 1706 A.D. there were five companies and thirty officers in the fortress.

The French government at Pondicherry started minting coins independently. It alarmed the Mughal authorities in Karnatak. They blockaded Pondicherry and so many inhabitants were taken as prisoners. Martin retaliated by organizing French troops and he could clear out the blockade. Afterwards the French government at Pondicherry was challenged by Daud Khan Panni, the faujdar of Karnatak. He raised objection to the erection of brick bastions around the fortress on the basis that it was an integral part of the Mughal Empire and not an autonomous administrative unit. When Daud Khan marched on Pondicherry, Martin paid 10,000 rupees as a present.[19] After Francois Martin the French trade on Coromandel suffered a set back for several reasons. The main cause was the non-availability of capital for investment in trade. At home the French East India Company deteriorated because of adverse policies of the French government. Gradually, the French lost economic and political influence beyond Pondicherry. They could establish only one factory at Yanam near Kakinada in 1731 A.D.

The Trading Methods

The internal and external trade was carried on by some commercial methods. The traders carried their wares in sacks large bags which open in the middle. Each end of these bags was filled with grain or other commodity and laid across the back of the animal. The traders who carried on trade in this manner were called Perike Setlu or sack-traders. Religious festivals gave enormous encouragement to trade. On such occasion certain articles which were generally difficult to get in the weekly Fairs and local markets could be obtained and business was conducted both wholesale and retail. Tolls were collected in different localities. Customs were collected on exports and imports.

The *Muster system* was one of the trading methods of the period under consideration. The European Companies considered all aspects of trade like prices of commodities, placing orders and taking delivery of goods, maintaining good relations with the native rules. The European factories in India adopted the *Muster system* to safeguard the standard of the product. The merchants made contracts with the companies eight to ten months before the ships reached India with their cargoes. In the contract all the necessary details pertaining to the textiles like the quality, the measurements, and the prices of the textiles, the date of delivery of goods and the names of the merchants were noted. After the clothes were transported to the warehouses, the officers concerned checked whether they tally with the samples showed to them earlier. If they found any deviation from the Muster, the cloth was either rejected or the price agreed in the contract was decreased. The clothe traders fell bitter about the Sample System as it resulted in heavy losses to them. Because they collect the textiles from a number of weavers, the differences in samples are bound to occur. While the European companies with their finances and organizational system exercised command over Indian merchants and markets, the Indian traders cleverly followed some tactics and troubled the companies. They used to delay the delivery of goods or waited for the nearing of the shipping to force the warehouse keepers to accept their goods without any option.

The *Advance contract system* was another commercial practice that was in vogue. The Andhra weavers manufactured some special varieties of textiles for foreign markets. They were in need of working capital to produce those special textiles. It was advanced to them by the merchants. This system of commercial advances was an adoption of the method called *Verlags system* or the 'putting out' method obtained in Europe. The wealthy merchants advanced money to the weavers either through their own agents or independent brokers working for commission at the port of shipment. The weaver was supposed to deliver the cloth to the contractor by the scheduled time as he was being paid a part of the total amount. The price was either fixed in advance or negotiated at the time of completion of the transaction keeping in view the market prices.[20] But this Indian system of commercial advance differed from the 'putting out' method obtained in Europe. As in this system the buyer gave the weavers all the raw materials necessary to manufacture the product and for a fixed price got back the finished product. But in the Indian system the merchant advanced finance to the weaver. This helped the weaver in supporting himself during the time of the production of the cloth.

The trade was conducted by another method known as *Bills of Exchange*. The expanding commerce and the need for the exchange of currency necessitated some sort of credit instrument which found expression in the bills of exchange in Medieval India. The most characteristic credit institution in India was the *Hundi* or *Bills of*

Exchange promising payment 'after a specified period, usually two months or less' at a particular place and allowing a discount which included interest, insurance (*bima*) charges and cost of transmission of money.[21] The *Bills of Exchange* enabled the merchants to get necessary credit in the long distance trade. Besides, it also reduced the hazards in the transmission of cash.[22] By using this method the Companies send cash from one port town to another. This business was mainly in the hands of the Sarrafs or Shroffs who were the professional money changers. They played an important role as bankers providing specialized service as suppliers of credit. They lent amounts to reliable persons at very high rates of interest and also accepted deposits both in cash and kind payable on demands. They judged the purity of the coins and controlled the rate of exchange between the currencies prevailing in different parts of the country.

The Shroffs were employed by the English Company to count coins and to procure bullion. The responsibility of the Shroff was to detect debased or counterfeit coins. He used to receive severe punishments for failing in discharging his duties properly. In 1717 A.D. one Perumal was punished for counterfeiting Fanams.[23] The other important commercial practice known as *Freight Business*. Merchants used to send their consignments of high value goods in different ships instead of in a single ship. In this way the merchants saved their goods from any unforeseen disaster like ship wreck or piracy. The freight charges are generally as follows:

Coast Bay Ships	...	£ 30 per ton gruff goods
Pepper ships	...	£ 32 ...
Mocha ships	...	£ 32 ...
China ships	...	£ 31 fine goods
Surat ships	...	£ 33 gruff goods.[24]

The freight voyages enabled the merchants to exchange their goods among different countries. The English sent their ships for freight voyages. In 1705 A.D. the English ship by name Queen was freighted for 8,000 Pagodas from Madras for a voyage to China and Persia.

Conclusions

The Commercial Communities gave enormous encouragement to trade and commerce of the period under review. Along with the indigenous traditional commercial communities, the foreign trading classes also contributed for the tremendous commercial development in Andhra Desa. The rise of these communities has to be attributed to the rise of cities and other entrepots of industry and commerce. The merchant classes banded themselves into a fraternity with a high developed community life.

Notes & References

1. N. Venkata Ramanayya, *Studies in the Third, Dynasty of Vijayanagara*, New Delhi, 1986, p.359.
2. Edgar Thurston & Rangachari, K., *Castes and Tribes of Southern India*, Vol. I, Madras, 1909, p.92.
3. *Ibid.*, p.93.
4. Vijaya Ramaswami, *Textiles and Weavers in Medieval South India*, Delhi, 1985, p.134.
5. M.V. Nanjundayya, *The Mysore Tribes and Castes,* Vol. II, Mysore, 1930, pp.104-105.
6. Saroj Cherian, *Seaports in Andhra with Reference to Later Medieval Period (17th & 18th Century),* Ph.D. thesis (unpublished), Osmania University, Hyderabad, 1993, p.184.
7. Edgar Thurston & Rangachari, K., *Op.Cit.*, Vol. VI, pp.191-192.
8. *Ibid.*, Vol. VII, p.15.

9. A.M. Siddiqui, *History of Golconda,* Hyderabad, 1956, pp.335 & 343.
10. *K.A. Letters*, LXXXVII, 22nd October, 1615.
11. C.S. Srinivasachari, *History of Madras,* Madras, 1939, pp.106-107 & 142-143.
12. H.K. Sherwani & P.M. Joshi (Eds.), *History of Medieval Deccan, (1294-1724),* Hyderabad, 1974, p.463.
13. *G.G. & Co to Directors,* 26th November, K.A. 1737, f, 244.
14. C.S. Srinivasachari, *Op.Cit.,* pp.1-2.
15. *Ibid.,* pp.4-5.
16. *RFSG,* Diary, 1711, 66.
17. Francois Martin, *Memories de Francois Martin,* Fondateur de Pondicherry, 1665-94, Paris, 1931-34, 11, 526, 528, 533, 546, 551, 556 & 574.
18. Paul Kaeppelin, *La Compagine des Indes Orientales et Francois Martin,* Paris, 1908, p.459.
19. *Ibid.,* pp.517-518.
20. Saroj Cherian, *Op.Cit.*, p.233.
21. Tapan Ray Chaudhuri and Irfan Habib, *The Cambridge Economic History of India,* Vol. I, Delhi, 1984, p.346.
22. *Ibid.*
23. Saroj Cherian, *Op.Cit.,* pp.236-237.
24. Court Minutes, Vol. 42, f, 14.

19

THE DYNAMICS OF URBANISATION: AN ECONOMIC ORIENTED PERSPECTIVE

Urbanisation is as old as human civilization itself. According to F. Braudel towns are "the turning points, water-sheds of human history" and "all major bursts of growth are expressed by an urban explosion".[1] Cities emerged as focal points in the socio-economic development of a people, who had achieved a certain degree of growth in a period of time. Interestingly, the towns had their roots in the surplus of agrarian economy. Advancement in agriculture supported by technology led to the growth of rural settlements both in spatial and demographic aspects. Further, this shift was supported by structural change in the settlements, mobility in occupational pattern and emergence of socio-economic, political and religious institutions. This gave settlements capable of integrating and organizing diverse social groups. So, urbanisation can be defined as the process by which rural economy expanded to evolve into urban economy. It is said that the primary characteristics of the town in Indian history are a high density of population concentrated in a limited space and predominantly non-agricultural nature of its population. This men-space ratio and occupational heterogeneity, with their consequential relationships, formed the main basis for the difference between the city and the village.[2]

Any approach to the subject of urbanisation differs depending upon the ideology concern on. V. Gordon Childe's concept of 'urban Revolution' that was developed in 1936[3] and in 1950[4] has stated that technology acts as the prime force in urban revolution. The other scholars like Park emphasized the law of ecological succession in urban frame work. Louis Wirth described urbanism as a way of life. Lewis Mumford examined the city from cultural and historical perspective.[5] Gideon Sjoberg in his study of the 'pre-industrial city' stressed on social and especially political authority as variables on which the city was dependent.[6] Both Lewis Mumford and Sjoberg placed undue emphasis on the role of political power in the rise of urban centres. After the Industrial Revolution, the focus shifted from physical structure to industrial factors. The Marxist scholars emphasised economic criteria rather than sociological factors. Karl Marx adopted an economic approach in his urban analysis. Later, Henry Pirenne laid emphasis on the development of trade and commerce for urbanisation.[7]

Though cities existed from the dawn of civilization, urban studies have been only of a recent origin and it is gaining popularity among the Social Scientists. Most of the scholars are influenced by western concepts and theories of process of urbanisation. B.B. Dutta, B.N. Puri, Stuart Piggot, A. Ghosh, R.S. Sharma and V.K. Thakur are some of the scholars worked on several aspects of urban history in ancient India. V.K. Thakur's work on *Urbanisation in Ancient India* is a comprehensive work, in which he assigns importance to the role of iron technology in the production of surplus. W.H. Moreland in his works observed that the urban centres in Mughal Empire in 16th century were based on craft production. H.K. Naqvi wrote works which dealt with the crucial role of industry and trade in the rise and decline of towns. The role of industries in urban growth process is being discussed by K.M. Ashraf in his works. J.S. Grewal and Indu Banga made notable contribution to urban history of North India.

In South India several historical studies are available in respect of political, social, economic and religious history, but not much research has been carried out on urbanisation. Talboys Wheeler, Henry Davison Love, Srinivasa Chary, S.K. Aiyangar, T.K.T. Viraraghavacharya worked on individual towns. R. Champakalakshmi made remarkable contribution to urbanisation in South India. In her work entitled *Trade, Ideology and Urbanisation – South India 300 B.C. to A.D. 1300*, she observes the importance of trade and ideology for the genesis and evolution of urbanisation mainly in Tamilnadu region of South India. In their works Burton Stein and Noboru Karashima discussed about urbanisation in Vijayanagara reign covering South India. The reputed scholars like Narayani Gupta, S. Arasaratnam, Aniruddha Ray, Manzoor Alam worked on Merchants and Sea-port, Masulipatam. Several scholars have published articles on various aspects of urbanisation in Andhra but no definite works on urban history in Andhra are available.

The urban history of India is marked with Harappan Civilization. In the medieval period, towns generally had a temple, market and a combination of people following different occupations. In the absence of demographic figures, the medieval Indian town can be defined as "a compact conglomeration of inhabitants within a delimited area, a centralized governing organism and industries as the materially productive unit, exist".[8] In medieval Andhra, Patnam with its variants Pattana and Pattinam enjoyed commercial importance. The famous dynasties like the Kakatiya (900-1323 A.D.), the Reddi (1324-1448 A.D.), the Velama (1361-1464 A.D.), the Vijayanagara (1336-1565 A.D.) and the Qutb Shahi (1518-1687 A.D.) mainly ruled medieval Telangana and Andhra. In the 17th century, the three European Companies namely the Dutch, the English and the French founded and consolidated their factories along the North Coromandel Coast of medieval Andhra.

Political Factor

Urban growth is an interplay of several forces/factors such as political, economic, social and religious. These factors contribute to the process of urbanisation. The policies of the rulers of the dynasties of medieval Telangana and Andhra regions contributed immensely for urban growth. If the creation of surplus is an economic necessity, its efficient handling is a political responsibility. During this period the rulers evinced keen interest in fostering agriculture, industry and trade. The Kakatiya ruler Ganapatideva, the Reddi ruler Anavota Reddi and the Vijayanagara king Devaraya-I issued a trade charter at Motupalli and promoted sea-borne commerce. Kings and ministers founded towns. In medieval times, cities, towns and administrative centres were strategically planned from the point of view of defence. Because of their geographical strategic position a number of forts emerged at several places. The rulers defended their kingdoms by means of well organised forts. The forts accommodated military barracks and this resulted in an increase in the size of the settlement. In medieval Telangana and Andhra, the towns with political and administrative importance were *Orugallu, Addanki, Kondavidu, Kondapalli, Rajamahendravaram, Vizayanagaram, Rachakonda, Devarakonda, Gandikota, Gutti, Udayagiri, Chandragiri, Golconda, Hyderabad, Medak, Panugallu and Elgandal.*

Social Factor

Social factor gave fillip to the urban growth. It relates to the size and density of population. Increase in urban population indicates the urban growth. This increase might be due to the process of migration from rural to urban. In medieval Andhra, migrations took place from Andhra to neighbouring countries like Karnataka, Tamilnadu, Kerala, Orissa and vice-versa. People enter the towns seeking livelihood and better employment opportunities. Trade in diamonds seems to have invited the Gujarati merchants to settle in Munimadugu in Kurnool district, where diamond mines situated. Further, traders from Orissa and Tamilnadu came to Andhra. A Telugu contemporary work, *Kridabhiramam*[9] refers to a Karnataka Vesya, who had come from Karnataka to Orugallu city.

In this period some Dravida Brahmins known as Puduru Dravidas[10] migrated to Andhra, perhaps after the establishment of Vijayanagara kingdom in 14th century. They migrated from a village called Kandra Manikya near Kumbha konam (Tanjore district) to Pudur, a village in Nellore. They were proficient in Vedas, Sastras and Puranas. So, the rulers of the Reddis of Kondavidu and Vijayanagara respected and patronized them. Later on the Agrahara, Pudur, which was donated to these Dravida Brahmins, developed into a full-fledged town by them. Among 44 families of Pudur Dravidians, the more famous are Mamidipudi, Nelaturu, Alladi etc. During the Qutb Shahi period, the Persians like Ulemas, poets, architects, scholars and others migrated to Golconda. In the beginning of the 17th century the Europeans established their settlements on the East Coast of Andhra. Due to the internal and external migrations many Persians, Mughals, the English, the Dutch, the French and the Portuguese were found in Hyderabad and contributed for its growth.

Religious Factor

In medieval period, religion played a distinct role in the process of urbanisation. The religious institutions like temples, Mathas and pontifical seats contributed for urban growth. The temple in medieval times dominated mainly the economic life of the people along with socio-cultural aspects. K.A. Nilakanta Sastri observes that the temple was a citadel of economic power enjoying a *status quo* equal to that of the state.[11] Temples received enormous gifts in cash and kind from the rulers and the people. The epigraphs available in the temples at Tirupati, Simhachalam and Rayachoti reveal us that the temple continued to grow with the patronage of individuals despite the political instabilities. K. Sarojini Devi in her work, *The Religion in Vijayanagara Empire*[12] states that the temples promoted agriculture in their owned lands, took up large scale irrigation works which contributed to agricultural settlements near temple centres. Temples also employed more skilled artisans, musicians, dancers, other artists and administrative staff. All of them lived in temple centres and so these centres developed into towns. In medieval Andhra the towns developed with religio-cultural importance were *Alampur, Bejawada, Bhadrachalam, Draksharamam, Srikurmam,*

Simhachalam, Lepakshi, Tirupati, Vemulawada, Srikalahasti, Manthani, etc. In the Qutb Shahi times the Muslim religious institutions like mosques, Khanqahs, Dargahs and Ashurkhanas contributed to the process of urbanisation.

Economic Factor

Economic forces tremendously contributed for the urban growth in medieval Telangana and Andhra. Surplus being a prime factor, it should be given paramount importance. According to R. Champakalakshmi "Agricultural expansion and intensification is necessary for the creation of surplus....".[13] Surplus is a necessary condition as it sustains the basically non-productive urban residents. Urbanites buy their food from peasants in turn for their manufactured products and professional services they provide. The surplus in agrarian commodities enters the towns and it brings towns in relation to the hinterland.

Medieval Andhra yielded a remarkable agricultural produce. The production of surplus depends on the technological advancement of the people. Extension of the cultivable land leads to the increase in production. In Telangana the Kakatiya rulers and their sub-ordinate chiefs took up the task of clearing the forests for cultivation with the cooperation of the people. They founded new villages at suitable places with water resources. The villages like *Ganapavaram, Mahadevapura, Bayyaram, Muppavaram, Kundavaram*, etc., came into being after the reclamation of forest lands by the kings and queens of the Kakatiya dynasty.[14] The Vijayanagara kings also formed new villages by clearing forests and brought fresh lands under cultivation that increased the gross yield from land.

Tanks excavation was taken up by both the government and public. Construction of a tank is included as one of the *Sapta-Samtanas* or seven acts of righteousness. There are several instances which refer to founding of new villages and excavating tanks by the Kakatiya royal family members. Some new townships developed around the irrigational tanks like *Ganapavaram, Kesarisamudram (Kesamudram), Bayyaram, Rudravaram, Mahadevapuram, Muppavaram, Kundavaram and Dharmasagaram*. The Qutb Shahi rulers constructed many tanks in and around Hyderabad.[15] A French traveller, Thevenot says that the land of Tilang-Andhra yielded "all things in abundance, especially fruits".[16] Another French traveller, Tavernier, who visited the kingdom of Golconda says that "even in the smallest villages rice, flour, butter, milk, beans and other vegetables, sugar and other sweetmeats dry and liquid can be produced in abundance".[17] Along with paddy, all kinds of millets, wheat, pulses, oil seeds and the commercial crops such as areca-nut, coconut, betel leaves, sugarcane and indigo were cultivated.

The rulers of medieval Andhra Desa appropriated the surplus in the form of various kinds of taxes, tributes and gifts. In all most all big villages the kings possessed *Rachagadelu*, i.e., royal granaries to store the king's share of grain.[18] This shows us the fact of agricultural surplus. Further, the irrigation was correlated with rapid population growth, nucleus of settlement and monumental construction. Infact, the economic life in cities centred round industry, trade and guild activities. The vigorous economic activity in the towns of medieval Telangana and Andhra is reflected in the enormous growth of numerous industries and brisk trade and commerce. The economy of medieval Telangana and Andhra was primarily of an agrarian base. But from 11th century onwards we find a progressive increase in the growth of industrial arts both quantitatively and qualitatively and this in turn, gave impetus to the process of urbanisation.

Metal industry is non-agricultural one. Metals like gold, silver, iron, copper, brass etc. were used for manufacturing different kinds of articles. The ornaments of gold and silver bear eloquent testimony to the excellent workmanship and creativity of the goldsmiths of those times. It is interesting to note that many temples permanently engaged goldsmiths and silversmiths.[19] The bright colours of enamel jewellery to the set precious stones came from Persia and was introduced in India in 14th century. The black enamel work is the speciality of Hyderabad. *Nirmal, Indur* and *Indalwai* possessed *iron mines* and developed into manufacturing centres. A town named *Indalwai* near modern Nizamabad was the centre of manufacture of swords, daggers and lances.[20] *Konasamudram* near Nirmal produced the best steel. *Dingurthi* mines in the Godavari areas were source of Damascus steel. Hyderabad supplied steel for making the Damascus blades. Many varieties of weapons were manufactured. Thevenot, who on his way to Golkonda visited Indur and Indalvai, wrote that the town Indalvai, of which nothing was to be said in particular but that great many swords, daggers and lances were made there, which were vended all over the India and that the iron was taken out of a mine near the town in the mountain of Calagatch.

In this period the manufacturing institutions were known as 'Kharkhanas' run by the State and private individuals. The Dutch East India Company began nail making centres at *Nagalwancha*, *Narsapur* and *Ramayapatnam* and employed a number of native artisans and labourers.[21] About 1600 A.D., the Dutch East India Company was active in developing the Iron industry in the Godavari Delta. A number of native artisans were employed. They produced fine quality nails and cannon-balls. Tavernier appreciates that the barrels of the muskets of Golkonda soldiers were stronger than those of any European muskets.

Diamond Industry was the most prominent one in medieval times. Perhaps the highly profitable industry during Qutb Shahi times was the mining, refining and cutting of diamonds, a process which made Golconda famous all over the world. Tavernier calls the kingdom of Golconda as 'a country of diamonds'. *Kolluru, Ramallakota, Vajrakarur, Gollapalli, Rajipenta* and *Gandikota* were the diamond mine centres which enjoyed international reputation. Koh-e-Noor, the world famous diamond is said to have come from the above mines. *Kolluru* grew into a town as the largest diamond mines located here. When Tavernier visited the place "there were nearly 60,000 persons working there, including men, women and children, who are employed in diverse ways, the men in digging, the women and children in carrying earth".[22] It shows the high level of concentration of population at Kolluru during this period. *Gollapalli* town rose to prominence on account of diamond mines and Streynsham master writes that it is situated with a mile and half of the mines. *Mellville* (Mallavilli) and *Rajipenta* mines were large and populous and 30,000 or 40,000 labourers working in those mines.[23] Gollapalli, Mallavilli and Rajipenta were forming parts of Kolluru or Paritala belt.

Wood carving and Ivory work industry flourished during this period. The carpenter was an important servant of both the society and temple. Different kinds of wooden furniture and palanquins were made by carpenters. They manufactured wooden temple cars for annual Kalyanotsavas and Vasantotsavas exhibiting excellent skill in art work. The contemporary Telugu works refer to various cots, couches and boxes used in those days. They were aware of the ivory work. Boxes and other articles were made of ivory.

Textiles Industry was the most prominent industry in medieval India. In the world of commerce, cotton was king and the best cotton, especially muslins and Bettilles (veiling) were produced in *Golconda* region exported mainly from the port of Masulipatnam. Dyeing and printing were the industries allied to weaving. *Masulipatnam* developed as a great centre for textile manufacture. The town was surrounded by a number of weaving villages. *Tuni*, which lies about 50 miles south of Vishakapatnam was the nucleus of weavers settlement on the coastal road from Masulipatnam to Vishakapatnam.

Warangal and 12 villages near by produced Bettilles, common Sarangs and fine cloth. At *Ellur* and 8 villages, nice Salempores and carpets were woven. The Chintz, a painted cloth in bright colours, was produced in *Palakollu* and *Masulipatnam*. The other centres of textiles manufacture with their clusters of weaving villages were *Mangalagiri* and *Ventapallem* (Vetapallem). Muslin which was as fine as that of Dacca was produced in north part of *Srikakulam*. In *Rajamundry* region Bettilles and Salempores were produced. Masulipatnam was also famous centre for Kalamkari industry. There was great demand that the production was not sufficient to meet the demand. It is because of the usage of the Kalam (or pen) in painting the designs that the name Kalamkari was given to this industry. But the Portuguese referred to it as 'Pintado', the Dutch called it 'Sitz' and for the English it was 'Chintz'. These Kalamkari clothes were in great demand in South-eastern Asia and even in far off Mozambique and Abyssinia.

Kalamkaris were also manufactured in Gujrat, Rajasthan and Madras areas, but none could match the brilliance of the colour of the Masulipatnam Kalamkaris due to the cultivation of the best quality of the Chay. (Telugu tsheri-vello known to the Botanists as Oldenlandia umbellata Linn). There is ample cotemporary evidence to confirm this fact. Tavernier said that the chites or painted cloths which were called calmendar, that was to say, painted with a brush were made in the kingdom of Golkonda, and particularly in the neighbourhood of Masulipatnam, but the quantity turned out was so small that when one made requisition on all the workers, who manufactured these cotton cloths, it was with difficulty that he could obtain as much as three bales. Thevenot tells us that the 'Schites' of Ahmadabad which were also painted cloths, were "nothing near so fine as those of Masulipatnam and St. Thomas". He further said that the painted cloths of St. Thomas were much finer and of better colours than those of the other parts of the Indies.

The actual centres of production of Kalamkari were *Petaboli* about 40 miles south of *Masulipatnam* and *Palakollu* about 80 miles to the north. *Kalahasti* and *Tadipatri* produced different varieties of this cloth. At Kalahasti, the painters specialised in producing religious Kalamkaris and the themes pertained to episodes of the *Ramayana* and the *Mahabharata.* The practice of Tirth Yatra and offering Kalamkaris to the main deity of the temple was the reason for the survival of Kalamkari craftsman at Kalahasti till recent times. A strenuous operational process was involved in the preparation of a large cloth with elaborate design in five or six colours in Kalamkari reveal the employment of several specialized skilled labour in the process of its manufacture.

Woollen and silk stuffs were produced in *Warangal. Mathwada, Urus, Rangasaipet* and *Karimabad* developed as centres of woollen carpets. These are popularly known as Warangal carpets. In addition to these places Hanamkonda, Parkal and Hasanparthi became famous for their silk manufacture. Cotton and silk weaving was done as a cottage industry at Wadepally and Kazipet near Warangal. Bernier observes that carpet making was one of the major industries of India, and in the Qutb Shahi dominions the centre of this industry was Warangal.

Building industry flourished in medieval Telangana and Andhra. Temple and building construction may be regarded as an industry of excellence during this period. Most of the temples built during this period are still in existence today. All the towns of medieval Telangana and Andhra had big temples and the capital cities had several temples. The rulers of the medieval dynasties followed a state policy of building new temples and maintaining the old ones. This created employment for a great number of masons, sculptors, architects and carpenters. The Uppalamulu (salt-pans) of *Peda Ganjam* and *Pina Ganjam* were producing centres of salt. Ship Building was an ancient industry in Andhra Desa. Ship-building naturally took place in Andhra, for it had a long coast line and the availability of the raw materials for the manufacture. Palakollu in Godavari region produced the ship building material like nails, ropes and coir. These were transported to Narasapore and Madapollam, the prominent ship-building centres in medieval Andhra.

Iron procured from mines near Nagulawancha was useful for ship building. Narsapur, at the mouth of the river Godavari, was a centre of the manufacture of many Indian and Portugues ships during 17th and 18th centuries.

The ship by name 'Globe' that was returned to Masulipatnam was taken for repairs at Narsapur. Masulipatnam was another important ship building centre. French travellers like Thevenot and Tavernier, who visited Andhra region in the 17th century, described Masulipatnam as a great shipping and trading centre, that had the best anchorage in the Bay of Bengal. Bangle and Glass industries also developed during the period under review. Making glass bangles was the secondary occupation of the Hakims in Hyderabad, who came from Persia to cure the Qutb Shahis carbuncles, in the 16th century. This flourishing industry consists of two stages as follows: (i) Making a surface of lac on glass bangles, (ii) Fixing stones to the lac surface. This was done by holding a wooden post of varying thickness with a cylindrical shape on the left hand with glass bangles of differing diameters on it. Lac melted and liquid was poured slowly on the rotating post. Then stones of different colours and sizes were affixed to the soft lac. Literary works and inscriptions refer to articles made of glass like winged-glass door (Gajurekkalatalupu) and mirrors.

Oil-crushing Industry is another flouring industry of the period. Oil is used by the people of all classes for cooking, for hair and for keeping perpetual lamps. An oil-mill was called Ganugu in Telugu and Tailayantra in Sanskrit. The oil-pressing industry was run mainly by the Teliki-Vevuru (the guild of one thousand oil-mongers). This industry in some areas was situated near the temple. An inscription from Srikurmam dated, 1394 A.D., states that the later Eastern Ganga king, Narasimha-IV donated to Kurmanatha a Tailakara (oil-miller) by name Talla. It means that this oil miller had to render his services to the temple by paying the tax in oil due to the government. Oil-mills generally drawn by bullock existed in towns and villages. There were women selling 'Sampangi oil' in the city of Orugallu.

Sugar-Cane Industry made considerable progress in this period. In fact many sweets and savouries were prepared by women folk with sugar and jaggery. For Naivedya or Prasadam i.e., for offering in the temples these articles were used extensively and so the temple encouraged this industry either by owning it or by taking contract in order to ensure a regular supply. The contemporary sources reveal the fact that sugar-cane was grown in West Godavari, East Godavari, Krishna and Guntur districts. There was a sugar-cane mill in Kopparam (Guntur district). Perfume, Minting, Leather, Bamboo-making industries developed in the period under consideration.

Trade formed as a potential force of urbanisation. More specialized production increases the need for mechanism to distribute it and it leads to the development of trade. Andhra had busy trade relations with far and near countries and continents since ancient times. The products of Andhra were in great demand in foreign markets. Favourable factors like the surplus, lofty development of money economy, growth of cash crops, a standard system of weights and measures, an efficient guild organization, banking system, better means of transport and communication, encouragement from the rulers and the rich, security provided to merchants and merchandise promoted the brisk internal and transcontinental trade. It has to be admitted that the advent of the Europeans served as a great impetus to the expansion of trade in medieval Andhra.

The market played a crucial role in the growth of towns. It has been considered as a prime ingredient of the town. Max Weber states that a city is a market place or a market settlement.[24] A market naturally requires a mechanism of distribution and thus trade becomes a primary motivating force in the evolution of urban forms. As a link between different systems of production and between rural agriculturists and urban producers, trade performed a supreme urban function. The market centres of medieval times may be classified into local, regional and inter-regional. A distinction was made between the *bazaars*, which were mainly retail markets and the *mandis*, or wholesale markets.

Trade either wholesale or retail was generally conducted at the select places usually called *Pemta, Adda, Santa, Qasba* and *Gunj*. Most of the village or town names ending with Peta or Pemta in Telugu and Karnataka regions were formerly the centres of fairs. The Pemta was provided with thatched sheds (Pakas) and there must have been market officers to collect Sunka (tax) in Pemtas. Sometimes, charters for markets (*Santa-sasana*) were issued and they helped in the efficient running of markets.

In the city of Orugallu a *Maila Santa*[25] (a fair for lower class people) was organized outside the city, where meat, fishes, etc., were sold and in *Madi Santa* (clean fair) within the city, vegetables, flowers and fruits were sold. The other marketing agency was the *Angadi*, (shop), through which the Vaisyas sold various articles. These shops, temporary or permanent, were established in villages, towns, temple towns and capital cities and gave fillip to trade. Narayanamatya in his work *Hamsavimsati* gives an elaborate list of market centres such as, *Gutti, Golconda, Bellamkonda, Devarakonda, Penugonda, Kadapa, Nellore, Vinukonda, Kondavidu, Nelakondapalli, Udayagiri, Mangalagiri, Bhadrachalam, Kalluru, Rachakonda, Tadipatri, Ramayapatanam, Palvancha, Gandikota, Chennapatnam, Kadiri, Kalahasti, Bhuvanagiri,*

Ramachandrapuram, Dharmavaram, Bejawada, Pakala, Macherla, Gadwal, etc.[26] These market centres were linked with agrarian villages.

In medieval Telangana and Andhra agricultural surplus had to be transported from one place to another place, commonly consumed commodities like salt and minerals had to be carried to all villages and also spices had to be imported from other parts. So the internal trade developed on large scale. The articles of inland trade were food stuffs, fruits, dyes, spices, metals, raw materials, manufactured goods, animals etc. During Qutb Shahi period the inter-regional trade was brisk. As there was a good network of roads connecting various capitals, industrial centres, markets and ports, the trade developed in medieval Andhra. The Vijayanagara city was connected with Udayagiri, Kondavidu, Kodapalli and along the coast to Simhachalam and Srikurmam. Another road led from Vijayanagaram to Dhanuskodi passed through Kalahasti, Tirupati, Kanchi, Tiruvannamalai, Cidambaram, Madhurai and Rameshwaram.[27] Hyderabad under the Qutb Shahis was connected by good network of roads with Surat, Goa, Madras via Gandikota, Ramallakota diamond mines and Masulipatnam port.

A brisk foreign trade flourished during this period. The goods manufactured in Andhra were in great demand in the markets of Asia and Europe. At this juncture Thomas Bowrey's words attract ones attention. To him "the great mass of riches these lands enjoyed, which caused the Christian Nations to settle and trade here, it is become a very glorious and potent kingdom, or rather Empire, of above two thousand English miles in circuit, very well populated and replenished with all things...".[28] The largest commodity for export trade was textiles. The woven goods were brought from the hinterland and through the ports of East coast were exported to other countries. A specialty of the Coromandal textiles was dyeing, painting and printing of textiles in beautiful colours and designs. Bettilles, Romals, Chintz, Kalamkari, diamonds, iron and steel, tobacco etc. were the items of export, whereas the imports were spices, precious metals, pearls, tin, porcelain, perfumes, lac, copper, arecanuts, dried fruits, elephants and horses. Andhra in medieval times maintained trade relations with South-East Asian countries, Ceylon, Burma, Manila, Arakhan, Maldives, West Asia and Europe. Because of vigorous trade activity, small and big port towns developed along the East Coast like *Motupalli, Nizampatnam, Masulipatnam, Karedu, Visakhapatnam, Bhimilipatnam, Coringa Bay, Krishnapatnam, Pulicat, Kumaragiripatnam* and *Madras*.

The Commercial communities gave enormous encouragement to trade. The trade of medieval Andhra was dominated by the Vaisya community and they were called in Andhra as Komatis. They were also known as Settis or Chetties. The Balijas or Banajigas, the Perikas, the Telikis, and the Golconda Muslim merchants of Andhra were the indigenous commercial communities. The Persian merchants, the Armenians, the European traders like, the Dutch, the English and the French were the foreign commercial communities. The trading methods that were followed by these communities like *wholesale* and *retail business, muster system, advance contract system, bills of exchange* and *freight business* helped the smooth and speed movement of business. These communities promoted the trade by undergoing perils and dangers.

Guilds played a key role in the economic life of the people. Guilds may be broadly classified into two kinds, viz., Craft or Professional guilds and Trade or Merchant guilds. The Craft guild *Teliki Vevuru* was the guild of oil-mongers. It is said that this corporate body consisted of one thousand families. From Teliki inscriptions it may be inferred that *Bezawada* must have been their centre of activities. Telikis organized units of their guild at *Bapatla, Kondapalli, Kondavidu* and *Rajahmundry*, etc. *Panchanamvaru* was a guild of artisan community. *Pemdota* in Palanadu appears their birth place and they worshipped Lord Kamatesvara of Dharanikota. They were known as Panchala in Karnataka. Usually they attached to the temples of their localities. *Salevaru* was a guild of weavers, who supplied clothes to temples and kings. The areas like *Mattewada, Bhimavaram, Nalgonda, Krishna, Guntur, Nellore, Cuddapah* and *Anantapur* were the centres of weaving community. *Kammatas* was a guild of coin minting workers. Thus, the rigorous industrial activity with social division of labour and the immense corporate activities of guilds contributed for the growth of urban centres in medieval Andhra.

The traders formed into guilds known as Trade or Merchant guilds. The guilds were powerful, possessed judicial and military powers and also acted as banks and thereby gave an impetus to the emerging urban economy. A trade guild, the *Vira Balanjya Samaya's* activities spread from Nepal to Kerala. The commercial bodies that constituted it were *Ainnuruvar, Nanadesi, Ubhaya Nanadesi Pekkandru, Ayyavole Swamins* (five hundred) and *Mummaridandas*. *Nakaramu* or *Nagara* was a significant guild of medieval times. It was a guild of Vaisyas and they styled themselves as lord-chiefs of Penugonda (West Godavari district). There were State guilds like that *Gangeyarajya Samaya* and *Rajaraja Samaya*. The chief of the Nagara was known as Nagaramukhya and Pattanaswami. His main duty was to conduct fairs and supervise markets. He collected tolls from merchants and made gifts to temples. The merchant guilds carried trade in commodities like cloth, indigo, areca-nuts, tin, copper, lead and other metals, oils, paddy, jowar, wheat, cotton, wool, pearls, camphor, etc. All these communities clamoured for some special privileges and honours which were to mark it off from others in the society.[29] Guilds made lofty contributions in kind and cash to temples, built temples and dug tanks. The commercial activities of these guilds promoted the growth of several towns.

Thus, it is obvious that the development of towns was primarily due to the growth of economic activities and manufacturing. The commercial centres emerged serving as collecting and distributing centres of raw and finished goods for local, regional, national and inter-national markets. The political and religious towns also became prominent centres of trade testifying the fact that it was the economic activity that dominated the most. Urban growth is a complex amalgam of several factors in which no individual factor can be singled out. However, the potential economic forces like the surplus, industries, markets, trade and guilds played a vital role in the escalation of the process of urbanisation in medieval Telangana and Andhra regions.

Notes & References

1. F. Braudel, *Civilization and Capitalism 15th – 18th Centuries*, Eng. tr. William Collins & Sons, London, 1985, I, p.479.
2. S.C. Misra, "Urban History in India: Possibilities and Perspectives", Indu Banga (ed.), *The City in Indian History*, New Delhi, 1991, pp.1-2.

3. V. Gordon Childe, *Man Makes Himself*, London, 1936.
4. V. Gordon Childe, "The Urban Revolution", *Town Planning Review*, Vol.21, 1950, pp.3-17.
5. Lewis Mumford, *The Culture of Cities*.
6. Aloka Parasher, "Social Structure and Economy of Settlements in Central Deccan (200 B.C. – A.D. 200)", Indu Banga (ed.), *Op.Cit.*, p.20.
7. Henry Pirenne, *Economic and Social History of Medieval Europe*, London, 1956.
8. H.K. Naqvi, *Urbanisation and Urban Centres under the Great Mughals*, Simla, 1972, p.3.
9. Vinukonda Vallabharaya, *Kridabhiramam*, published by V. Prabhakara Sastry, Hyderabad, 1960, vv.86 and 87.
10. Vedamu Venkataraya Sastri, *Puduru Dravidulevaru*, Madras, 1978, pp.3, 4, 11, 14 & 15.
11. K.A. Nilakanta Sastri, *The Cholas*, part-II, Madras, 1937, p.504.
12. K. Sarojini Devi, *The Religion in Vijayanagara Empire*, New Delhi, 1990.
13. R. Champakalakshmi, *Trade, Ideology and Urbanisation South India 300 BC to AD 1300*, Delhi, 1996, p.3.
14. P.V. Parabrahma Sastry, *The Kakatiyas*, Hyderabad, 1978, p.199.
15. R. Varalakshmi, "Tanks in Golconda and Hyderabad Areas 17th & 18th Centuries A.D.", *Proceedings of the DRS Seminar*, Department of History, Osmania University, Hyderabad, 1997, pp.176-185.
16. Thevenot Jean de, *Indian Travels of Thevenot and Careri*, (ed.), Surendranath Sen, New Delhi, 1949, p.145.
17. Jean Baptiste Tavernier, *Tavernier Travels in India*, Vol. I, London, 1925, p.238.
18. H.K. Sherwani and P.M. Joshi (eds.), *History of Medieval Deccan (1295-1724)*, Vol. I, Hyderabad, 1973, p.542.

19. K. Sundaram, *Studies in Economic and Social Conditions of Medieval Andhra (A.D.1000-1600)*, 1968, p.19.
20. Tapan Raychaudhuri and Irfan Habib (eds.), *The Cambridge Economic History of India,* Vol. I, Delhi, 1982, p.310.
21. S. Jaikishan, "Metallurgy and Industry of Arms in Andhra Desa in 17th & 18th Centuries", *Proceedings of DRS*, Department of History, Osmania University, Hyderabad, 1995, p.93.
22. Jean Baptiste Tavernier, *Op.Cit.*, Vol. II, p.58.
23. R.C. Temple (ed.), *Diaries of Streynsham Master*, Vol. I, London, 1911, pp.174-175.
24. Max Weber, *The City*, London, 1960, pp.65-66.
25. Vinukonda Vallabharaya, *Op.Cit.*, vv.76-77.
26. N. Venkataramanaiah, *Studies in the History of the Third Dynasty of Vijayanagara*, Delhi, 1986, p.301.
27. T.V. Mahalingam, *Administration and Social Life under Vijayanagara*, Part-II, Madras, 1975, p.161.
28. Thomas Bowrey, *A Geographical Account of Countries round the Bay of Bengal*, Cambridge, 1995, pp.109-110.
29. P. Sree Rama Sarma, *Saluva Dynasty of Vijayanagar*, Hyderabad, 1979, p.277.

20

INLAND AND OVERSEAS TRADE

Linked up with the growth of specialization of crafts is the development of trade. More specialized production increases the need for mechanisms to distribute what is produced. The medieval Telangana and Andhra regions had continued busy trade with far and near countries and continents since ancient times. The products of medieval Andhra Desa were in great demand in foreign markets. Andhra yielded good harvest in almost all cereals and pulses, cotton, tobacco, mangoes and grapes and supplied articles to the local as well as to the foreign markets. Consequently, there was a tremendous progress of trade on the East Coast.

Coinage and Banking

The sources of the period under study refer to various coins that were in circulation. The reign of Abdullah Qutb Shah witnessed a veritable plethora of coins current in the kingdom. They testify to the spread of an extensive monetary system, especially in the urban areas. Yet, the Barter system continued in the countryside. Gold, silver and copper coins of several varieties were in vogue. The coins of those days were as follows:

Gold Coins	:	Mada and Dinar, Gadyana, Varaha, Pon or Honnu, Nishka.
Niskha	:	Kalanju, Dala and Panam.
Silver Coins	:	Ruka, Tanka, Tara and Rupee.
Copper Coins	:	Chinnamu, Dramma, Kasu, Paraka, Visamu, Panam, Bags, Keni, Adduvu, Duggani, Drona, Paisa, Gazers, Obv., Sultan Abdullah Qutb Shah Rev., Zuriba Haidarabad, and Obv., Sultan Abdullah Padshah Rev., Zuriba Muhammadnagar.

Among the silver coins Ruka was in common use. *Kridabhiramam*[1] states that a good meal was provided in a Brahmin hotel in the city of Orugallu for only one Ruka. Allada-vendi Tankas and Vendi-Alavim-tankas,[2] minted in the name of Allada Reddi, were in use in Kalinga country, which he conquered during the time of Kumaragiri Reddi. Tara was a silver coin being 1/6 of gold Panam.[3] During the Qutb Shahi period the silver coin was the Mughal rupee. In medieval Andhra Desa, copper coins were in wider circulation. An inscription[4] from Bhimavaram gives the equation of 28 Chinnalu for one Mada. The other copper coin Kasu and its half division Ara-kasu were referred in *Kridabhiramam.*[5] Visamu was a copper coin of a small unit. Kesari Visamu and Kanari-visalu were varieties of it. There was Ara-visamu or half a Visamu coin also. Paisa was a copper coin, and 55 paisas made a rupee when Thevenot was at Golconda.[6] Thevenot says that Gazer was a small copper coin minted by the Dutch at Pulicat, and it was as big as a Fanam in size.[7] From the times of Ibrahim Qutb Shah, there were distinct varieties of the copper coins in the kingdom, such as:

1. Obv., Sultan Abdullah Qutb Shah Rev., Zuriba Haidarabad.
2. Obv., Sultan Abdullah Padshah Rev., Zuriba Muhammadnagar etc.

In addition to these metal coins, shells called 'cowries' were current as small money. Tavernier tells that these shells had 'edges inverted' and were in vogue in the kingdoms of Bijapur and Golconda.[8] In the coastal areas, one paisa fetched 80 cowries, but in the interior places like Agra it used to get only 50 to 55 cowries. These were imported from Maldive islands.[9] Thus, the extensive money economy gave a fillip to brisk trade and commerce.

Money-lending must have stood on a firm ground, though epigraphical evidence to this effect is meagre. The temples, the guilds and some rich individuals acted as banking agencies. From the inscriptions, it is known that the borrower executed a loan-deed (Patramu), which was deposited with the creditor. The principal amount (Modalidhanamu) and the interest rate (Vaddidhanamu) were clearly stated in them. Sometimes, a third person stood surety (Punta) for the borrower. The temple treasury acted as a bank. It used to lend money to the needy peasants, priests, artisans and merchants on the payment of normal rates of interest. The professional crafts and merchant guilds had some banking activities during the period under study. Banking was certainly in a progressive stage, when Tavernier visited India. One Shroff, professional money changer at Aurangabad, who had to receive payment of a letter of exchange on Golconda, assisted Tavernier in receiving some money in new silver coins at Golconda.[10] At the diamond mines in the kingdom of Golconda and Bijapur, bills of exchange on Agra, Golconda, Bijapur and mainly Surat were readily accepted in lieu of cash.[11]

Inland Trade

During the study period villages were self-sufficient in regard to food and clothing. But the agricultural products had to be carried from one place to other even in those days. Particularly, the surplus of produce had to be transported from one place to another place. Commonly consumed commodities like salt, minerals and forest products had to be carried to almost all villages. Further, spices like, pepper, ginger, and cloves were to be imported from other parts. Animals like horses, camels, cows, oxen, sheep and buffaloes are also commonly mentioned in the records of the period as items of trade. Special fairs or Pemtas were conducted for the trade of animals.[12] During the medieval Telangana and Andhra, various kinds of towns served as busy centres of trade. The following were the important trade centres of the period under review:[13]

1. Orugallu the capital town deserves to be mentioned first. There seems to have been the Samta or Pemta of the capital town and that particular place was called Mathiya. It was located between the old town Anumakonda and the fort town Orugallu and at present it is called Mattewada which forms the heart of the modern Warangal, where all business activities still take place.
2. Panugallu, near Nalgonda, which was the capital of a branch of the Choda chiefs of Kanduru, was a big trade centre.
3. Jadcherla in the Mahbubnagar district, was another centre of business and this town enjoys the same status even today.
4. Alampur on the bank of the Tungabhadra was another trading centre.

5. Manthena in Karimnagar district was a trade centre.
6. Perur in the Nalgonda district.
7. Tripurantakam in the present Prakasam district.
8. Penugonda in West Godavari district.
9. Pedaganjam salt Pans in Prakasam district.
10. Nellore.
11. Macherla.
12. Tangeda.
13. Kopparam.
14. Enamadala.
15. Upparapalle.

The Rajadhani and Rajadhani Pattanas, the religious centres and commercial towns all served as centres of trade. Generally, in these towns many kinds of articles such as sarees, clothes, jaggery, arecanut, salt rice, paddy, gingily, grains, pulses, vegetables, fruits and animals were sold. An inscription of Krishnadevaraya's time at Kondavidu and other lithic records furnish a list of articles of inland trade, as mentioned below.[14]

Articles of food	:	Paddy, rice, millets, jaggery, ragi, jowar, wheat, tamarind, pulses, mustard, gingily, coriander, cumin, royal cumin, salt, vegetables, ghee, sugar, onions, green and dried ginger.
Fruits	:	mangoes, lime, pomegranates, sweet berries, black berries etc.
Dyes	:	Dammer, gall-nuts, clearing-nuts, myrobalan and Sangadi-nuts.

Spices	: Cardamom, cloves, turmeric, saffron, musk, pepper, arecanut, perfumes, mace, nutmeg, coconut, sandal, betel-leaves and drugs.
Metal	: Iron, lead, tin and copper.
Raw Materials	: Cleaned and uncleaned cotton and yarn.
Manufactured	: Textiles, silk clothes, cotton thread, blanket (Gongadi), steel, chisels and gunny bags.
Animals	: Horses, cattle like sheep, goats, bullocks, cows and buffaloes.
Miscellaneous goods	: Pots, leather wares, garlands, curds, butter, milk, ghee, butter milk, meat and fishes.

During the Qutb Shahi period the inland trade or the inter-regional trade was brisk. Even in small villages also commodities were available in plenty. In urban bazaars a wide variety of domestic and foreign commodities were reported by all foreign travellers. For instance, in the capital city Golconda, oxen, fowls, spotted deer, butter and wheat of a fine quality were sold.[15] Rice, millets, pulses, butter, oil and potatoes were produced in Andhra region in such abundance that these articles were transported in Sampans to Pulicat and nearby Gugarazupatnam and other places in the South Coast.[16] From Masulipatnam, mangoes which were considered to be items of delicacy were sent as far as Delhi.[17] It is quoted that the best mangoes in the Delhi market came for Golconda.

Golconda was a renowned centre for iron and steel all over the world. From the celebrated port of Masulipatnam, Junks (large Chinese ships) carried iron to Bengal. Steel was exported to Punjab and the world famous Damascus swords were made out of Golconda steel.[18] Besides this, the diamonds of Golconda were exported to Surat and Gujarat and also to the imperial cities of Agra and Delhi. They also found market in the various parts of the Vijayanagara kingdom. Commercial crops like tobacco were also exported to other places from the port of Masulipatnam.[19] It is clear from the above discussion that the regional trade in medieval Andhra Desa was primarily an exchange of food stuffs, wide range of textiles but not highly valued luxury goods.

Trading Centres

Many towns and cities developed into trading centres in Medieval Telangana and Andhra. Palakol (Palakollu) is a trading centre of considerable significance. It is also famous for export of rice and coconut. Palakollu was noted for its long cloth, salempores and moris. Tuni, which lies about 50 miles south of Visakhapatnam was the nucleus of weavers settlements on the coastal road from Masulipatanam to Visakhapatnam. Udayagiri was a good internal trading centre. Various kinds of grain, Rasavargas (ghee, sugar, oil, etc.) and perfumes like sandal, camphor, musk and other articles were in transit at this town. Guntur is situated on the Vijayawada-Madras trunk road, 9 kilometres east of the picturesque Kondavidu hills. It has grown into an important commercial centre. It supplied to the markets allegias, rumals sellas and varieties of painted and dyed red goods. Tripurantakam is a trading centre in Kurnool district, located on the north-eastern side of the Nallamalai hills. It was a significant centre of the Ubhayananadesi trading corporation. It lies between the regions of Andhra and Karnataka, and controlled the trade routes to the south and to the Deccan. Yenamadala is an important centre of trade in Guntur district. A temple was constructed for the worship of God Gopalasvami. It was an important trading centre of the Ubhaya-nanadesi.

Another town Konidena in Guntur developed as a commercial centre on account of Santa-sasana (market charter) dated 1435 A.D. Tangeda was a business centre in Guntur district, located at the mouth of the river Krishna. Bapatla, a business centre, situated 5 kms., from the seashore on the East Coast, is said to have been named as Bhavapatla or Bhavapuri after Bhavanarayanaswami, the presiding deity. This trading centre was associated with the reign of the Kakatiyas, Reddi Kings, Gajapathis and Vijayanagara kings.

Alampur is a reputed religious centre and also large commercial centre. The town witnessed glorious days during the time of Badami Chalukyas with the temple building activity and acquired prominence under Kalyani Chalukyas by becoming a capital town under their administration. Later, the town grew commercially attracting people from various areas, far and near. In 1299 A.D. the heads of the Samasta-pekkamdru, who were called the protectors of the Vira-Balanjya-Samaya-Dharma namely, Alampur Mummedi Brammisetti, Prithvisetti Prithavaya Timdaka Vadi Brammisetti, Koduri Hegada Gessetti, Revaka Nagisetti etc., and others made a gift of land for the personal and public enjoyment of the God Gaureswara and the Jaina saints.

Perur is another commercial town of importance flourished during the period of the Kalyani Chalukyas and the Kakatiyas. In this town there were quarters of the Brahmans, Arava merchants, Telugu merchants, Telikis Lata (Gujarati), local officials and others. These merchant communities had their own guilds as well as the temples for the presiding deities of the guilds. Eighteen Nagarams or towns formed a federation with headquarters at Penugondanagara, presided over by Penugonda Nagarasvami. All the eighteen towns were situated between the rich region of the rivers Godavari and Krishna. The chief city Penugonda located on the river Gautami, consisted of twelve Suryavidhis, sixteen Somavidhis, lofty buildings, houses and gardens, (a Vidhi being a street).

The other towns of the Nagaram were Dharma, Dhanadapura (i.e., Tsandavole in Guntur district), Pancala, Niravadhya (i.e., Nidadavolu in West Godavari district), Jagannadha (Draksharamamu in East Godavari district), Kshirakasara (Palokol in West Godavari district), Dendulur (a place of the same name in West Godavari district), Ela (Eluru in West Godavari district), Ghantasala (Krishna district), Trigunita, Ghanabhima (Bhimavaram in West Godavari), Visala (present Visakhapatnam), Kalinga (present Kalingapatnam), Nrusimha, Viranarayana, Acanta (West Godavari district), and Nagaramu (East Godavari district). All these towns developed into medium sized towns. Anantapur was known as Hande Anantapuram after the Hande chiefs. This place and a few other places were gifted to Hanumappa Naidu of the Hande family by the Vijayanagara rulers. The town developed under the Vijayanagara kings.

Vajrakarur was a town of diamond mines. The very name indicates that it is associated with diamonds. It is located in the present Anantapur district of Andhra Pradesh. The other towns and cities like Anumakonda, Bhadrachalam, Devarakonda, Dharmapuri, Elgandal, Eluru, Golconda-Hyderabad, Koilkonda, Lepakshi, Medak, Nirmal, Rachakonda, Vemulavada, Srikakulam, Warangal etc., developed as trading centres in this period.

Overseas Trade

The oceanic trade forms a most fascinating aspect in the history of medieval Andhra Desa. The ocean with all its perils was a perpetual attraction with the lure of rich rewards to compensate for the enterprise involving insecurity. From the early centuries of the Christian era, the Andhra country including Kalinga, kept up its distinction as one of the foremost states of India that had sea-borne trade with countries and islands far and near. The trade with the East was exclusively in the hands of the countries of Eastern India, while that with the West was carried on chiefly by the Arabs and the Moors. The long coast-line of the Andhra country was responsible to a large extent in making the Andhras a sea-faring nation from early centuries.[20]

The Andhra Satavahana rulers inaugurated the trade with the countries in the East. This intercourse was carried on in the later period by the Eastern Chalukyas of Vengi. But in the middle of the eleventh century A.D., the sea-borne trade of Andhra Desa suffered a set-back, as it became a hotbed of battles place among the Eastern Chalukyas, the Cholas, the Western Chalukyas and the Eastern Gangas. It was the illustrious Kakatiya king Ganapatideva who encouraged oceanic trade by issuing a charter of protection to both the native and foreign merchants by fixing the rates of export and import duties and extending some facilities to them.[21]

The decline of the Kakatiyas affected adversely the sea-borne trade of Andhra Desa. It was revived by the Reddi kings, the successors of the Kakatiyas. Anavota Reddi (1353-1364 A.D.) issued a charter[22] in 1358 A.D., which gave a fillip to the foreign trade again. The charter was included in Tamil and Telugu languages on a pillar in the Virabhadraswami temple at Motupalli. It is interesting to note the fact that the inscription containing the instructions in Tamil proves that many of the merchants coming there were from the Tamil country. This trade charter promised to give the garden land which was under their enjoyment previously to those who deserted Motupalli, not to collect Aputrika dandam and kaddayamu (forced import) and to remit tax due on gold and silver etc. Further, the high import duties and low export duties indicated in this charter reveal the sound principles of foreign trade laid down by the ruler to protect internal industries and to bring in a favourable balance of trade. Anavota's charter of rights issued to the merchants of Motupalli is a ratification and continuation of the earlier charter of Ganapatideva. Later, Motupalli was conquered by the Vijayanagara king, Harihara-II (1377-1404 A.D.). He sent his son, Devaraya-I to govern that territory. Then Devaraya-I, like Anavota Reddi issued a charter[23] at Motupalli in 1390 A.D. fixing the rates of custom duties and amending the former's charter of 1358 A.D. Because of these three marvellous charters Motupalli became a great port and emporium.

Imports and Exports

The commodities of the foreign trade of medieval Andhra may broadly be described under two categories: imports and exports. It is beyond doubt that Andhra country had rich resources, still, to pacify the requirements of some of the classes and the State, it imported some items from abroad. The prolific poet Srinatha enumerates in his *Haravilasam*[24] various countries and islands with which the Andhras had trade transactions. In the post-Reddi period, lac, tin, pepper and sealing wax were imported into Andhra Desa from the Eastern counties. Regarding exports, printed and plain clothes, iron and steel were exported from Andhra to the south-eastern islands. Food stuffs like rice and pulses and other things like teak and sandal wood etc., were exported to the neighbouring and foreign countries. Finally, precious stones like diamonds called "the stones of fire", which were available in the Kollur mines and the Vajrakarur mines were also exported to China and other countries.[25]

During the Qutb Shahi period there was a spectacular growth of trade concentrated on the East Coast. The largest commodity for the export was that of textiles. The production for export was due to the specialization at some of the manufacturing centres. Textiles had extensive export market in Asia for centuries and later in Europe. The peculiarity of the Coromandel textiles was the dyeing, painting and printing in beautiful colours and designs. In addition to them, the other cloths like Bettilles (veiling cloth), Sucatoons (heavy cotton cloth) and Rumals (cotton or silk pieces) etc. were also exported. Animal skins were exported to Batavia and Japan, whereas saltpetre[26] was exported to Europe and West Asia. Iron and steel were exported to Pegu, Tenasserim, Arakan and Acheh to Arabia and Persia. The diamonds of Golconda were exported to South East Asia and also to Europe and the diamond trade grew largely in the 17th century. Leather was exported to Arabia and south-East Asian countries. Tobacco was grown in the later part of the 17th century in the Godavari area. Methwold recorded export of tobacco to Mocha and Arakan.[27] Redwood was exported to Persia. Lac from the hinter land of Masulipatnam was exported to Arabia.

In the 16th and 17th centuries India witnessed a widespread demand for certain varieties of foreign articles. In fact, these imported articles catered to the needs of the rulers, ministers, officials, nobles and the upper classes of the society in the Golconda kingdom. A major part of imports consisted of pepper and spices. They were sold more in the Muslim kingdoms like Golconda and Bijapur, as they were consumed more by the Muslims, than the Hindus. Spices were imported from Moluccas and cinnamon was imported from Ceylon. Precious metals like gold were procured from Acheh, West Sumatra, Burma, Europe and Persia.[28] These imports included tin from South East Asian countries; copper from Tenasserim and Burma; perfumes mostly from West Asian countries; coconuts and coir from Ceylon; porcelain from China. Silks, carpets, brocade, dried fruits, rosewater, wines and dry roots were imported into Masulipatnam from Persia and Arabia, while elephants were imported from Acheh, Tenasserim, Tailand, Pegu and Ceylon. Elephant tusks from Ethiopia and horses from Arabia, Persia, Uzbekistan and Ethiopia were imported.

Trade with South-East Asian Countries and Ceylon

Andhra witnessed flourishing trade with the countries of the East and the West during the Qutb Shahi period. India in general and Andhra Desa in particular, had good trade transactions with South-east Asian countries over centuries. During this period the rulers of Ayuthya established close links with the Andhra merchants and diplomatic ties with the Golconda rulers and later with the Mughals. From the port of Masulipatnam the major ware of export to this region were textiles specially long cloth, salempores and moris. Another variety, Kaingulong was exported to Tenasserum and Siam,[29] whereas the Dupathy had good market in Siam. The other items like animal skins, leather, iron, steel and diamonds were exported to the port of Tenasserim and from there Andhra imported tin and copper in great quantities.

The Dutch conquest of Malacca in 1641 A.D., inaugurated a sprightly trade with Malacca. Apart from textiles, rice, round pepper, vermilion, iron and steel, were exported to Malacca and items such as copper, brass, tin, ivory, sandalwood, spices, gold, rubies and emeralds were imported from that country. A good number of elephants were transshipped to Andhra from Tennaserim and Pegu. The Andhra merchants fortunately found Acheh, a great trading emporium of South East Asia as heaven for their trade.[30]

Trade with Acheh and Bantam

Owing to the generous policy of the rulers, the port Acheh was opened to the Andhra merchants. Vessels reached Acheh from Masulipatnam, Pulicat and San Thome and traded in rice, pepper, tin and gold. Masulipatnam had excellent trade relations with Bantam, and important commercial ports situated on the Western tip of Java. Andhra exchanged textiles for pepper, copper, tin and Chinese goods in Bantam.[31]

Trade with Burma

In the Burmese kingdom, Andhra had trade contacts with Syriam, Martaban and other ports. Interestingly, the Dutch and the English competed with the Andhra merchants for the expansion of trade in Burma. The Burma rubies were in great demand in the kingdom of Golconda. Tin, copper coins, lead, zinc, sappan wood, long pepper, precious stones for which Burma was famous, were imported to Andhra.[32]

Trade with Manila

In the early 17th century the Andhra trade with Manila developed. The exports from Andhra contained textiles, both long cloth, painted and dyed items. Tobacco, sugar, wax, copper, limestone, silver, silks and chinaware were imported from it.[33]

Trade with Arakan

The famous port of Mrohaung, the capital of Arakan and the centre of ship building, was another trading place to the Andhra traders. The vessels of Golconda from Masulipatnam carried textiles to this port.[34]

Trade with Ceylon and Maldives

Andhra had prosperous trade with these countries, especially with Ceylon since ancient times. After the Dutch conquest of Ceylon, about 250 boats used to travel in a year from Jafna to Masulipatnam, Nizampatnam and Bhimilipatnam. The boats used in this trade were built at Narsapur and Madapollam. Rice and coarse cloth were the important items in this trade. Rice was exported from Bhimilipatnam and Krishnapatnam. The Golconda merchants brought spices from Ceylon and transshipped them to Surat and West Asia. A large number of elephants, huge quantities of arecanuts, coir for preparing cordage and ropes in ship building were imported from Ceylon.[35] Trade with the Maldives was generally part of a long voyage to Ceylon and Malabar.

Trade with West Asia

A bulky trade from Masulipatnam with the ports of Bandar Abbas, Basra in the Persian Gulf, Muskat in South Arabia and Mocha in the Red Sea flourished more in the 17th century. Mir Jumla, the Governor of Karnataka and of Golconda, carried on lively trade with the Persian gulf in 1640 and 1650 A.D., making the Masulipatnam port as the centre.[36] There were some hardships in this trade, due to Dutch restrictions and the danger of piracy all along the West Coast of India and at the entry points to the Red Sea and the Persian Gulf. Inspite of it, trade grew mainly due to the large investments made by the ruling elite of Golconda. The wave of exports to West Asia were fine muslins, chintzes, iron and steel, tobacco, ivory, indigo and sandalwood.

Trade with Europe

India carried on extensive trade both maritime and overland with Europe. The goods manufactured in Andhra were in great demand in foreign markets. Abdul Majeed Siddiqui accurately pointed out:

When the foundation stones of the Golconda kingdom were being laid, nations were searching for sea routes to reach the sub-continent and some of the Western nations had already set their foot on some of the coastal towns. It has to be admitted that the advent of the European nations served as a great impetus to the rise of Indian trade.[37]

During the 17th century, a great bulk of the trade to Western Europe passed from Portuguese to the Dutch and the English. The Dutch ships which left from Masulipatnam to Europe sometimes went to Batavia, the Dutch Company's Eastern headquarters, or went directly with cargo.

The trading guilds like the Vira Balanjya Samaya, Nakaramu, Ubhaya-nanadesi, Svadesi-paradesi and the State guilds such as the Gangeyarajya Samaya and the Rajaraja Samaya played key role in the development of trade and commerce. Thus, there was flourishing inland and overseas trade in medieval Telangana and Andhra regions.

Notes & References

1. Vinukonda Vallabharaya, *Kridabhiramam*, published by V. Prabhakara Sastry, Hyderabad, 1960, v.166.
2. *South Indian Inscriptions*, VI, Nos.789 & 970.
3. *Ibid.*, VII, No.673.
4. *Ibid.*, V, No.66.
5. Vinukonda Vallabharaya, *Op.Cit.,* Introduction, p.69.
6. Thevenot, *Indian Travels of Thevenot and Careri*, Surendranath Sen, (Ed.), New Delhi, 1949, p.136.
7. *Ibid.*, p.148.
8. Jean-Baptiste Tavernier, *Tavernier Travels in India*, Vol. I, London, 1925, p.23.
9. *Ibid.*
10. *Ibid.*, p.28.
11. S. Sakuntala, *Travels of Tavernier and Thevenot in the Golconda Kingdom,* M.Phil. dissertation, Osmania University, Hyderabad, 1980, p.147.
12. P.V. Parabrahma Sastry, *The Kakatiyas*, Hyderabad, 1978, p.25.
13. *Ibid.*, pp.252-253.
14. R. Varalakshmi, *Urban Centres and Urbanisation in Medieval Andhra (A.D. 1300-1687)*, Ph.D. Thesis (unpublished), Osmania University, Hyderabad, 1998, p.164.
15. Saroj Cherian, *Seaports in Andhra with Reference to Later Medieval Period (17th & 18th Century)*, Ph.D. Thesis (unpublished), Osmania University, Hyderabad, 1993, p.157.
16. W.H. Moreland, *Relations of Golconda, in the Early Seventeenth Century 1608-22*, London, 1931, p.68.
17. Bernier, *Travels in the Mughal Empire 1656-68,* Delhi, 1968, p.249.

18. A.M. Siddiqui, *History of Golconda,* Hyderabad, 1956, p.351.
19. R. Varalakshmi, *Op.Cit.*, p.165.
20. M. Somasekhara Sarma, *History of the Reddi Kingdoms*, Waltair, 1948, p.403.
21. Epigraphia Indica, XII, pp.183 ff.
22. Epigraphia Collections, Nos.601 and 602 of 1909.
23. *Reddi Samchika*, p.196 and p.199-200.
24. M. Somasekhara Sarma, *Op.Cit.*, p.408.
25. R. Varalakshmi, *Op.Cit.*, p.169.
26. W.H. Moreland, *From Akbar to Aurangzeb*, London, 1923, pp.96, 97, 192, 118 & 122.
27. *Ibid.,* pp.80, 81 & 189.
28. S. Aresaratnam, *Merchants, Companies and Commerce on the Coromandel Coast 1650-1740*, Delhi, 1986, pp.99-102.
29. Peter Floris, *His Voyage to the East Indies 1611-1615*, London, 1934, pp.41-42.
30. R. Varalakshmi, *Op.Cit.*, p.171.
31. I.O.L., Factory Records, Masulipatnam, G/26/12.
32. Saroj Cherian, *Op.Cit.*, p.226.
33. S.D. Quiason, *English Country Trade with the Philippines 1644-1765*, 1966, pp.34-40.
34. Memoir of Pit, 25th June, 1663; Mack Collection, Private 47.
35. S. Arasaratnam, Dutch Power in Ceylon, Amsterdam, 1958, pp.150-153.
36. M. Alam, "Masulipatnam, A Metropolitan Port in the 17th Century", *Islamic Culture,* 1959, pp.173-175, 117-118.
37. A.M. Siddiqui, *Op.Cit.*, pp. 353-354.